Managing
As If Faith
Mattered

Catholic Social Tradition Series

VOLUME ONE

Preface to the Series

In *Tertio mellenio advenient,* Pope John Paul II poses a hard question: "It must be asked how many Christians really know and put into practice the principles of the church's social doctrine." The American Catholic bishops share the pope's concern: "Catholic social teaching is a central and essential element of our faith . . . [and yet] our social heritage is unknown by many Catholics. Sadly, our social doctrine is not shared or taught in a consistent and comprehensive way in too many of our schools." This lack is critical because the "sharing of our social tradition is a defining measure of Catholic education and formation." A United States Catholic Conference task force on social teaching and education noted that within Catholic higher education "there appears to be little consistent attention given to incorporating gospel values and Catholic social teaching into general education courses or into departmental majors."

In response to this problem, the volumes in the Catholic Social Tradition series aspire to impart the best of what this tradition has to offer not only to Catholics but to all who face the social issues of our times. The volumes examine a wide variety of issues and problems within the Catholic social tradition and contemporary society, yet they share several characteristics. They are theologically and philosophically grounded, examining the deep structure of thought in modern culture. They are publicly argued, enhancing dialogue with other religious and nonreligious traditions. They are comprehensively engaged by a wide variety of disciplines such as theology, philosophy, political science, economics, history, law, management, and finance. Finally, they examine how the Catholic social tradition can be integrated on a practical level and embodied in institutions in which people live much of their lives. The Catholic Social Tradition series is about faith in action in daily life, providing ways of thinking and acting to those seeking a more humane world.

Michael Naughton
University of St. Thomas

Todd David Whitmore
University of Notre Dame

Managing As If Faith Mattered

Christian Social Principles
in the
Modern Organization

HELEN J. ALFORD, O.P.

&

MICHAEL J. NAUGHTON

University of Notre Dame Press
Notre Dame, Indiana

Manufactured in the United States of America

Reprinted in 2006, 2008

Library of Congress Cataloging-in-Publication Data
Alford, Helen, 1964–
Managing as if faith mattered : Christian social principles in the
modern organization / Helen Alford and Michael Naughton.
p.   cm. — (Catholic social tradition)
Includes bibliographical references and index.
ISBN 10: 0-268-03461-3 (cloth. : alk. paper)
ISBN 13: 978-0-268-03462-7 (pbk. : alk. paper)
ISBN 10: 0-268-03462-1 (pbk. : alk. paper)
1. Business ethics. 2. Management—Religious aspects—Catholic
Church.   3. Sociology, Christian (Catholic)   I. Naughton, Michael,
1960– . II. Title.   III. Series.
HF5387 .A58 2001

658—dc21   00-012821

∞ *This book is printed on acid-free paper.*

Contents

Foreword

Robert Wahlstedt
Founder and Chairman of Reell Precision Manufacturing

I first met Michael Naughton and Helen Alford when they made a presentation with the intriguing title, "The Genesis Model of Product Development." We at Reell Precision Manufacturing Corporation were especially curious because our Direction Statement includes a commitment to "the practical application of Judeo-Christian values for the mutual benefit of co-workers, customers, shareholders, suppliers, and the community." It was not possible to ignore someone who is able to find guidance for product development in the Bible.

From this beginning a relationship has developed—particularly with Michael (Helen spends most of her time in Europe)—that is both enlightening and affirming: enlightening, because Michael has introduced us to the rich resources of Catholic social thought; affirming, because many of the practical innovations inspired by our commitment to Judeo-Christian values have been independently posited by Michael and Helen as they have pursued a theological understanding of moral management. It is as though, searching our way through an uncharted forest, we have come to a clearing and met a person with a map that confirms we are on the right trail!

Let me give you just one example of this alignment between practice at RPM and the understanding developed by Michael and Helen. Catholic social thought teaches a principle called "subsidiarity." Subsidiarity means that decision making should be pushed down to the lowest possible level, so that all concerned can contribute to the fullness of their ability. Compare this excerpt from the "History of RPM."

> In 1983, we faced a problem that led to revolutionary changes in our people relationships. It didn't seem like a revolution at first;

ix

we simply had a problem to solve. Our set-up procedures called for an independent evaluation of set-up samples by Quality Control after the set-up was complete and before the job was run. The problem was the time that often elapsed before the set-up was approved.

When the set-up was finished, the set-up person would submit samples to Quality Control and it would usually take several hours before an inspector was free to do the evaluation. Of course, by this time the set-up person had gone on to the next job so, if the samples were not satisfactory, more time would elapse before the adjustments could be made. In some cases, this process would have to be repeated several times before the job was approved. Manufacturing found this understandably frustrating because they could set-up a job and not be able to run it for several days.

Someone asked the question, "What if we taught the set-up people to do their own inspection and *trusted* them to do it right?" At this time we had no objective other than to improve the efficiency of the set-up procedure. We decided to buy a complete set of inspection tools for the set-up people and assigned one of the quality control inspectors to the manufacturing department to train set-up people in inspection techniques. This would allow the set-up person to stay on the job, without interruption, until it was ready to run.

The results were surprising! Not only did we achieve the expected improvement in efficiency, but the quality of production improved as well! This was the first step in a philosophical evolution from a Command-Direct-Control style of management (CDC) to a Teach-Equip-Trust style (TET). By *teaching* the set-up people in inspection procedures, *equipping* them with inspection instruments and *trusting* that they would do things right, greater productivity, better quality and growth for the individual were achieved.

This positive but limited experience with the benefits of trusting people prepared us for even more significant improvements when we were exposed to training in Statistical Process Control (SPC) and Just-In-Time manufacturing (JIT) provided by a major customer. These new techniques were exactly what were needed to allow us to extend the Teach-Equip-Trust philosophy to our entire manufacturing operation.

This change was truly revolutionary! Previously, our assembly process required 5 weeks making, inspecting and stocking sub and final assemblies. Now, *all* sub-assemblies *and inspections* are done in one continuous flow process *by production people*. The entire process takes less than 2 minutes and the finished unit is ready for shipment without further inspection when it comes off the assembly line! In fact, it is placed directly into the shipping carton.

As promised by the proponents of JIT, we have experienced the positive financial effects of reduced inventory, inspection and assembly costs, better quality and better utilization of space.

More importantly, assembly positions are enriched. Assemblers can move up in responsibility and pay to Senior Assembler and Line Leader positions as their skills increase through training and experience.

This experience . . . this revolution has shown us that the biggest misconception of American manufacturers is the belief that production workers are not dependable and must be motivated and/or constrained to do quality work. We have been amazed by the self-motivation and dedication to quality and productivity that are demonstrated when they are *freed* to develop and use their full potential.

You can see that our completely pragmatic effort to improve the logistics of our process is a direct application of the principle of subsidiarity, even though we were unaware of it at the time. Furthermore, we learned how the integration of our faith and our work could become more than a theoretical concept. As we have allowed our actions to be informed and energized by our beliefs, an organization has developed that helps people to grow.

Michael's previous book, *The Good Stewards*, pulls together concepts from papal writings of several centuries to form a "blueprint" for a spiritually based organization. In addition to "subsidiarity," this book introduced us to the principles of "participation," "common use," and "justice." We came to realize how closely our pragmatic attempts at applying Judeo-Christian values had brought us to the Catholic social tradition. Reading Michael's book was like looking in the face of God and hearing Him say, "Well done, faithful servant!"

In this book, Michael and Helen combine the results of their theological inquiry with the experience of practitioners to make a compelling case for the integration of spiritual principles, values, and insights with management theory. As you make this integration, I believe that you will be encouraged, enlightened and affirmed, as you find more energy, more meaning, and more virtue in your work.

Preface

Jean-Loup Dherse
Former CEO of the Eurotunnel, former Vice President of the World Bank,
and Member of the Pontifical Council *Cor Unum*

God and business. Business and God. Both of them are potentially present in the manager's personal "control center," deep down in the core of his person. Both God and business are candidates for the manager's time and attention.

Are God and business competitors? Well, if they are, we must admit that business takes precedence most of the time. Indeed, time seems to be in very short supply, and God can wait. He is very patient. Business is not.

The attitude "God can wait" is common and can last throughout a manager's life. This is typically the case when business is challenging and rewarding, and as long as the manager does not meet major problems in his work, in his family, in his life. But such problems do arise, very often, even when success is there. Indeed, success itself brings fear that it may not last.

Business is usually very demanding on the manager's time even outside business hours. Time for "relaxing" is precious: the manager needs it for making his way up into society, for meeting the right people in the right atmosphere. As his business grows, he has indeed to make himself known in society and to befriend rich, influential, and discreetly admired elites. Business tends to feed personal desire for power, reputation, and financial means; the more these three goods are acquired, the more the desire for them seems to grow. There is no saturation, no self-induced limitation in the process. Along this dangerous route, the manager finds it more and more difficult to realize that his motivation is becoming more and more exclusively selfish. He forgets more and more that his action has consequences on people who cannot reward him or, conversely, hurt him. He would be amazed at the thought that it is not right to consider other people as mere instruments with which to fulfill his otherwise legitimate goals, and that he should assess the consequences of his decisions on people at large, on those who cannot help him or fire back.

Our manager would find it hard to believe that many of his decisions, which may be quite legal, have indeed been costly, in economic terms, for the world at large, while possibly profitable to him—even in the long term—and to the institution he works for. He will want to put a figure on everything, although accounting cannot reckon strictly human improvement or debasement. He feels committed to the bottom line and to nothing more.

This may be an extreme case, but it is not a caricature. Many such examples abound. Happily, many other managers (at all levels) think and act otherwise. In any institution, this more thoughtful manager will look at reality around him more thoroughly when he is about to make a business decision. He will look at the proposed decision from four different viewpoints and ask himself four sets of questions:

- Are the figures right and is our technology appropriate for going this way? Scientific, technical skills are always critical, and not to rely enough on them will deprive the institution and the world at large of potential additional riches.
- Is the structure or organization appropriate? All structures are less than perfect and therefore can always be improved. His question will be: *Am I accepting to cooperate in spite of such structural limitations, and am I also willing to try to help improve the structure as I go along?*
- In what I am going to do, will I be a promoter of mutual trust between all those concerned, at all levels, or will I have to trick some people into believing something that is in fact untrue? Will I have to betray anyone?
- In what I am going to do, my motivations usually boil down to personal motivations (in terms of money, authority or responsibilities, public image), and to institutional motivations (the good of the people for whom I work). But am I also looking at the consequences of what I am going to do for those who will be adversely affected but cannot weigh in on me? Am I considering these people, who are outside the scope of my corporate respon-

sibilities, as important? Am I doing my best to find other ways to achieve my purposes that do not have the same negative effects on people at large?

The seasoned and more thoughtful manager knows by experience that these four sets of questions are very much at the core of his daily life. In particular, the last set of questions is not marginal, but can lead him toward doing quite different things from those he had first in mind. Without being able to prove it, he will nevertheless be convinced that his more thoughtful approach is not a handicap, but a positive factor in institutional performance. That conclusion will never be proven, because accounting does not integrate all the facts taken into consideration. In other words, this thoughtful manager will experience that the world is much more sensitive to each decision he makes than is generally perceived. He will even accept that forgetting about the consequences on others (however distant) of what he does has tremendous hidden costs:

- cost to oneself, as one tends to become more and more blind to the fate of other people;
- cost to one's immediate environment, since newcomers find it much more difficult to come in with their values and be accepted. If the main local actors have no such values, the newcomer is placed in the very unjust position of having to either drop those values or be ousted;
- cost to the planet, since acting with lack of care for consequences on humans has large macroeconomic consequences, compared to the scenarios where care for people is fully taken into consideration (we know that excessive self-protection on the part of one individual can have a huge cost to the community and to the world at large).

Last, but not least, the thoughtful manager will find through experience that this downward spiral can be reversed. By seeing others as human beings and not as mere instruments to his own career path, he will discover that his vision gets sharper as it relates to what he is really working for. The thoughtful manager will, within what is possible, reconcile his bottom-line approach and his responsibilities vis-à-vis the world at large. His approach is in fact a way of life that will apply to everything he does, within or outside his institution.

I know this struggle personally. I know firsthand the pathologies of success. The lures of money, success, power, and fame are not always easy to detect in oneself. I have been prone to let God wait on the proverbial sidelines, which has caused me to miss opportunities to develop as well as to help others to develop. And yet, the power to live not merely for the self alone but for the human community never leaves us completely.

I believe that God is the Uncreated Love, a Trinity of three persons in one, having created the world—in an ongoing process—out of pure love. He has entrusted you and me with the role of steward of the whole creation, left absolutely free to perform as God's agent, with His support and help. God has also given us the profound freedom to turn our back on His promise of eternal union. This radical decision is in part made in the work we do. It has come to me in the clearest of terms that my work either enhances His creation or deteriorates it. There is no neutral ground.

It is in this context that I recommend this book to the reader. Helen Alford and Michael Naughton provide an important contribution to an indispensable discussion in life: faith, what we believe to be true, and work, what we do. All too often, many of us fail to engage our faith with our work, because, as I have indicated above, we get too busy, too distracted by money, success, and the rewards of our career. We also have a culture that creates obstacles to taking faith seriously in the work we do, imposing on us the belief that faith should be left to the private domain of the pew. This book counters these personal and cultural temptations by examining the question of faith and work within the Christian social tradition. This is a tradition rich in resources and insights, of which, unfortunately, too many Christians are unaware. While I do not agree with everything Helen and Michael have written, I am indebted to their work of recovering a faith tradition which I hold to be true to and their integration of this tradition with work in which I have spent most of life.

The reader of this book, whether student or manager, can begin to deepen her understanding of business beyond the narrow, wealth-maximizing formula found in finance. The Christian social tradition can help us to explore the social and spiritual desires deep within every human person and to connect these human desires to an understanding of business that can help people develop in the fullest sense of that term. If we want a better world, which is at the tip of our fingers, we cannot sell ourselves short on the meaning of our work and our organizations. God does not leave us alone, although He respects our freeom so much that sometimes we may regret He is so discreet. He is going to teach us, with our own participation, how such a call can be implemented in business life, in political life, in work life, whatever the work, and wherever in society it may take place.

While this book is directed toward Christians, particularly those who have yet to explore the social dimension of their faith, its content will be worth considering by all people, since all—irrespective of cultural, ethnic and religious differences—are entrusted with a corner of the planet. The relative roles of God, of humanity, and of society are here put in a new light. Please help yourselves to this light.

Acknowledgments

If it takes a village to raise a child, it takes a community to write a book. We have given drafts of this book for comment to a wide range of managers and scholars. They have responded with helpful and insightful critiques and additions: Donna Adler, Robert Ashford, Gary Atkinson, Tom Bausch, Bernie Brady, Anthony Brenninkmeyer, Don Briel, Jeanne Buckeye, Brian Campion, William Cavanaugh, Francesco Compagnoni, Jean-Loup Dherse, Dan Rush Finn, Michael Flood, Jeff Gates, Jim Grubs, Stewart Herman, Jim Jensen, Bob Kennedy, Norman Kurland, David Lutz, Ray MacKenzie, Bill McDonough, Mark Nolan, Michael Papesch, Dan Pekarske, Ernest Pierucci, John Pimenta, Deborah Savage, Mick Sheppeck, Colleen Striegel, and Bob Wahlstedt. We are especially indebted to our students, in particular to Thérèse Cullen, Mara Hobday, Kelly Gass, Amanda Osheim, and Gretchen Shively who read through various drafts, questioning our logic and improving the clarity of our thought. We owe a special debt of gratitude to Steven Cortright, whose editorial skill and philosophical insight has strengthened the argument of this book and has harmonized the writing styles of an American and a European, which is no small feat. We would also like to thank Sharon M. Van Sluijs, our copy editor, whose comments helped to bring greater clarity to the book.

This book could not have been written without the generous institutional support at the University of St. Thomas, which speeded its composition with summer grants and course releases. We are especially indebted to Msgr. Murphy and The Aquinas Foundation, the John A. Ryan Institute for Catholic Social Thought, the Center for Catholic Studies, and the Faculty Development Office. We are also grateful for the generous financial and intellectual gifts of John Murray, and of an anonymous donor.

Finally, we would like to thank Mike's family: Teresa, Clare, Noel, Mary, Eamon, and Annie; and Helen's fellow Dominicans, especially those of her congregation, The Dominican sisters of St. Catherine of Siena, Newcastle, Natal ("Bushey" Dominicans). By their encouragement, all these people have challenged us to our best efforts, and helped us toward integrating our own faith and work.

Helen Alford, O.P.
Michael Naughton

Introduction

Our title, *Managing As If Faith Mattered,* was inspired by the subtitle of E. F. Schumacher's famous book, *Small Is Beautiful.* Through his ironical subtitle, *Economics As If People Mattered,* Schumacher wanted to indicate how far economic thinking had strayed from its real object and purpose, and how he hoped that his book was a step toward redirecting economics back toward its goal. Our contention in this book is similar: much management theory and education has lost sight of the fundamental reasons for which we go into business, and our book is an attempt to reorient management thinking toward the realization of management's fundamental goals. Furthermore, most management courses treat management as if faith did not matter, just as Schumacher saw that most economic theory treats economics as if people did not matter. Even in religiously based universities, one is often hard-pressed to find anything in the curriculum of the business school that could connect the practice of management to the religious tradition of the university.

We have been educated and trained, by default usually, to work as if faith is in a category completely separate from our work. While we may adhere to a religious tradition, we tend not to see the relevance of that tradition to our work. If anything, we actively think of things the other way around: we cannot let the ethical or religious principles of our faith interfere with the way we manage the perplexities of organizational and professional life, in case this could compromise our efficiency or our return on capital. In this book, you are challenged to consider seriously that it might just be possible to manage as if faith mattered, where organizations are created to serve the common good and promote the dignity of the human person, all for the greater glory of God.

The first thoughts for this book began in the summer of 1994 when we began meeting with Gary Atkinson, Robert Kennedy, and Bernie

Brady to discuss the relationship between Christian social thought and management. The impetus for this discussion came from several sources. The first and foremost was a questioning of our vocation as teachers. Were we adequately fostering a genuine integration of faith and work in the education we were giving our students? Were we helping them overcome the gulf that is so often encountered between their liberal and their business education? Were we enabling them to penetrate the connections between the philosophical and theological traditions we have come to call the Christian social tradition with the discipline of management? Our answer was clear: we still had a long way to go.

Similarly, we were also concerned about the mission of our universities. In 1990, John Paul II issued a document called *Ex Corde Ecclesiae (On Catholic Universities)*, which articulated the importance of integrating the faith of the Church into the whole of Catholic university curriculum. Since management students form a significant number of students at Catholic and Christian universities, it was clear that if this call were to be taken seriously in the university as a whole, it had to be taken seriously by these faculties.

Initially, the lack of teaching material on this topic hindered our progress. As people who were teaching theology, philosophy and business in a Catholic university, we felt this dearth of classroom material as a great hindrance to our ability to communicate the links between the Christian social tradition and the management disciplines. These links provide the basis for regarding the work of the Christian manager as a vocation, and since their role in the curriculum is crucial to the fulfillment of the mission of a Christian, and in particular a Catholic, business school, this lack of teaching texts and aids had much wider consequences for management and theological education. In response to this acute lack of teaching material, we wrote this book.

In the last several years, the landscape of questions regarding the intersection of faith and work has changed dramatically. Something has happened. Ten years ago, questions of faith and spirituality seemed confined to the private realm, discussed publicly only in churches or during retreats. Now, conferences, seminars, and workshops reveal an awakening to the importance of the religious and spiritual dimension in all realms of life. As part of this awakening, this book offers a particular contribution: connecting the richness of one religious tradition—the Christian social tradition—with management theory and practice. Our hope for you, our reader, is that the ideas and practices discussed here will help foster a deeper integration of faith and work in your life.

This book is the first volume of a series on the Catholic social tradition to be published by the University of Notre Dame Press. It provides a broad introduction to the connections between Christian social thought and management by focusing on such leading principles as the common good, solidarity, subsidiarity, the universal destination of material goods, and the cardinal and theological virtues as they relate to critical questions in management: organizational purpose, job design, wages, ownership, product development, and the like. The second volume will address the foundational question, *What is the nature and purpose of business?* It will comprise papers collected from the disciplines of law, finance, theology, management, economics, and philosophy, each addressing this critical question, with particular emphasis on the Catholic social tradition. The third volume will also be an interdisciplinary work within the Christian social tradition, but it will focus on the topic of wealth creation and distribution, a crucial issue as we face increasingly disparate distributions of wealth, and the globalization of business.

Until we have a robust, realistic, and interdisciplinary engagement of managerial questions with the riches of the Christian social tradition, we will neither do justice to the profound implications this tradition has for management, nor will we as teachers adequately fulfill the mission of our Christian and Catholic universities.

This book is in three parts. The first part concerns *establishing the engagement* between the Christian social tradition and management. Chapter 1 begins by tying the discussion of Christian social thought and management to the existential problem so many of us face in our work: the context of a divided life, and suggests ways that Christian thinkers and managers have used to overcome this division. In chapter 2 we provide a critique of the two dominant concepts of organizational purpose, the shareholder and the stakeholder theories of the firm, from the perspective of the common good. Next, in chapter 3, we examine the reemergence of virtue as a theme in organizational literature, and consider the virtues needed in business in the light of the

Christian moral tradition. Throughout this section, our discussion revolves around the two fundamentals of the Christian social tradition that provide the basis for an engagement with the management disciplines: the nature, value and development of human virtue, and the promotion of the common good. Lacking virtuous members, organizations fail to flourish in a humane way; without a deliberate, common pursuit of the good, the human person at work is unable to pursue more than a "divided life," where the implications of faith cannot be lived out at work.

The second part of the book *makes the engagement* between Christian social thought and management by examining specific management issues. Chapters 4 through 7 are devoted to the *skills*—broadly defined—that are the prerequisites for realizing a vision of the common good in today's business organization. In this section, therefore, we relate the pursuit of the common good to four critical management functions, and we attend to specific issues within each function's purview. In chapter 4, we consider the reasons why operations/production management has paid so little attention to designing jobs that allow people to grow, and we discuss possible ways of redirecting job design to be more consonant with the Christian tradition. In chapter 5, we explore the tendency of human resources management to instrumentalize human relations when determining employees' pay, and ways to place strategic concerns in a wider perspective, in light of the Christian tradition. In chapter 6, we examine the role of finance, its failure to promote an equitable distribution of capital ownership, and possible alternative mechanisms for promoting such distribution. In chapter 7, we discuss various philosophies of marketing and marketing practices within this function, providing critical evaluations of several approaches.

In part three, we explore what is necessary to *sustain the engagement*. This part serves what G. K. Chesterton might have called an "Afterword, In Defense of Everything Else." In chapters 8 and 9, we consider the question of an authentic spirituality of work in both its personal and communal dimensions. We are fully cognizant that apart from an authentic spirituality of work, our argument for the integration of faith and work is a dead letter.

Establishing
the
Engagement

1

Making Us Whole

Avoiding "Split Personalities"

Compromise is said to be the way of the world and yet I find myself feeling sick trying to accept what it has done to me.[1]

—Douglas Coupland

FOR MANY OF US, COUPLAND'S STARK WORDS RING TRUE. Like the ever-compromising prince heeding the words of Machiavelli, we are inclined to believe that "how we live is so far removed from how we ought to live, that he who abandons what is done for what ought to be done will rather bring about his own ruin than his preservation."[2] Machiavelli's observation can be directly applied to the demands of our work. Yet unlike Machiavelli's prince, who to be a successful leader must "learn how not to be good," we try not to give up on the good completely. Therefore, we tend to accept a divided life, acquiescing to an apparent necessity to maintain a *"split personality."* That is, often we act as one person, following one set of goals and standards in our private lives, while we become a strikingly different person—someone molded by expediency and necessary compromise—at work.

Of course, the problem of personal integrity or wholeness does not reside exclusively in the disparities between our "private" and "working" selves. In moments of clarity, most of us can recall reasons to regret the gap between who we ought to be and who we actually are. Nevertheless, one's working life is a powerful source of the fragmentation and estrangement of self from self that Coupland laments. It is

7

not merely because work occupies so many of our hours. It is also because work is central to the practical life of goal-setting and decision-making, of personal and interpersonal achievement. For many of us, it is the fount of our well-being, for we as creatures are, above all, *doers*. We fear that if our working lives spawn inner division and conflict, our search for happiness beyond the transitory satisfactions of success must fail. The measure of our need for personal integrity or wholeness, then, is our overriding desire for personal happiness.

Our desire for wholeness or integrity has both a personal and communal, or organizational, component. "Integrity" comes from the Latin adjective *integer:* whole, complete, single (in the sense of "pure"). As an abstract noun, "integrity" thus signifies the condition of being one or whole, whether the thing in question is a whole number, a whole person, or a whole institution. Integrity also means the state or quality of being complete and unimpaired. At the personal level, integrity refers to our ability to be wholly consistent in ourselves and in our actions. At the organizational level, integrity requires that conditions or structures exist that allow us, as workers, to become and to remain whole.

These aspects of integrity pose two questions which drive the argument of this book: The first question, at the level of personal integrity: *What kind of person should I as a manager or employee strive to become?* The second question, at the level of organizational integrity: *What kind of organizational community should I as a manager or employee, strive to build and maintain?*[3] As teachers of management, philosophy and theology in Catholic universities, we face students who are concerned about these questions, and are wary of the all-too-common experience of the "split personality." Similarly, when we talk at business seminars, churches or community groups about the nature and vocation of work and management, practicing managers and professionals frequently ask how they can integrate their faith with their work. If you ask these questions, do not think you are alone; you are one among a great number of people for whom this rift between their so-called public and private lives is unacceptable or even unbearable.

Writers and social commentators have begun to respond to this problem. Book publishers have recognized a new market. Titles concerned with the "soul of business," the "virtuous manager" or "spirituality and management" are beginning to crowd the shelves—not to mention the wealth of material on the more familiar "business ethics." While many of these books provide helpful, even profound, insights into the meaning of work, few offer a strong connection to any particular moral or religious tradition. More often than not, authors try to construct a business ethic or spirituality of work from scratch. Some authors simply "mix and match" useful ideas from different, and even conflicting, traditions of thought. Consequently, many authors fail to address seriously the ethical and spiritual traditions that have formed the managers and employees to whom their writings are ostensibly addressed. While it is true that some managers and employees are not inspired by religious faith, the fact remains that many are. Many others are influenced by the ethical principles of a religious tradition, even if they may only inconsistently accept the tradition from which these principles are drawn. In the face of this, it is striking that many management thinkers involved in ethics and spirituality still attempt to "reinvent the wheel" instead of engaging existing moral and spiritual traditions. These traditions are centuries older than the new managerial disciplines, and, unlike today's homemade ethical theories, have stood the rest of time.

Many of these management theorists would perhaps argue that none of the ancient religious and moral traditions allow for a genuine dialogue, and that is why they need to create their own models. They would be right to raise the question, for a true and vital (that is, living) tradition must be constantly developing through engagement with other traditions, the fruits of other cultures. However, when one considers how deeply the Christian tradition is established, with millions of Christian believers worldwide all participating in the dialogue between faith and culture in large and small ways, this argument can hardly be sustained. At the same time, however, the fruitful engagement with other traditions never comes automatically. Christian thinkers may be tempted by *triumphalism*, using Christian doctrine to repress "alien" cultural expression, or by *assimilationism*, defining Christianity's distinctiveness away in the search for a rapprochement with the prevailing culture. In this book, we take up that struggle regarding the culture and literature of management. In doing so, we ask questions of the Christian social tradition[4] and of the management literature to initiate and facilitate a critical dialogue. In doing this, we hope to help students, managers, and employees enter into this dialogue, so that they may find a means to overcome the "split personality" syndrome.

However, before proceeding to our three positive models for integrating faith and work, we need to inquire further into the nature of the "split personality" and the divided life depicted briefly above. Two paradigms that foster the divided life exist in present-day Western culture. We call their proponents "secularizers" and "spiritualizers." Our use of these terms is not meant to classify people, but rather to name positions that many of us take to our work. By dissecting these two models, we begin to understand that we come to this issue of faith and work not with a clean slate, but with many unstated cultural presuppositions, and that the engagement of faith with work is inescapable. We need to clarify how we relate faith and work, and to clarify what is at stake in their relation, both for the kind of people we want to become and for the kind of organizations we want to build.[5]

SECULARIZERS

It is often noted that we live in an increasingly *secularized* world, that is, a world that is tied to temporal and material things and disassociated from religious or spiritual things The secularization of society is not necessarily a denial of the truth or value of religion itself; it merely aims to confine religion to the private sphere of one's life. When so-called "public" issues of work or of politics arise, a secularized mind rules out the possibility that any insight might be gained from a religious perspective. Thus, secularizers argue that while religion can have "private" meaning for individuals, it cannot directly have "public" bearing on political or economic issues.

Tom Peters displays several characteristics of this secularizing attitude. The co-author of the former bestseller, *In Search of Excellence,* Peters' commentaries on various trends in business treat everything from individual creativity to commercial globalization. In response to the deluge of literature on the spirituality of management and leadership, Peters accuses proponents of blurring "the borders between church and corporation." Spiritual or religious language makes him nervous, he writes, because it makes larger moral claims on the organization than he considers reasonable. Peters complains, "It should be enough if I work like crazy, respect my peers, customers and suppliers, and perform with verve, imagination, efficiency, and good humor. Please don't ask me to join the Gregorian Chant Club, too." He concludes that religious or spiritual talk simply has no place in the "secular corporation."[6]

Peters' dismissive attitude toward spiritual meaning in the workplace stems from his own *belief* concerning what a corporation is. He explains that corporations are liberating institutions "aimed at enhanced competitiveness—which is the point . . . of our secular corporations." To be competitive in today's global markets, an organization must be productive and efficient, concerns about which, Peters insists, religion and spirituality have nothing to say. For him, if the corporation exists to enhance competitiveness, then, any rational person will say, as he says, "let's leave the Bible, the Koran and facile talk of spiritual leaders at home."[7]

Why is Tom Peters so averse to talk of religious and spiritual meaning at work? Why does he (in his words) "want to run . . . when the talk turns to the spiritual side of leadership"? If the engagement of faith and work leads to a distorted evangelism, or a misguided enthusiasm that threatens the freedom of others, we would agree that that sort of faith should be left at home. However, there is something deeper in Peters' reaction, which reflects a modern attitude toward religion, particularly in the West. Although he would probably not admit it, rather than defending an accepted notion of work, Tom Peters is proposing a diminished notion of religion, which is that *religion and spirituality have nothing to do with work, precisely because religion by its nature is a private affair, to be left at home.* It is ironic that Peters, who is so loudly "nervous" about managers imposing their religious beliefs on the corporation, preaches as dogma the belief that religion and spirituality have nothing to do with corporate life.

To say that religion and spirituality have nothing do to with public issues, with economics or politics, is to define a "religion" at odds with most actual religious life. Gandhi is credited with the view that those who say religion has nothing to do with politics do not know what religion means.[8] Similarly, to say that religion and spirituality have nothing to do with work and economic organizations is to "privatize" religion into insignificance.

Peters' misunderstanding of religion, his insistence that faith itself calls for its own relegation to the private spheres of life, denies the fullness of what faith means (and, for that matter, of what work means). His ideas reflect a popular sentiment in our culture that "reveals a decapitated faith," a faith without consequence in public affairs.[9] Yet, to accept the popular premise that religion and spirituality have no role in the corporate workplace is to accept the death of religion and spirituality as believers of most world religions daily live them, since most believers' understanding of "good" work is informed by their understanding of what is "true"—that is, spiritually sound—work.

From a Christian perspective, this brand of secularism subverts the essential, social dimension of membership in the church, and virtually imposes a divided life on believers who must work in that secular realm. For the church is no private enclave dedicated to the self-seeking consumption of "spiritual goods." It is at once the community and crucible of faith *within* which Christians are first transformed by Word and Spirit, directly or sacramentally, and *from* which Word and Spirit send them out to transform the world through the virtues of justice and charity. Moreover, as an incarnational faith—one which discerns God's presence in all human affairs—Christianity must call into question the culturally accepted distinction between the so-called "public" and "private" spheres of life, just as individual Christians must grow to recognize God's redemptive action in all their work. To call on Christians to divorce faith from work is to urge the church, as a body, toward scandal, and to foist on its individual members the absurd notion that they have a kind of public moral or political duty to shirk their religious duty. That Peters should propose such a thing as if thinking Christians could take them seriously is a measure of how poorly he understands Christian faith![10]

Contrary to Peters' assertions, many people seek a complementary relationship that may unite and *complete*, rather than fragment, two very important aspects of their lives: faith and work. As Bill George,

CEO of Medtronic Corporation, writes in response to Peters: "After all, we spend more time at work than in any other part of our lives. Shouldn't we find significance in our work and the opportunity to use our mind and feeling while appealing to 'the animating or life-giving principles' within us?"[11] If we discount our spiritual nature at work, we deny one foundation of our humanity, and blind ourselves to one of an organization's important foundations as well: the human aspirations of its members. As David Whyte puts it, "Whatever strategy we employ, or whoever we choose to speak with, we are eventually compelled to bring our work life into the realm of spiritual examination. . . . We simply spend too much time and have too much psychic and emotional energy invested in the workplace for us to declare it a spiritual desert bereft of life-giving water."[12] People do not want more separation and more privatization, and consequently less meaning; rather, they aspire to lives *whole* and clear of even a hint of fruitless division, of a "split personality."[13]

SPIRITUALIZERS

Unfortunately, the current spiritual awakening in the West does not always lead to a full engagement of faith and work. People can exclude God from the workplace by over-personalizing faith at the expense of examining the organization's policies and systems in the light of justice. For some, faith lacks an intellectual component that one can use to evaluate and, when necessary, to criticize the way corporations function. The tendency of some Christian managers to leave nuts-and-bolts practicalities to one side as they consider the relation of their faith to their work leads us to call them "spiritualizers."

While many Christian managers speak of the need for the conversion of our materialistic and secularized culture, they rarely address the larger structural problems within business that contribute to such cultural ills. Marketing plans that show little consideration for their wider effects, job designs that dehumanize workers, ownership structures that reserve wealth to the few, compensation policies that pay below family wages, work hours and travel policies that keep managers away from home, and downsizing policies that fail to address the problems of transitions: these practical realities are rarely addressed by spiritualizers from the point of view of their faith.

A classic case of this overly spiritualistic view can be found in the life and work of Andrew Carnegie (1835–1919). Carnegie was extremely generous with the money he made from his industrial endeavors. He once said that the person who dies rich dies disgraced. Yet, the way in which Carnegie made his money exhibited no principle beyond wealth-maximization. In his pursuit of increased efficiency and decreased costs, he broke unions, reduced wages, and increased work hours. While his contributions to concert halls, museums, and libraries enriched communities throughout the United States, and manifested Carnegie's personal, spiritual commitment to a "Gospel of Wealth," his managerial practices, influenced by Herbert Spencer's social Darwinism, were at their root unjust, and worked against the common good by creating distrustful, hostile and fragmented communities of workers.

A wall of sorts between how he *made* his money and how he *spent* his money permitted Carnegie to live by two incompatible standards: maximization of profit for the first, and promotion of the commonweal for the second. Philanthropy toward people whose lives have been dashed by one's business decisions cannot undo the initial harm.[14] As Thomas Schaffer and Robert Rodes point out, "If you spend the day on corporate takeovers and plant closings without thinking about the people you put out of work, you cannot make up for the harm you do by giving a woman free legal advice in the evening when her unemployed husband takes out his frustration by beating her."[15]

A survey of two thousand managers gives us further insight into the spiritualizers' view of faith and work. Fifty percent of the respondents claimed that religion "had a significant impact on business decisions." Those who regarded themselves as more religious reported that religion had a greater effect on their professional decisions than those who regarded religion less seriously. The managers influenced by religious faith saw their religious values manifested in prayer and personal virtue, such as honesty and generosity. Yet, when it came to issues such as plant closings, only 16% of the respondents perceived any religious or ethical connection to the issue at hand. They perceived plant closings largely in market and economic terms, and found the United States Catholic Bishops' criteria for morally defensible plant closings (adequate notification, employment transition assistance, fair compensation, etc.) irrelevant to their business practice. Ninety-five percent of the respondents wanted the clergy to abstain from any social critique of corporations.[16]

At root, spiritualizers avoid judging business policies in light of their faith by ignoring "structural sins"—those policies which begin as someone's personal failing, but achieve institutionalization and so become features of the organization, its permanent structural obstacles to human development.[17] For the spiritualizers, faith becomes so exclusively personal that public, organizational policies (such as compensation or marketing) seem to fall naturally, almost necessarily, outside its authority. Consequently, for spiritualizers business policies can be neither sinful nor "grace-full"; they respond only to strategic criteria of efficiency and profitability. (In chapters 4 through 7 we examine these policy questions.)

Throughout the Christian social tradition, a "spiritualizing," nonstructural engagement of faith and work has been criticized precisely because it fails to develop the whole person. Those in this tradition attend closely to questions of business policy—to wage rates, the distribution of ownership, job design, work conditions, distribution of decision-making authority, plant closings, and so forth—precisely because such policies and structures determine whether people can develop integrally through their work. Spiritualizers omit this dimension from their integration of faith and work, and consequently fail to be true to *a faith that does justice.*

Although they are professed and believing Christians, spiritualizers tend to become like the secularizers in practice. Religious faith serves them well as a source of personal meaning and help, but it has no place in organizational structures or decisions. In the last analysis, spiritualizers' public and private lives, their faith and their work, cannot be united. Both spiritualizers and secularizers inevitably end up living fragmented lives.

THE ROLE OF TRADITION AND THE UNIVERSITY: AN IMPORTANT INTERLUDE

Here we must pause to ask two pressing questions. The first is: *Why do secularizers and spiritualizers agree on a 'separation of work and faith' that decrees that to manage in light of one's faith is either to manage utterly unprofessionally (secularizers) or to overreach one's faith itself (spiritualizers)?* Although a full response to this question demands more space than we can give, the short answer is that both secularizers and spiritualizers embrace, though differently, a peculiar feature of modern culture, and that they do so largely because they have been taught to do so in universities.

The cultural feature in question stems from the liberalism of the Enlightenment. Its sources and its meaning for our own cultural conflicts have been the study (among other fascinating questions) of Alasdair MacIntyre, in a recent series of brilliant (and controversial) books.[18] Classical, liberal thinkers of the seventeeth and eighteenth centuries offered a solution to the problem of public conflict over first principles, a problem made acute by the division of Christendom. Beliefs, especially traditional religious beliefs, on the nature of the good life for human beings were to be declared matters of conscience—inviolable and private, beneath (or above) the concern of public authority or public debate—by *all* parties. Civic and economic life, it was felt, should be reestablished on the basis of common consent to sets of moral, legal and economic principles. These principles would command consent neither by appeal to existing tradition nor to any other "authority"; rather, these new foundations would express the findings of free rational inquiry, subject only to the direct evidence of human experience.

Instead of one set of compelling, rational principles, however, the liberal philosophy of the Enlightenment produced a number of incommensurable, conflicting principles, none of which included rational grounds from which to refute the others. In the realm of morality, for example, the Enlightenment saw Hume's utilitarianism, Kant's deontology, Smith's theories of moral sentiments, and so forth, all disagreeing—as every undergraduate student of ethics knows—right down to our day. So also in politics and economics, unfettered reason turned out to be the sovereign source of multiple, inconsistent sets of "first" principles.[19]

While failing to provide a consistent set of shared principles, the movers and shakers of the Enlightenment did succeed to a degree in marginalizing spiritual and religious concerns from public life. This is particularly evident in the changing university education of professionals. Over the past hundred years, professionals (including, recently, managers) have been initiated into their disciplines within a university setting. Many professional educators have increasingly sought to ground their fields within the confines of empirical claims.[20] This has brought them to identify the progress of their professional knowledge with the progress of the means of their trade, with its technical dimension—with the "How?" of things.

This focused search for the "How?" of things has produced a wealth of information and knowledge, and has revolutionized the world of work. There is little doubt that the benefits of technical progress make the world more habitable for humankind. Yet, technical know-how alone cannot answer the human question, "For what purpose?" Hence, as professional education, and in particular management education, becomes more specialized and technical, it also becomes more and more *instrumental*, that is, it becomes increasingly concerned with the features of organizations that make them superb means, and increasingly disposed to equate problem solving with the manipulation of organizational structure. It also increasingly shunts moral or spiritual explanations to the realm of "opinion," and accords them little value in the search for truth. The predominance of empirical methods, especially in the social disciplines (now known as "social *sciences*"), has greatly influenced the way in which the humane and social professions, which rely upon the research in those disciplines, are now taught.

Students of the professions in today's university can hardly escape exposure to the strong belief that organizational and societal problems, as well as their solutions, so far as they are knowable, are merely technical in nature.[21] That is to say, they can hardly escape the belief that professional knowledge solely addresses the means— the "How?" leaving to the realm of opinion the ends: the "Why?" and the "Wherefore?" Without a robust, deeply philosophical and theological discussion over "why we do these things," even the most thorough technical education recommends, by default, a privatized professional ethic. By default, the all-important question of ends collapses into merely a question of asserted or perceived interests, and inevitably of self-interest.[22] Ultimately, the view that professional knowledge can only be the technical knowledge of means generates the desperately shallow conclusion that institutions exist "to serve the private ends of individuals."[23]

By relegating religious knowledge to the domain of mere private opinion and mere personal practice, university education begins the process of isolating students "from the major force that connects most adults to the common good."[24] As Christopher Dawson aptly explained, "Instead of the whole intellectual and social order being subordinated to spiritual principles, every activity has declared its independence, and we see politics, economics, science and art organizing themselves as autonomous kingdoms which owe no allegiance to any higher power."[25]

The foundations of these autonomous kingdoms are laid in universities where academic disciplines are compartmentalized as "schools" and "departments" that suggest rows of storage silos rather than threads in a web of interconnected knowledge. For example, in their study of business schools in the United States, Lyman Porter and Lawrence McKibbin find that "the typical [business] school sees itself as pretty much a 'stand alone' operation; there is little interaction—or perceived need for interaction—with other academic units on campus."[26]

That spiritualists and secularists see little or no relationship between faith and work should not surprise us in light of their educational formation. Studies have shown that even religiously affiliated universities face the problem of a fragmented curriculum that "plagues personal integration and the development of moral maturity."[27] When it comes to their Christian faith, secularizers and spiritualizers are unable to give full expression to the integrity of faith and work, because they have assimilated a moral outlook from their education, and from the culture at large, that demands they privatize their faith and insulate their professional judgment from questions of common and of ultimate purpose.

But whose Christian faith is to guide? Catholic? Baptist? Quaker? I'm not so sure the philosophies of the enlightenment were unsuccessful as authors assert (p. 16). I think they did give us universal principles—honesty, integrity, etc

This brings us to our second question: *Why is the Christian (or another religious) tradition so important in overcoming the divided life?* We argue throughout this book that a more thorough understanding of the Christian social tradition provides a basis for authentic integrity; it helps develop the whole person through the integration of faith and work. The Christian social tradition promotes integrity by clarifying the goals or ends to which human beings are called to aspire, and the ways of living toward those ends that follow the Gospel. These goals and the means to them are synthesized in the Christian tradition in the *virtues*. Developing in virtue, that is, connecting ways of life with proper human ends, is a necessary part of developing fully as a human being. This tradition persistently asks the questions, "What is the *end* and purpose of my work?" and "How does this end influence *how* I work?" It examines how we focus our work toward a unified end or purpose for our whole lives. These questions are not merely private matters of self-improvement; they go to the heart of the human condition. The history of how wise women and men have grappled with them is a large part of the Christian social tradition.

Human beings are social beings. To affirm this is to admit that individuals lack in themselves the resources to integrate or unify their lives in a fully moral and spiritual way. Integrity—the integration of parts to a greater whole, that which makes us one—is a tall order that can only be achieved communally, in a community both of the past and the present. While many people associate the word "tradition" with old-fashioned and rigid thinking, with sectarianism and exclusivity, we contend, with MacIntyre, that tradition is a condition of human development. If we are to be, to know, and to appreciate more than the bare experience that a single, brief human life can afford, traditions are as indispensable as they are inescapable.

A vital tradition forces narrow and individualistic views on human success to answer to the best thinking of our forebears. As G. K. Chesterton explained it:

> Tradition means giving votes to the most obscure of all classes, our ancestors. It is the democracy of the dead. Tradition refuses to submit to the small and arrogant oligarchy of those who merely happen to be walking about. All democrats object to men

being disqualified by the accident of birth; tradition objects to their being disqualified by the accident of death.[28]

If we are concerned exclusively with the thoughts and practices of "those who merely happen to be walking about" we will become mere fodder for the fad-makers.

What makes for a vital tradition, one that promotes growth toward human wholeness? We believe that any moral tradition that cuts people off from religious and spiritual resources will result in a divided, and thus a stunted, life. Far from being dogmatic, rigid and confining, in our experience, the Christian social tradition insistently draws out our ability to see ourselves as part of a larger community, to discern common ground, and to recognize our differences. As expressed in many sources—Scripture, the traditions of religious communities, the teachings of bishops and popes, the reflections of theologians and other academics, the critiques of prophetic voices within (and without) the church, and the practice of faithful workers and managers— the Christian social tradition is big enough and broad enough to engage both managers and employees on a level that goes to the heart of their existence and self-understanding.

The rest of this chapter explores different models of engaging faith and work within the Christian social tradition. But before we move to these models of engagement, we should offer a few clarifying remarks about the Christian social tradition's relationship with contemporary western culture.

Hypothesis of Book — Our working hypothesis is the following: in order to overcome the contemporary privatization of faith, and the resultant splitting of lives and personalities over work, we need to reevaluate working life and its management in light of a tradition. Before we can do this, however, an objection could be raised. Is the Christian social tradition (or any other religious tradition) simply too esoteric, or too sectarian, to be of help to managers and employees? We may expect Christian managers to be in sympathy with our approach. However, part of our aim in writing this book is to make the Christian faith and its social implications more accessible, intelligible, and credible to our non-Christian contemporaries.

For at least three reasons, we believe our project deserves attention from diverse Christians (whose theological doctrines may, at times, be at variance with our own) and from non-Christians alike. First, in this era of multiculturalism in which we gradually learn to appreciate the richness of each other's traditions and cultures, a book that makes the Christian tradition accessible to non-Christians can only help to advance understanding and mutual cooperation. For example, we may point to illuminating connections between Confucian social thought and Christian social thought. Second, anyone living in the Western hemisphere is inescapably influenced to some extent by Christianity, just as those brought up in the Middle East are influenced by Islam and Judaism even if they are of neither faith. For those whose acquaintance with Christianity is casual, this book's reliance on the Christian tradition may illuminate the sources of familiar values or beliefs. Third, the engagement of the Christian social tradition with work provides an important basis for ecumenical discussion among Protestants, Catholics, and Orthodox Christians.

We are aware, of course, that the Christian tradition has at times been abused. Christians have sometimes fallen into "integralism," reducing every sort of knowledge to a subset of theology and all authority to a function of religion. As a result, talk of "engagement between faith and work" makes some people wary of being imposed upon by others' zealotry. Clearly, this integralism is an unacceptable basis upon which to propose an engagement of faith with work. An encounter with the Christian social tradition need not be an experience of the extremes of an integralism that distorts work or that of a secularism that distorts faith. The Second Vatican Council, one modern source for this tradition, clearly recognizes the legitimate autonomy of secular politics and economics, while at the same time maintaining that there is an integral relationship between the sacred and the secular.[29] Similarly, the Christian social tradition seeks an engagement of faith with work that respects and preserves the goods proper to each realm.

MODELS WITHIN THE CHRISTIAN SOCIAL TRADITION

Examining both the ways managers attempt to integrate authentically their faith and their work, and at the witness of the Christian tradition in its writings and in the lives of its saints, we can discern three main models of linking faith and work. Each model has advantages and disadvantages. While there may be occasional conflicts among their different proponents, overall, the models complement each other and each is necessary if the Christian tradition is to maintain a full and flexible connection with the management disciplines. The three models also represent quite broad categories, so that the actions or writings of some people may seem to cross the apparent boundaries between them. The important thing is not to categorize, but rather to recognize the possible diversity of methods while maintaining an authentic engagement between management and the Christian tradition. Unlike the two extremes of secularizing and spiritualizing that are rigid and limiting, the authentic forms of linking faith and work are diverse and flexible, able to encompass and support new circumstances creatively.

A MODEL OF IMPLICIT ENGAGEMENT: THE NATURAL LAW APPROACH

A *natural law model* presupposes that all human beings share some broad, basic notions of what is good and bad, of what ought to be blamed and what ought to be praised, and so on. This natural law model addresses Christian employees of those organizations in which the institutional culture excludes explicitly religious language. Christians in these institutions need not, and ought not, insulate their faith from their work. They are challenged to live their faith within an organization that is frankly secular in language and inspiration.

Of course, not all organizations are equally secular, or secular in the same way. There are secular organizations whose policies and practices are compatible with, or at least amenable to, Christian social principles (and the Christian social tradition will have much to learn from some of these). However, there are also organizations with policies or practices that stand in sheer contradiction to Christian social teaching, to Gospel values, or even to plain moral standards. Companies that pursue shareholder wealth to the exclusion of all other considerations, or that systematically overwork employees, or that market socially dubious or dangerous products, for example, are problematic for Christian managers and employees. Christian managers cannot suppose that they will somehow be unaffected by cooperation with an organization's abuses, even if they privately deplore them. People are formed in part by the institutions they inhabit. Managers and other employees whose responsible attempts at correcting a company's abuses are ignored or rebuffed may find themselves in moral and spiritual danger. If so, they should seek other work.

In practice, the natural law model supposes that Christian managers' own perception of the rightness or wrongness of their organizations' standards will suggest the contributions they can make to the ethics of the workplace. At the same time, because institutional pluralism means that the Christian message will have no special standing, this model supposes that Christian managers must communicate their principles in a vocabulary that anyone of good will can understand, regardless of religious or other belief.[30] Without emphasizing their ideas' origins, Christians must try to bring their tradition into the public sphere of work by demonstrating how their own concepts of the human person and of work provide a more robust basis to their understanding of work and management. Thus, a philosophy of management will supply the vehicle for a dialogue between faith and secular thought. All Christian managers in pluralistic workforces should keep before them this question: "How do I, as a Christian manager, live a life of Christian integrity in a culture where Christian language and inspiration are not the common language and inspiration?"

An incident from the early history of the United Nations may help to illuminate the role of the Christian manager in a secular and pluralistic setting. Jacques Maritain, the French Thomist who stressed the contemporary relevance of natural law theory, was involved in formulating the United Nations Declaration of Human Rights in 1948. The UN's agenda included the difficult task of inducing the members of an international body—many of whom professed inconsistent and even contradictory first principles—to agree on a common list of fundamental human rights. The members' differences notwithstanding, Maritain believed that their common human experience could lead them to agreement on "practical truths regarding their life in common." For Maritain, this achievement represented no small step toward human development across diverse societies. Had he insisted on a clear philosophical statement establishing the basis of human rights, let alone their theological basis, progress toward this genuinely common good would have certainly been derailed. Maritain credited the "neutral" language of practical truths, which we might call the common sense of human action, with enabling the diverse U.N. participants to agree, even though they could not agree on why they could agree! As Maritain explained, "We agree on these rights, *providing we are not asked why*. With the 'why' the dispute begins."[31]

Of course, Maritain did not recommend keeping the principles behind our actions obscure as a rule. He believed that understanding the first principles of our actions is indispensable to overcoming a divided life; we should only consent to actions we believe to be true to principle. Faith without an intellectual basis leads to the problems of both the secularists and spiritualists, but under conditions of pluralism, the existence of shared principle is precisely what is most in question. Agreement on what Maritain called "practical truths" is thus a condition of the very possibility that we may come finally to agreement on first principles, be they theological or philosophical.

For the Christian manager as for Maritain, the Christian social tradition, aided by the language of natural law, can supply terms which articulate the pluralist organization's human and moral character, and which rest directly on "convictions concerning actions."[32] For example, at the manufacturer Borg-Warner, Jim Beré (then CEO) championed a mission statement called "The Beliefs of Borg-Warner" (see the Appendix for the full text). While Beré's Christian faith influenced the statement's tone and content, "The Beliefs" avoided explicitly religious language and "they held to sound management analysis,"[33] so that Beré's coworkers of various faiths or of none could both grasp and accept them.[34]

In order to keep his statement intelligible and accessible, Beré had to start with beliefs that were already embedded in Borg-Warner's corporate culture and were familiar to the company's employees.[35] He had to relate those accepted beliefs to principles which at once extended and developed their meaning. The natural law language of human dignity, justice, and common goods (that is, shared purposes and achievements) served Beré well, both in overcoming the cynicism which organizational change often arouses, and in winning positive commitment from employees.

The strength of this natural law model is its ability to move people of widely differing beliefs into practical, active agreement with some essential aspects of Christian social teaching that reflect our shared human experience without labeling them "Christian." The natural law model attempts to make the pluralistic culture of the organization itself into the vehicle of principled, common action. Natural law concepts offer managers a language of principle that people within and without the theistic community can accept, albeit on different grounds.

The disadvantage of the natural law model—and it should not be underestimated—is that Christians who seek to change the secular organization may find that, instead, the organization has changed them. The richness of the interplay between faith and work is partly obscured, except in a fully integrated, theological vision. To the Christian worker, the natural law principles that can ground and guide corporate policy require theological grounding in their turn. Those who use natural law principles and natural law language risk their ideas being co-opted by competitive pressures running through the corporate culture and the larger economic system, with the unfortunate consequence that proponents of natural law diction may discover that their attempts to meet others on common ground may actually lead to the dilution or surrender of Christian essentials.[36]

Managers in pluralistic settings may be tempted to treat notions of personal dignity or the common good as if these were universal concepts understood by everyone in the same way. However, this is not at all the case. For the Christian manager, their meaning and their power to inform judgment depends upon their remaining vitally linked to the wider Christian tradition. Cut off from the theological context in which they were formed, Borg-Warner's "Beliefs" concerning human dignity and the common good are at risk of "death by slogan." They were meaningful to Beré, and through his work became meaningful for others, owing to the spiritual and intellectual culture already in place which inspired his efforts. The natural law model cannot sustain itself unless it is nurtured by a moral and spiritual culture grounded in a mature, theological vision.

Apart from suffering slogan death, isolated natural law principles may degenerate into a "checklist" of corporate "dos" and "don'ts." This makes principles into instruments, rather than sources, of corporate policy. Moreover, it may degenerate into a second, wearily familiar form of instrumentalism: doing things deemed "good" merely as a better way of doing well. Many companies proclaim their determination to put people first and to be good corporate citizens as the conclusion of a crassly materialistic logic: If we are good corporate citizens, we will make more money. Instrumentalism of this kind is unacceptable in the Christian social tradition, and ultimately fails on the practical level, as we will see in more detail in chapter 2.

Christian managers are not strictly obligated as Christians to introduce religious language into their workplace. Their first obligation in the workplace is to treat others justly and to respect others' dignity as the beloved of Christ. Nevertheless, Christian managers working in a secular environment must find means for sustaining their hold on the basic Christian principles that give their work meaning, and that form the basis upon which to build an authentic spirituality of work. Failing this, the Christian manager may suffer the alternative, that is, to be drawn into the compromised faith of the spiritualizers or the secularizers.

AN EXPLICIT MODEL OF ENGAGEMENT:
THE FAITH-BASED APPROACH

Many companies have been founded explicitly on faith-inspired values. Some are not well-known: Reell Precision Manufacturing, Lincoln Electric, and the Mondragon Cooperatives. Some, such as Herman Miller and ServiceMaster, have begun to attract attention, at least within the U.S., and still others, such as Dayton Hudson, Johnson and Johnson, Cadbury (and other Quaker companies), have long been household names, although their religious origins often have been forgotten. Many non-profit organizations active in education, healthcare, and the social services, were founded to serve religious purposes.[37] In their mission statements, their welcoming messages, and official symbols, these organizations reveal first principles drawn from

Christian revelation. Explicit, faith-based models often guide Christian entrepreneurs as they develop new businesses. That such organizations exist, and that still more are being created, suggest that contemporary Western culture, secular as it may seem, nevertheless remains open to explicitly Judeo-Christian principle and practice, both in business and among nonprofit providers.

One of the most difficult challenges that those who found religiously guided organizations face is to express their faith in the workplace in a way that is both forthright and specific without being rigid or exclusive.[38] Christian managers and entrepreneurs struggle over how to preserve the sources of their inspiration as their organizations acquire employees, partners, shareholders, suppliers and customers, who are not committed to that faith, even if they can respect it. In other words, "How does one articulate the unifying spirit of an enterprise inspired by one's faith while at the same time respecting the diversity that its success ushers in?"[39] At Reell Precision Manufacturing, for example, some employees expressed discomfort at the explicitly religious language in the firm's direction/mission statement (see the Appendix for the full text). These few employees (at the time, 95% of Reell's employees were expressly committed to the firm's spiritual mission) endorsed and accepted the moral convictions of Reell: Do What Is Right, Do Your Best, etc. (see "Our RPM Direction"), yet, they did not share the theological vision that inspired and grounded those moral principles. Like Maritain's colleagues at the United Nations, they seemed to be saying: *Let's not ask why we believe in this vision; let's simply agree on the actions themselves.*

In the ensuing discussion over the religious character of the mission statement, Bob Wahlstedt, then president of Reell, raised a critical question: How do you guarantee a commitment to the moral convictions of the company and the just treatment of stakeholders without articulating the spiritual vision that inspired these convictions in the first place? He believed that if all references to the core beliefs that had inspired Reell's purpose were withdrawn, it would be difficult to resist reduction of the company to a mere collection of various stakeholders' interests. Wahlstedt wanted to avoid a financial philosophy that focused only on wealth maximization for shareholders. He was also attempting "to move beyond the sterile chessboard of stakeholder analysis,"[40] and to lead the parties beyond their own narrowly defined interests in the organization and into the confidence that others would do the same.

For Wahlstedt and the other founders of Reell, the firm's mission is focused on human development, not because it will make Reell more profitable (although it may), but because each individual is made in the image of God and deserves to be accorded the dignity of that image. It is this transcendent belief that supports an organizational culture of moral confidence that each person will work for the other's good. For Wahlstedt, to lose that religious grounding would be to lose Reell's essential character; it would risk undermining its moral commitments. For Wahlstedt and Reell's other founders, the transcendent language found within the Christian tradition serves to strengthen their commitment to the common good by constantly calling them beyond the "minimum" of the law to the "maximum" of justice and charity.

Like our other two models, this model also has its weaknesses. It cannot be used as widely as the natural law model, and lacks the incisive critique of the prophetic model (to which we will turn presently). Yet, its major strength compared to the other two models is that where it is practiced, it represents a form of engagement that can bring the riches of the Christian faith to bear directly on daily working practice, creating the maximum possibility of developing a virtuous workplace.

It is important here to recall that not all business organizations are alike, and to avoid the error of treating a Reell and, for example, a Borg-Warner in the same way. Borg-Warner differs decisively from Reell in that religious commitment never informed its corporate culture. Just as nothing compels Borg-Warner to imitate Reell, there is no reason why Reell should follow the same path of development as Borg-Warner. Companies like Reell Precision Manufacturing reveal the real possibility of existing as an expressly Christian organization in the pluralistic world of work.

The Christian vision championed by Reell and similar firms mandates just treatment for all stakeholders and respect for the religious liberty of employees. It welcomes dialogue with the world, recognizing that insight and truth may come from many different sources. However, it also affirms that one can undertake an authentic exchange of views only if one has a clear understanding of one's own. It is a vision that attempts the integration of faith and work in both *deed* and *word*, in practice and in theory.

When a case on Reell, written by Kenneth Goodpaster, was discussed in an MBA strategy class, some students argued that faith and spirituality do not belong in the corporation. They argued that since we live in a diverse and pluralistic society, Bob Wahlstedt and the other founders of Reell should keep their religious beliefs strictly "private," and that they should eliminate all theological language from Reell's official documents.

There is an obvious irony in these students' responses. If, in the name of diversity and pluralism, Reell must forfeit its forthrightly Christian character, then "diversity" and "pluralism" have become mere code words for secular conformity. It is puzzling, Michael Buckley points out, "to see distinctiveness ruled out in the name of pluralism. Pluralism is precisely the admission and celebration of distinctiveness and difference on every level of unity."[41] The MBA students understood pluralism only in individual terms. They failed to understand institutional plurality. Reell, as a business institution, contributes to a wider pluralism and diversity among business organizations by remaining an explicit work of Christian faith, maintaining the firm's integrity through its unique set of principles.[42] Christian entrepreneurs do not have to become clones of their secular counterparts. In an age of diversity and multiculturalism, Christians can make the business world more diverse precisely by infusing their explicit, Christian beliefs into the work they do.

A Prophetic Model of Engagement

All Christian managers and professionals, whether they work in a Christian or secular organization, must face squarely the paradox of their vocation: *to be in the world but not of the world*. The prophetic model which addresses this paradox needs to be a part of Christian workers' daily encounter with the workplace, as well as the primary form of engagement with the world of work for churches, grassroots movements, and self-help groups of the poor and marginalized.[43]

From its Jewish roots, the Christian tradition has inherited a prophetic edge: *to comfort the poor and marginalized and to challenge the rich and powerful*. The prophets were often ostracized and persecuted during their lives, but later generations realized the value of their words, thus preserved, especially, in the prophetic writings of the First Testament and in the early Church Fathers. The prophetic voice of the church today still aims to recall people to just dealing, to living in love and, ultimately, to a right relationship with God. People who assume a prophetic stance often seem critical and harsh, but it is their awareness of what is at stake and their desire to bring people back to a realization of the need for a real engagement between faith and work that makes the prophetic model a crucial complement to the other two models, both within the work organization and within the church. Those making a prophetic stand often aim to shock people so they might stop and reconsider what they have unthinkingly accepted as normal.

The prophetic model by its very nature challenges and often gives rise to conflict between the "prophet" and those he addresses. For this reason, those within the organization cannot routinely use this model, as it would make their lives impossible. Yet, there are important circumstances when a prophetic stance is necessary in business itself, even though one may risk losing one's job. Sometimes "whistle-blowing" can be a form of prophetic engagement between faith and work, such as when products or working practices are dangerous, and attempts to persuade the firm to change things have failed. The case of the Ford Pinto car is an example of unchallenged bad design. People died unnecessarily as a result. A prophetic denouncement of what Ford was trying to do—saving money at the expense of safety—would have been an appropriate response from the professional engineers in this situation.[44] Whistle-blowing is only one form of prophetic critique, however. A prophetic stance can also work within the organization when those in the lower echelons of the organizational hierarchy challenge those higher up and more powerful to live up to their moral principles and "practice what they preach."

Tension is inevitable when outside institutions such as the church make public a prophetic critique of business. Tensions are unavoidable even as a result of the actions of managers trying to integrate their faith and work by means of the faith-based or natural law models.

Such tension was present at a meeting of the International Christian Union of Business Executives (UNIAPAC) that convened in Monterrey, Mexico. One of the sessions was entitled "Church/Enterprise Dialogue." The dialogue began with many Latin-American businesspeople expressing their dissatisfaction with the sharp criticism Latin American bishops had directed against modern corporations. The bishops had consistently criticized businesses for oppression of the poor, unequal distribution of wealth, horrendous work conditions, and environmental degradation. While not denying these realities, the business leaders felt the churchmen underestimated positive contributions of commercial businesses: creating new wealth, providing necessary goods and services, creating a tax base, and contributing funds to charitable projects. The business people felt that rather than call into question the business community's integrity, the church should support businesses' efforts to achieve a more equitable level of development.

Some of the bishops responded that they could not remain silent while business people who professed to be Christians oppressed large numbers of people. As Isaiah criticized the religious employers of his time—"Behold, in the day of your fast you seek your own pleasure and oppress your workers"[45]—the bishops must provide a critique of present-day oppressors. While the bishops admitted they did not have concrete solutions to corporate problems, silence on such matters would be a denial of their prophetic charism as bishops, a failing too common in Latin America's history. If they failed to speak for the poor and suffering, who would speak in their place?[46]

This exchange highlights both the strength and weakness of the prophetic perspective. Prophetic voices such as those of the Latin American bishops denounce the moral and social evils ignored by the spiritualizers. They announce the possibility of a new society, a more humane life.[47] The bishops confront the corporate world with the proclamation of God's Word: no exceptions, no excuses—justice must be shown to each and all. This is not triumphalism, but clear proclamation of what the Gospel requires of corporate life. The bishops are authentically *radical:* they get at the root—the *radix*—of the real conflicts that the Gospel calls managers to examine. God's ways are not always the corporation's ways, and Christian managers must realize that they must face the problem when the two conflict.

The prophetic critique has certain limitations. Prophets, such as the bishops, often emphasize the conflicts between faith and work, but they rarely discern means to achieve the new life they champion. Moreover, prophetic criticism presents a potential danger to the integrity of the Christian social tradition itself in its tendency to fall into moralisms, that is, ethical-seeming or charitable-seeming prescriptions which fail to consider the real, concrete complexities of the situation. As Joseph Cardinal Ratzinger, a bishop himself, has pointed out, "A morality that believes itself able to dispense with the technical knowledge of economic laws is not morality but moralism. As such, it is the antithesis of morality."[48] Prophetic criticism must be joined with competent technical expertise if it is to succeed in realistically promoting justice.

CONCLUSION

We have argued that both the secularizer and the spiritualizer signally fail to integrate faith and work authentically. Neither has the capacity nor the resources to resist the compromising effect that the world imposes. Because it distorts Christian faith, the secularizing model cannot be considered a legitimate way of bringing the Christian social tradition to bear on management theory and practice. This model is fundamentally opposed to any Christian understanding of the relation between a secular discipline and the realm of faith, and exists as the theoretical underpinning for the kinds of workplaces that cause people to experience the divided self or "split personality" we discussed at the beginning of this chapter.

The spiritualizing approach, on the other hand, often appeals to Christian managers. It makes demands on managers' personal virtue, and to that extent it undeniably promotes the engagement of faith with work. However, it is deficient in that it discounts the structural dimension of management and the need to develop technologies and forms of organization that promote the common good. While not as far from the genuine models of engagement as the secularizer, the spiritualizer neglects the other-regarding components of the work/faith engagement, such as organizational policies and strategies, and so limits it in an unacceptable way.

With the faith-based, natural law, and prophetic models in mind, we will continually return to the two questions we posed at the beginning of this chapter. First, there is the question of virtue and individual character: *What kind of person should I as a manager strive to become?* Second, there is the question of the common good and organizational character: *What kind of organizational community should I as a manager strive to build and to maintain?* These two questions address the twin pillars of Christian social thought: the common good, which we will discuss in chapter 2, and personal virtue, the topic of chapter 3. They address the keys to building economic organizations that deliberately promote the common good and human virtue through individual agents taking personal responsibility for shared purposes.[49]

Study Questions

1. How do we live a life of integrity; that is, how do we make ourselves whole?
2. What moral tradition have you been formed in? What are the presuppositions of your moral tradition?
3. Would you want to work for a company like Reell or Borg-Warner? Why or why not?

Video Suggestion

See The NewsHour with Jim Lehrer: interview with CEO of RJR Nabisco Steven Goldstone at http://www.pbs.org/newshour/bb/health/jan-june98/goldstone-1-29.html. The interview exposes the tensions between private and public moralities.

Course Suggestion

For some examples of how one might teach a course on the relationship between Christian social thought and management see http://www.stthomas.edu/cathstudies/cst/mgmt/curriculum/theo.htm.

APPENDIX

The Beliefs of Borg-Warner: To Reach Beyond the Minimal[1]

Any business is a member of a social system, entitled to the rights and bound by the responsibilities of that membership. Its freedom to pursue economic goals is constrained by law and channeled by the forces of a free market. But these demands are minimal, requiring only that a business provide wanted goods and services, compete fairly, and cause no obvious harm. For some companies, that is enough. It is not enough for Borg-Warner. We impose upon ourselves an obligation to reach beyond the minimal. We do so convinced that by making a larger contribution to the society that sustains us, we best assure not only its future vitality, but our own.

This is what we believe.

We believe in the dignity of the individual.
However large and complex a business may be, its work is still done by people dealing with people. Each person involved is a unique human being, with pride, needs, values, and innate personal worth. For Borg-Warner to succeed, we must operate in a climate of openness and trust, in which each of us freely grants others the same respect, cooperation, and decency we seek for ourselves.

We believe in our responsibility to the common good.
Because Borg-Warner is both an economic and social force, our responsibilities to the public are large. The spur of competition and the sanctions of the law give strong guidance to our behavior, but alone do not inspire our best. For that we must heed the voice of our natural concern for others. Our challenge is to supply goods and services that are of superior value to those who use them; to create jobs that provide meaning for those who do them; to honor and enhance human life; and to offer our talents and our wealth to help improve the world we share.

1. John Bowers Matthews, Kenneth E. Goodpaster, and Laura L. Nash, *Policies and Persons* (New York: McGraw-Hill, 1991), 184.

We believe in the endless quest for excellence.
Though we may be better today than we were yesterday, we are not as good as we must become. Borg-Warner chooses to be a leader—in serving our customers, advancing our technologies, and rewarding all who invest in us their time, money, and trust. None of us can settle for doing less than our best, and we can never stop trying to surpass what already has been achieved.

We believe in continuous renewal.
A corporation endures and prospers only by moving forward. The past has given us the present to build on. But to follow our visions to the future, we must see the difference between traditions that give us continuity and strength, and conventions that no longer serve us— and have the courage to act on that knowledge. Most can adapt after change has occurred; we must be among the few who anticipate change, shape it to our purpose, and act as its agents.

We believe in the commonwealth of Borg-Warner and its people.
Borg-Warner is both a federation of businesses and a community of people. Our goal is to preserve the freedom each of us needs to find personal satisfaction while building the strength that comes from unity. True unity is more than a melding of self-interests; it results when values and ideals also are shared. Some of ours are spelled out in these statements of belief. Others include faith in our political, economic, and spiritual heritage; pride in our work and our company; the knowledge that loyalty must flow in many directions, and a con- viction that power is strongest when shared. We look to the unifying force of these beliefs as a source of energy to brighten the future of our company and all who depend on it.

Our RPM Direction

RPM is a team dedicated to the purpose of operating a business based on the practical application of Judeo-Christian values for the mutual benefit of: *co-workers and their families, customers, shareholders, suppliers,* and *community.* We are committed to provide an environ- ment where there is no conflict between work and moral/ethical val- ues or family responsibilities and where everyone is treated justly.

The tradition of excellence at RPM has grown out of a commitment to excellence rooted in the character of our Creator. Instead of driving each other toward excellence, we strive to free each other to grow and express the desire for excellence that is within all of us. By adhering to the following principles, we are challenged to work and make decisions consistent with God's purpose for creation according to our individual understanding.

Do What Is Right We are committed to do what is right even when it does not seem to be profitable, expedient, or conventional.

Do Our Best In our understanding of excellence we embrace a commitment to continuous improvement in everything we do. It is our commitment to encourage, teach, equip, and free each other to do and become all that we were intended to be.

Treat Others as We Would Like to Be Treated

Seek Inspirational Wisdom by looking outside ourselves, especially with respect to decisions having far-reaching and unpredictable consequences, but we will act only when the action is confirmed unanimously by others concerned.

We currently manufacture motion control devices for a world market. Our goal is to continually improve our ability to meet customer needs. How we accomplish our mission is important to us. The following are fundamental to our success:

Co-Workers People are the heart of RPM. We are committed to providing a secure opportunity to earn a livelihood and pursue personal growth.

Customers Customers are the lifeblood of RPM. Our products and services must be the best in meeting and exceeding customer expectations.

Shareholders We recognize that profitability is necessary to continue in business, reach our full potential, and fulfill our responsibilities to shareholders. We expect profits, but our commitments to co-workers and customers come before short-term profits.

Suppliers We will treat our suppliers as valuable partners in all our activities.

Community We will use a share of our energy and resources to meet the needs of our local and global community.

We find that in following these principles we can experience enjoyment, happiness and peace of mind in our work and in our individual lives.

2

The Purpose of Business

Working Together for the Common Good

So guide us in the work we do that we may do it not for the self alone, but for the common good.
                    —Episcopal Book of Common Prayer[1]

WHY DO WE GO TO WORK? A DECEPTIVELY SIMPLE question, to which many people give the simplistic answer: to make money. But how many people *really* think that making money is the whole point of working? Many would refuse work that manipulated or exploited others, no matter how well paid. Many want their work to contribute to society, and expect great personal satisfaction from it. Some who claim they work "just for the money" may say so because they are unhappy in their work; they feel trapped in meaningless or dead-end jobs, but see no alternative way of supporting their families or of meeting their other obligations.[2] They would get out if they could and try to find more rewarding work. Their thinking is fundamentally different from that of people who hold on principle that the sole *genuine* purpose of business is to make money. People in the first group speak out of their own difficult circumstances, and their unhappy experiences underscore rather than contradict the contention of this chapter, namely, that "making money" is not the sole reason we work. Money-making is certainly an important part of why we are in business, but it is not the whole story.

In one of the most influential management books of recent years, *The Seven Habits of Highly Effective People*, Stephen Covey emphasizes the habit of "having the end in mind."[3] All too easily, our actions can become routine. We slip into doing things just because we are accustomed to doing them. Keeping the end in mind requires questioning why we do what we do. Habitually asking, "What am I working for?" makes us consider and clarify what is the end or goal of our daily work.

To be able to answer why we are in business, first we may need to ask a more fundamental question: "Why do we do anything at all?" The obvious answer to this question is that we do things because we want to gain something we do not have. For instance, we may want to supply our material needs or to develop our abilities. The fact that we never do anything without a goal in mind is something so obvious that most of the time we do not even think about it.

Aristotle, one of the foundational thinkers of Western civilization, called what we seek in order to fill a need a "good." It is for "goods" or "good things," and ultimately "the Good," that we seek and strive. Aristotle's definition of a "good," therefore, is something that perfects or fulfills a living being (such as a human being). He proposed that we are naturally inclined to pursue things that we judge to fit a certain measure or meet the name "happiness," and we apprehend it in a general (sometimes confused) way as our complete fulfillment, as "a state of being well and doing well in being well."[4] Accordingly, Aristotle identified happiness as the human end or purpose.

The main point here is the premise that everything we do is mo- ✗ tivated by a desire for something good. Without such motivation, we would not act. For Aristotle, rational desire is the *pursuit* of a thing following the *judgment* that obtaining or achieving it will contribute to complete fulfillment or happiness. From the context of the pursuit, the thing is called the "end," and from the context of the judgment, the "good."[5] Aristotle calls "*a good*," then, some one thing or achievement that appears to us under the color of "good" in the foregoing sense: that is, we judge something to *be* good, and to be *a* good, whatever seems capable of promoting *our* Good, happiness, whether by meeting our need or increasing our abundance. If there were a singular good apart from all others that could completely fulfill us, that would be *the* human Good and *the* human End in itself. Of course, in many of our human activities, even the simple ones, we actually aim simultaneously at more than one end. We eat a meal with our family to satisfy our hunger, but also to share conversation and conviviality with those we love. In these connections, our sense of our activity's oneness—or fragmentation—reflects whether one among our several proximate ends informs and orders the others.[6]

All this is relevant to management. In a business organization, we need to work together toward many goals, such as giving a fair return to shareholders, serving the customer well, and providing jobs and benefits for employees. Once we have determined which goods we are pursuing, we must decide how to *prioritize* them in a way that is consistent not only with "doing well" in the usual sense, but that is also consistent with promoting "being well and doing well in being well," that is, human fulfillment or happiness. Thus, to consider seriously our end in business, we consider two questions: "What are the goods that we pursue?" and "How do we prioritize these goods?"

In order to address these questions methodically, we have organized this chapter into three levels of analysis, which we call the "common good model of the firm." In the first level, we introduce the idea of a "hierarchy of goods." We distinguish and rank two types of good pursued through business activity: "foundational goods" (such as profits, capital, technology) and the other we call "excellent goods" (such as human development). In some ways, foundational goods, like profits or efficient methods, are the most important because they directly support the economic viability of the firm in a market environment. They are necessities, and they influence everything else the firm undertakes. In other ways, however, our own development and that of others are most important, because as ultimate motivations they inform and render meaningful all of our work.

We argue that in order to work well and to do well in working well, we must pursue both types of goods. To illustrate how the very character of the firm is affected by how each type of good relates to its ends, we use the first part of our analysis to critique the *shareholder model* of the firm. Under this model, the controlling purpose of the firm is defined as the maximization of shareholder wealth. We attempt to show that under the shareholder model, the firm is hindered from pursuing excellent goods, while conditions that make the workplace uninspiring, and even harmful, tend to be encouraged.

At the second level of analysis, we explore relationships among various meanings of *private*, *individual* or *particular*, and *public* or *common* goods. Historically, a common good is considered to be a human perfection or fulfillment achievable by a community, such that the community's members all share it, both as a community, and singly, *in* their persons. A common good, then, is *neither* a mere amalgam of private and particular goods *nor* is it a good of the whole that disregards the good of its members. While we argue that business is not responsible *for* the common good, it is, like all communities, responsible *to* the common good.

With these variations of "good" in mind, we offer a qualified critique of the *stakeholder model*, which understands the firm as a "balancer" (by means of negotiation) of the interests of its stakeholders. The stakeholder model, in its well-known forms, brings under management's purview the "interests" (as we understand them—the private and particular ends or goods) of the members of the groups connected to the firm. From this stem both its superiority to the shareholder model and the ground for our criticism: the stakeholder model does not limit the firm to the single end of promoting the shareholders' wealth, but neither does it makes room for the genuinely common goods of the firm.

At the third level of analysis, we raise the classical question of the distinction between real and apparent goods. This distinction is perhaps the most dubious to those raised and educated in modern Western cultures, who may profess, "Only I know, and only I have the right to say, what's best for me." Yet, we all know that people can and do sometimes bring a blunted or corrupted judgment to the task of discerning their own good. Hence, whatever the difficulties, we must attempt to draw and defend the distinction between real and apparent goods, or witness the collapse of the "common" in "common good" into a mere accounting of what most individuals most often, or "normally" pursue. At this level of analysis we discuss how we can try to ensure that the goods we pursue both *seem* and *really are* perfective or fulfilling.

A final introductory note is in order here. Of all the chapters in this book, we found this chapter the most difficult to write, and from the reader's perspective we suspect it will be the most difficult to read.

Yet, it is probably the most important chapter. Without the common good as an integral part of our thinking and action, we will fail in our attempt to integrate our work with the insights of the Christian tradition, and will all too easily fall into the trap of the secularizers or spiritualizers. Also, as the human community becomes more global, we may find that what we call the "common good model of the firm" will be more closely attuned to Islamic and Oriental sensibilities than are the shareholder and stakeholder models, which are forged in the individualistic liberalism of the modern West.[7] The model we present contains little that is specifically Christian, and so there is little that will impede dialogue or obstruct a practical consensus across religious lines. Such a dialogue and such a consensus must occur if we are to live at peace and flourish in the fast developing, one global community.

A Hierarchy of Goods: Foundational and Excellent Goods[8]

The distinction between the foundational and excellent goods of the organization is a simple and powerful one. A foundational good is one that we need in order to obtain other goods. As a good, it interests us principally as "good for 'X'," in employing it to gain something else. We would be likely to ignore it altogether if "X" were available without it. Many material and practical goods whose use involves their consumption, occupation or exchange—such as money, real estate, capital equipment—fall into this category. They are as necessary to the firm's functioning as are air, food and water to human functioning: without the latter goods, we die; without the former, the firm "dies."

Nevertheless, we might well say that breathing, eating and drinking are things human beings do (as do other animals), but they are not fully human actions unless they serve also to support the self-conscious rational and deliberate development that distinguishes human life from animal life—for example, friendship, personal cultivation, moral self-possession. These latter are among the "excellent" goods that we pursue more for their own sake rather than for the sake

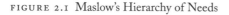

FIGURE 2.1 Maslow's Hierarchy of Needs

of eventual exchange for other things. They may, indeed, serve some further purpose in our lives,[9] but if so, they also impress us as worthy of pursuit in any case. Similarly, we can talk of an "ennobling" of foundational goods when they are incorporated into our pursuit of excellent ends. Thus, eating may become the exercise in civility called "dining," and four walls and a roof may be elevated to the art of architecture. In this way, both may become nourishment for the spirit, as well as sustenance or shelter for the body.

A useful model for prioritizing foundational and excellent goods can be found in Abraham Maslow's well-known "hierarchy of needs." As the pyramid in Fig. 2.1 illustrates, Maslow describes human needs in a hierarchical order, ascending from the physical to the spiritual. These needs include physiological requirements, safety, belonging, self-esteem and ultimately, self-actualization. While no one can live without taking nourishment in some form, self-actualized people do not live to eat. Similarly, while it is true that good health promotes and poor health obstructs nearly every sort of activity we may propose for ourselves, it is also true that we are almost certain to achieve nothing admirable in our lives if we put our health and our physical well-being first on absolutely every occasion. Thus, Maslow's hierarchy illustrates clearly that those needs which claim priority *as* needs, and whose claims on us are broadest, are nonetheless (and quite literally) "not the point."

Maslow's hierarchy of needs suggests an unstated corresponding hierarchy of personal fulfillments or completions—of "goods," in our idiom.[10] Here, Thomas Aquinas may be of assistance, with his suggestion that what we experience as "needs" are really the "tugs," "inclinations," or natural promptings to apply our intelligence to the service of our flourishing: self-preservation, procreation, participation in society, and the knowledge and the love of God. We can see in this hierarchy a framework for a rational structure of life for most human beings: work, marriage, friendship (personal and political), religious practice and experience—a fair list of the things we may undertake in our progress toward maturity.[11] We do not generate the good of wealth as an end in itself, rather we generate wealth as a means to obtain what we really want: for our families, for supporting others in need, and so on. While some people who focus on the good of financial success are motivated by pure greed, many more are motivated to achieve the good of security which those financial goods in part provide, and which is a foundation for relationships.

Similarly, behind the lists of organizational "needs," that is, of conditions thought to be necessary for corporate success in business, there is an analogous hierarchy of organizational goods, foundational to excellent. A practical example may help here. The founders of Reell Precision Manufacturing address the relation between foundational and excellent goods in a welcoming message to new employees:

> We do not define profits as the purpose of the company, but we do recognize that reasonable profitability is necessary to continue in business and to reach our full potential. We see profits in much the same way that you could view food in your personal life. You probably do not define food or eating as the purpose of your life, but recognize that it is essential to maintain your health and strength so you can realize your real purpose.[12]

The founders of Reell recognize that if the pursuit of profits and other foundational goods is not taken seriously, a workplace will soon collapse. Adequate revenue, adequate profit, efficient use of resources: these and their like are necessary ends—and real goods—because they are the necessary means to organizational survival. However, if an organization is dedicated solely to profitability, then even if it happens to pay good wages and to produce socially useful products, the organization is deficient. The clue to this deficiency lies in the phrase "happens to" produce socially useful products, etc., as opposed to "deliberately pursues" a socially useful product.

Profitability and efficiency are worthy goals because their realization is foundational to the development of the business as a whole. Nevertheless, foundational goods are not the full story. They account neither for the ultimate motivation of our work nor for the first principles of the business organizations in which we do our work. The excellent goods of human development are what really motivate us.[13]

Simple observation tells us that in no human activity, business or otherwise, can we easily separate efficiency from development; in every human action, we are at once forming ourselves and others and effecting results. The founders of Reell are among the contemporary business leaders who have recognized what their employees' (and their own) self-formation needs, and that it ought not be left to happenstance: that the "integral development of the person" is the most excellent—hence, the controlling—end of the organization. Since the acquisition of foundational goods is for the sake of gaining excellent goods, the goal of human development must inform all the ends for which the company is organized and run.

Thus, sound management involves planning and organizing for the promotion of excellent goods, as an integral part of the business operation. The competitive market environment guarantees that the pursuit of foundational goods nearly always seems urgent. Attention to excellent goods must, therefore, be deliberate and sustained in season and out, lest management's attention simply give way to the claims of foundational goods' urgency. More important, people do not develop steadily unless they are part of an organization that allows them to pursue the goods of their development in a regular and orderly way.

The distinction between foundational and excellent goods gives us the basis for a working definition: the organizational common good is *the promotion of all the goods necessary for integral human development in the organization, in a such way as to respect the proper ordering of those goods.*[14] We use the term "promotion" advisedly, for the organization's pursuit and realization of excellent goods, while it is necessary for human development, cannot ensure the development of individual persons. Like gardeners, managers may cultivate the conditions for growth, but these conditions cannot guarantee that employees will take advantage of them. Good organizational conditions can only provide the possibility for human development to occur.

A Critique of the Shareholder Model of Organizational Purpose

Thus far, we have sketched the first level of analysis of the common good model. Although we will develop this model further, we already have ground enough to begin our critique of the shareholder model.

In both practice and theory, the shareholder model has been largely influenced by the field of finance. Most financial theorists identify the firm's reason for being as the *maximization of shareholder wealth*.[15] Typifying this approach, Brigham and Gapenski's textbook *Financial Management* treats the ends of the organization in the following way:

> [M]anagement's primary goal is stockholder wealth maximization. . . . This translates into maximizing the price of the firm's common stock. Firms do, of course, have other objectives; managers, who make the actual decision, are interested in their own personal satisfaction, in their employees' welfare, and in the good of the community and of society at large. Still . . . stock price maximization is the most important goal of most corporations, and it is a reasonable operating objective on which to build decision rules.[16]

Brigham and Gapenski invite two important observations. First, both types of good are recognized in their account of the firm's purposes: management is expected to be cognizant of multiple ends, including the foundational or economic goods of shareholders (and the need to promote them by increasing the share price) and the excellent goods of employee and community welfare. Second, and more important, the relationship these authors describe between these two types of goods *inverts* the order we have so far discussed: maximizing shareholder wealth is the first and controlling end, while the excellent goods comprising employee welfare are regarded as foundational (or instrumental) goods, ancillary to the shareholders' economic benefit.

The difficulty with the shareholder model lies not with the goods the model includes, but with the way it *prioritizes* them. In other words, it controverts the second part of our working model of the organizational common good, which requires that all other goods be ordered in light of human development in the context of the firm. The shareholder model instrumentalizes the excellent goods of employee and community development and directs them to one foundational good—profits—and their effect on share price/shareholder wealth. By elevating shareholder wealth to the status of the ultimate good, the shareholder model in effect erects a "tyranny of foundational goods," inhibiting managers from considering more excellent goods except as instruments to increase profits.

An illustration may help here. Proponents of the shareholder model would probably join us in the conclusion that it is unacceptable to market malt liquor with a high alcohol content to young, low-income inner city males. We doubt, however, that they would conclude this because to market such a product in such a way would take unjust advantage of a poor, largely uneducated and vulnerable group of people. It is more likely that proponents of the shareholder model would caution against risking the firm's image, as marketing such a product in such a way would invite public criticism, tarnish the corporate image, and indirectly depress the share price.

Under the shareholder model, managers are not responsible to customers or employees in the same sense that they are responsible to shareholders. They may make demonstrations of respect for employees or customers one of the organization's goals, but not because of a belief in customers' or employees' human dignity. They will do this because they know attention to customer-relations or employee-relations generates greater gains (or ensures more effectively against loss) in shareholder wealth than indifference in these areas. Many proponents of the shareholder model maintain that although the excellent good of human development is an inseparable feature of vital business organizations, it is not to be pursued for its own sake, but only for the sake of maximizing shareholder wealth.[17]

"Well, so what?" the counter-argument may go. "Does motivation really matter all that much when we are all interested in results?" Here, we reach the heart of the matter: *the end that motivates one's actions makes the meaning and outcome of apparently similar acts quite different.*[18] One's intention shapes an action's outcome no less than one's actual efforts, and financial outcomes are no exception. Let's suppose that management is proposing an organizational change, and that they're calling it a chance for greater "empowerment." But strategically, management is really attempting to intensify employee workload as the prelude to selective layoffs. Can anyone doubt that employee attitude toward the change—and their subsequent performance—will be significantly worse than if management enacted the very same change with entirely clear, above-board intentions?

The view that employees, customers or suppliers ultimately matter to the firm only as factors influencing shareholder wealth is unlikely to replace any manager's ordinary habits and her belief that human beings are more important than business theory suggests. Consequently, most managers will continue just as Brigham and Gapenski describe them, that is, concerned for their employees' welfare as for their own; anxious that their firm both be, and be perceived as, a "good citizen." To the degree that the shareholder model is actually effective in her organization, however, a manager's personal and professional intentions may directly conflict, and the manager may well be haunted by T. S. Eliot's famous maxim: ". . . the greatest treason, [is] to do the right deed for the wrong reason."[19] Thus, under the shareholder model, managers may be called to pay a steep emotional and ethical toll to a corporate culture which tends to set organizational demands against personal integrity.

We can agree that we are all interested in results. However, to us the results that matter go beyond whether a profit is made. If the task of turning a profit sends habitually manipulative managers out to face a chronically suspicious workforce, we have a result that none of us wants to see day after day. Business practices have profound effects on society at large, and those social effects should be judged as seriously as the effects of productivity or profit.

Finance alone among the business fields explicitly defines the overall end of the business organization through the shareholder model. In doing so, it steps into the arena of social philosophy. It no longer merely articulates "value neutral" techniques, nor does it function as a descriptive science. Rather, it prescribes what a business ought to be, and that prescription is philosophically charged. We

argue also that it is deficient, because the *telos,* or purpose, it postu-
lates for business activity fails to respect the nature of human community. It thus promotes a business culture at odds with itself, for
businesses themselves are a form of community.

The strength of the shareholder model lies in its emphasis on the
foundational goods, its deficiency in its exclusive emphasis on those
goods. That it remains, as Brigham and Gapenski observe, the practical wisdom of most corporate organizations, demonstrates how
crucial it is to consider financial and similar instrumental goods as essential and *foundational.* As a foundational good, profit is a necessary
means to other ends, and serves as a regulator of organizational policy.[20] However, it must remain a *means to* and not the ultimate end of
business activity.[21]

Distributing Goods: Common and Particular Goods

So far, we have presented excellent and foundational goods as the initial elements of the common good model. Now we turn to another
and more difficult question concerning the firm's purpose: *How do we
promote both the good of each person in the firm, the good of the firm as a
whole, and the good of the wider society of which the firm is a part, all at
the same time?* At this level of analysis, the governing issue overall is
the *relationship* among the ends and goods of individuals and the
ends and goods of the various communities to which individuals belong. Within the firm, if there is too much emphasis on the good of
the individual, we risk rampant individualism through the loss of a
common mission, destructive internal competition for personal rewards and benefits, and at best, erratic performance. Conversely, if
there is too much emphasis on the good of the organization, we risk
bureaucratization, hostility to individual initiative and innovation,
and at best, sluggish performance.

We will address this question in three stages. First, we will discuss
how different goods are shared or distributed, either through "participation" or "allocation." Second, we will discuss possible priorities among participated and allocated goods. Third, we will discuss
how pursuing a private end (such as one's personal good within the

organization, or the good of the business organization in the wider community) can be linked to the promotion of the public or general common good. Throughout this discussion, it is important for the reader to remember that the meaning of "common good" varies analogously,[22] depending on how people share the goods they attain cooperatively, and on the kind of community through which they pursue and attain them.

1. Distribution of Goods—Participation and Allocation

By *allocation* we share a pizza, a bench at the museum, profits from a product or service; by *participation* we share a conversation over pizza, the view from the museum bench of van Gogh's "Sunflowers," the fairness of the distribution of the profits. *Allocation* is the sharing of a whole by dividing it into, and distributing, its parts; *participation* is the sharing of a whole by its distribution as a whole.[23]

From experience, we know that consumable goods that exist as "amounts"—water, food, money—can be made common to the members of a community by division and allocation. It is also possible that a good, which is in itself a mass and not divisible into parts, may also be made common by allocation. Our figurative museum, for example, may stand as a genuine common good if access to it is distributed so that all in the community are able to enjoy its benefits (for example, with reasonably priced admission, "free" days, etc.). For similar reasons, roads, aqueducts and other such community utilities are often called common goods when their benefits are made accessible to all equitably.

Knowledge is perhaps the best example of a good that is distributed by participation, rather than by allocation. For example, if I explain to you how a piece of software works, and you grasp my explanation, we both participate in this knowledge while it remains whole to both of us. It is not diminished in being distributed, and is thus shareable without limit. Those who participate in it do not so much acquire a material possession, but rather a personal enrichment, because goods distributed through participation typically touch us in who and what we *are*, rather than in what we *have*.

Because participated goods can be distributed among indefinitely many (and in principle, among all) persons, benefiting all wholly, they are sometimes called "common goods" without qualification. By the opposite token, allocated goods are sometimes called "particular goods," to emphasize that they can go as a whole to one owner only by being denied to all others. Nevertheless, participated goods and allocated goods are alike in this: they must be *made* common by deliberate means. The deliberate, cooperative *pursuit and distribution* of various goods for the sake of human fulfillment is the basis of community.

2. Holding Goods in Common—The Priority of Participated Goods

Communities that are at least as complex as a family will involve both participated and allocated goods. It is a mark of community that its goods are allocated according to some consistent standard of distributive justice, which (as a virtue) is itself a participated good. As a corollary, then, it is also a mark of community that its members' participation will determine how goods are allocated to them. In other words, a genuine community of allocated goods depends upon its prior history as a community of participated goods.

The reason for the priority of participated goods in a community is that equitable allocation depends not only on the will to allot to each whatever is owed to each (the formal virtue of distributive justice), but also on *knowing* what or how much is owed. In business exchanges, this knowledge is a matter of contractual agreement and bookkeeping, but in other cases we allocate according to need and contribution, that is, according to the distribution of participated goods: For example, a teenager's access to use of the family car (an allocated good) will depend on her sharing in family standards of responsibility (a participated good); a college student's place in an upper-division mathematics course (an allocated good) depends upon sufficient knowledge of integral and differential calculus (a participated good).

3. Promoting the Common Good—The Role of Private Ends

Community may be shaped by the *comprehensive end* of attaining, by and for all, the good life of human fulfillment.[24] The community shaped in this way is political, and is known by an array of suggestive names—civil society, the commonwealth, the commonweal. Its common good is often called the public good, which does *not* subsume the goods of individual citizens, but as gesture toward the classical Latin concept, *res publica*, which interprets the public good as "what belongs to the whole people."

A particular community may also be shaped by ends that are less than comprehensive, and reflect specialization in meeting human needs and in the promotion of human growth. This is all to the common good. One measure of a commonweal's success is its expansiveness coupled with a richness in the texture of life, so that one feels there is no facet of potential human excellence which is not the subject of someone's special attention. It is in the light of their contributions to the reach, abundance, and intensity of the common pursuit of the good that we speak of the *educational community*, the *arts community*, the *business community*, and so on.

Nevertheless, whatever their size or influence and whatever the scope of their contribution to the commonweal, communities of special, limited ends are essentially private. We use the term "essentially private" advisedly, and in a sense best explained through an examination of its origins. Like "public," "private" is from the Latin: *privatus*. In Latin, *privatus* contrasts with *publicus* in much the way the English "private" contrasts with "public." However, the Latin word carries a more precise meaning that is sometimes lost in English. *Privatus* also signifies a "lack" in both the positive sense of "freed from" and in the negative sense of "deprived of."

Private ends are partial, and as guides to action they tend inevitably to encourage partiality in those who pursue them. They ignore the comprehensive perspective that is part of political wisdom or prudence and is the mark of successful statesmen and their legislation. Yet, those who pursue private goods, whether in common or individually, pursue them as participants in common, public goods, in the institutions of ownership, in the prosperity of the commonweal, in the security of the laws, and so on. Without these common goods, an individual or a corporation could not pursue its private good. To conceive of personal goods, or the goods of an organization, without reference to their dependence upon the public good is simply incorrect and ignores the reality of the situation in which every person and every business functions.

Still many do try to deny this reality. To accept it involves accepting the responsibility to respect and promote these common goods, and not merely to exploit them for private gain. All too often in business, one can find examples of people who avoid the responsibility of promoting these common, public goods while maintaining their right to avail of the opportunities that such goods give them. For example, George Soros made a billion dollars speculating against the British pound, leaving the British economy severely damaged, but he denied any responsibility for the wider effects of his actions:

> I am sure that speculative activities have negative consequences but I never think about them and cannot afford to think about them. If I stopped doing some things because of moral scruples, I would have to stop being a speculator. I feel no remorse whatsoever about having won money when the pound was devalued; I did not speculate against the pound to help England or hurt her; I did it to earn money.[25]

In the end, the actions of people like Soros—those with great power but no sense of the responsibility that must accompany great power—weaken and undermine the social fabric that holds society together and makes private gain possible. If too many do as Soros did, society would soon collapse into anarchy, and the pursuit of private good would be severely curtailed. For the sake of both common, public goods *and private goods*, private ends must be recognized and pursued because of their essential participation in the common good.

Considering this, one must ask, "What further good can be expected of the firm than that it obey the letter and spirit of the laws, and in addition serve as a vehicle of private, personal ends, including those of its owners and employees, as well as those of its suppliers, creditors, customers?" The concept underlying this question includes an assumption that the firm exists to lend itself to private and public ends—that it is itself only a useful good. We should not, then, worry ourselves over a supposed "organizational common good," but over whether the firm's activities are consistently of service to the real communities whose interests the firm's activities influence. In this view, "integral human development" is not considered a purpose of the firm, nor is it considered a participated good that shapes the firm into a community. It is, instead, an aspect of "working conditions," i.e., one of the many interests of the firm's employees, which they may use to bargain or negotiate against other interests as a kind of private currency.

The view of the firm as a locus of public concerns, and especially of private interests, underlies the stakeholder model to which we will next turn. Our qualified criticism of the stakeholder model must be coupled with a strong argument that the firm is or can be an authentic community of ends and goods in itself.

We have already touched lightly, but repeatedly, on a point which now bears emphasizing: business organizations are standing witnesses to what Yves Simon has called the "antinomic" or the unruly character of "intermediary ends," that is, objects of decision and action that count as ends in one respect and means in another. The distinction we drew earlier between the foundational and excellent goods of the firm is a case in point. Managers must treat foundational goods as necessary ends, but they must do so remembering well those foundational goods' further function as a means to realizing excellent goods. At the same time, the excellent good of human development must be pursued with an eye to its effects, such as its effect on productivity; that is, it must be regarded in the context of means. Harmonizing these various ends, and the yet more complex relations that make up business activity, is a task that cannot be reduced to a set of simple rules (Gapenski's and Brigham's wonted "decision-procedures"); nor can it be eased by a consensus reached by negotiation (the "balancing act" of stakeholder theorists). It requires a kind of wisdom, the ability to see the firm's dynamics as a whole, and in the realm of shifting markets. It requires the self-possession to act temperately, justly, and courageously on one's best judgment. It requires managerial virtue, the subject of the next chapter.

Seen in this light, our initial question becomes less thorny: Why can't the firm be treated as something simpler and less demanding—something more manageable—than a full-fledged community of work? The answer, of course, is that it can, and very often is. The stakeholder and especially the shareholder models of the firm prevail, and they do not wholly fail to advance the common good.[26]

Are business organizations, based on whatever model, able to move toward a community of work? A positive answer seems to be twofold. In the first place, however its purposes are conceived, no business organization thrives when its members see themselves as, and perform as, mere functionaries. Organizations thrive by gifts of human excellence—skill, industry, and a spirit of cooperation that does not stop to count costs. These gifts are consistently and freely elicited when the worker knows he is working for himself, when he experiences his gifts of skill, industry, loyalty as "communions," as contributions to a common purpose that return to him as participated goods. So generous is the human spirit that almost any organization can count upon some degree of spontaneous community, and enjoy its gifts in some measure.

The common good model rests on the principle that business organizations, like individual persons, ought to cultivate their excellences deliberately, and offer them as their unique contribution to human growth.[27]

Thus, in the second place, the provisions mentioned above are themselves matters of organizational choice; firms will choose them if they can be judged consistent with the organization's financial necessities. That judgment must rest in turn on a careful review of particular provisions a firm can make for a community of work. Consequently, the present argument, then, depends upon a whole series of arguments on the roles that wages, structures of ownership, job design and marketing can play in promoting human development through a community of work. We will turn to these arguments later in the book.

4. A Qualified Critique of the Stakeholder Model of Organizational Purpose

The stakeholder model is somewhat more difficult to characterize than the shareholder model. Its proponents do not entirely agree on what criteria one must meet to qualify as a stakeholder or precisely what sorts of claims stakeholders may make on the business organization.[28] Nevertheless, the stakeholder model differs clearly from the shareholder model by raising groups with stakes in the firm's activities, such as employees, suppliers, or even local residents, to the status of quasi-shareholders. In the shareholder model, management has a fiduciary relationship to shareholders alone, but under the stakeholder model, management's relationship extends to multiple classes of stakeholders.

The stakeholder model is indebted to contemporary rights theory, which supports the view that the property rights traditionally invoked in support of the shareholder model are intrinsically limited. Recent examinations of property rights, for example, conclude that the right to use property includes the obligation to refrain from "harmful" uses.[29] Of course, such an obligation supposes the right of some non-owner to demand that an owner desist from uses alleged to be harmful. Members of employee, shareholder, creditor, consumer and similarly interested groups are regarded as rights-bearers in this sense, and their diverse claims must be respected by the organization's management.

Proponents of the model also argue more generally that today's large business organizations wield such power that no one interest (such as the interest of shareholders) can be allowed to dominate in the determination of its purposes. Rather, management must weigh the interests of multiple constituencies. Because stronger versions of the stakeholder model propose that management's duties to a variety of stakeholders are the same as those that management has traditionally been thought to owe to shareholders alone, the stakeholder model is sometimes called the "multi-fiduciary model." As stated in a Council for Economic Development (CED) document, which represents the stakeholder perspective, the manager is a "trustee *balancing the interests* of the many diverse participants and constituents in the enterprise."[30]

From the perspective of the common good, the stakeholder model is clearly preferable to the shareholder model, since it at least permits expansion of the concept of organizational purpose to include promoting human development. As a model, it permits the articulation of and recognition of human aspects, such as livable and equitable wages, distributive structures of ownership, human-centered job design, and so forth. Nevertheless, as we have already argued, the model invites an inadequate description of organizational purpose. First of all, it may fail at the first hurdle, as the shareholder model does, if it defines its organizational purpose as the maximization of stakeholder (as opposed to shareholder) wealth. In this situation, it would prioritize foundational over excellent goods and invert the proper order of these goods no less than the shareholder model.

Even if the stakeholder model does not invert the hierarchy of goods, it may be deficient by treating all goods within the organization as particular goods for allocation. We saw this in the characterization of the manager as a "balancer of interests" in the CED definition cited above. The idea of balancing interests against one another is practically impossible unless all are individual, independent, and comparable. That is, the stakeholder model cannot account for the distinct character of participated goods or for their role in shaping organizational purpose and in motivating the allocation of particular goods.[31]

The stakeholder model discounts participation because it accepts in principle an individualistic view of the human person. The model supposes that stakeholders are "interest maximizers" similar to shareholders under the shareholder model. Managers are enabled to "balance" interests when stakeholders advance them in an "enlightened" fashion. If each stakeholder pursues his own interest in a manner that also advances the interests of all others, the interests of all will be maximized. What results is a strategic calculus by which managers-as-referees attempt to maximize the sum total of particular goods for each stakeholder. The good of the firm, that is, the good that one expects of the firm, is just this maximizing effort.

Since the stakeholder model views the organization as a group of autonomous individuals who affect or are affected by the organization, an analysis of it begins from what the person *has* as a "stake" in the company. By contrast, the common good model begins with who each person *is*—a social and spiritual being whose development is intimately connected to the good of others through a complex of shared ends. Because the stakeholder model begins with *having*, and not with *being*, its view of the corporation tends to be utilitarian.

That is, it presumes that human beings are united only through external things they can exchange.[32]

It is important to remember that the defining feature of the common good, which sets it in opposition to any form of utilitarianism, is that it is realized "among those who pursue it . . . [as] a common life of desire and action."[33] Because of our social nature, we develop authentically only through our participation in an array of communities: family, school, church, commonwealth, *and work*. This requires "a firm and persevering determination to commit oneself to the common good."[34] If we fail to align our pursuit of our personal and private good to a common life, we are not left as neutral "nonparticipants," but are rather left in the fragmented and immature position of the husband who believes in his "growth as a man" apart from his growth as a husband. As Aquinas put it, "[A] man's will is not right in willing a particular good, unless he refer it to the common as an end."[35]

Conversely, when people begin to align their particular goods to a common life of desire and action, they begin to establish relationships that are real communions and not merely contracts or mutually self-serving exchanges. They bestow on one another "'communications' or signs aimed at producing 'communions'" such as the virtues of solidarity, justice, loyalty, trust, patience, and so forth.[36] In these communions, which we call a "community of work," an employee develops as a whole person and not merely as a functional part.[37] These communions do not happen automatically or through some applied technique; rather, they happen through a lifetime of deliberate and intentional interpersonal relationships—that is, of "me" relating to "you" as an other.[38]

While we find the stakeholder *model* problematic as an answer to organizational purpose, we view the stakeholder *analysis* as critical to the common good. It has enormous value as an exercise for moving a firm's management toward a detailed, circumspect appreciation of the extent and variety of the ends that are implicit in the firm's activities. Moreover, the stakeholder model itself points to a real risk that could accompany the implementation of the common good model, that is, a distortion of the idea of community which would hold the community above the person, and a demand for individual service to a specious common good which could never be distributed.[39] Historically, nations have abused the idea of the common good outrageously in this fashion. Josef Pieper, for instance, writes about his political coming of age in Nazi Germany: "The new masters' slogan, 'the common good before the good of the individual,' which was proclaimed at all turns and like everything [the Nazis] took up, was quickly worn-out and denatured, rapidly unmasked itself as a mere pretext and a propaganda trick."[40] However, apart from such abuses, the notion of the common good entails the primacy of the whole (the community) over the parts (the community's individual members) in a way that the stakeholder model avoids. The common good model must face this problem squarely. In one sense, individual persons are ends in themselves, and their development is an inherent good, not to be sacrificed to anything else. Yet, insofar as the individual person's development and fulfillment follows from participation in the common good—in fact, *is* a participated good—the community may call upon the individual to make outright sacrifices for its preservation.[41]

One would have to take individualism to a doctrinaire extreme in order to argue that personal sacrifice for the sake of the family is an unjust imposition. Few would argue that blood is thinner than water. But is citizenship thicker than blood? Families who have sacrificed husbands, sons and, more recently, wives and daughters to defend the declared interests of the political community are a tacit argument that it is so. If the firm constitutes a genuine community, it possesses analogous authority to require of individual employees the sacrifice of redundancy or downsizing, *if* that measure will preserve the firm as a whole. We should add that, downsizing could never be justified as an ordinary business practice. It would represent the alternative of last resort, and so—like the resort to war—would be hedged with extraordinary safeguards.[42]

Finally, we must point out that the stakeholder and common good models may be closer in practice than they seem in theory. Jean-Loup Dherse has suggested to us that the stakeholder model can be conceived as a transition to the common good model, since it rejects the narrow "mechanism" of the shareholder model and insists that the firm's management "navigate" by a deliberative process, rather than by adhering to financial formulae. The common good may appear to be a more profound development further in the direction in which the stakeholder model is already moving. Bob Wahlstedt has suggested that the idea of the common good supplies the "rootedness" that prevents stakeholder analysis from "drifting" into utilitarianism and individualism.[43]

REAL AND APPARENT GOODS:
GOD AS THE ULTIMATE COMMON GOOD

In the introduction to this chapter, we put forward the premise that human beings act always for the sake of an end they judge to be desirable, that is, "good" in the simple sense that achieving it will improve their lives. We argued further that we are naturally inclined to seek our own fulfillment or perfection as "happiness"; our wills are designed to do so. Properly speaking, we do not choose happiness; rather, the desire for happiness shapes our choices; and they are our choices. We are the authors of our actions: we plot them; we execute them. In plotting them, we rely on our judgments that a certain thing is good, and that having or realizing it will in some way fulfill us.

We are concerned here with two aspects of our situation: First, to aim at the good is a necessary condition of right action, and to aim we must first *see*: our judgment that an end is good precedes and informs our actions. Second, we make mistakes in judgment. The first aspect, gaining clarity about what is good for us, is our overriding concern here. But we must begin from the second concern: we make mistakes; therefore, we must learn to distinguish the real from the apparent good.[44]

Conceptually, the distinction between the real and apparent good could not be simpler. A real good is something we pursue in the belief that achieving it will perfect or fulfill us, and which really will perfect or fulfill us if we achieve it. An apparent good is something we pursue under the belief that it will perfect or fulfill us, but which, if achieved, would do neither. In practice, we need to distinguish the real from the apparent good *for ourselves* in every action we contemplate. The need is real; for if we do not make the distinction in judgment before the fact, we are likely to suffer its consequence *as* a fact.

The judgment that an end really will (or will not) fulfill us in some respect is *for* ourselves: it must be drawn in the light of who and what we are. It is also *of* the end: it must be drawn according to our knowledge of the end as something with attributes that can serve us. Thus, to say that we can be mistaken in our judgment about whether a thing is good for us or not is to say that we can fail in self-knowledge, or that we can fail in the knowledge of our object. The possibility of failure in the second respect—that of fully knowing the thing we judge—is something most of us would probably concede. But the possibility that we may fail in our own self-knowledge, and the consequent possibility that we could be *corrected* in our self-knowledge may invoke resistance.

First, let us examine the easy case: What sort of situation would involve a failure in knowledge of our object? Not so long ago, cigarettes were widely regarded as a good thing: their use was (and remains) pleasurable, and perhaps for that reason smokers attributed other benefits to them. They aided digestion and concentration, helped in weight control, and so forth. As we now know, they also contribute to heart disease, emphysema, cancer, and stroke, to name just a few maladies. No one considering smoking now can pretend to do so rationally without making their health effects the primary consideration. A failure in knowledge of our object has been corrected with new knowledge.

The second case is not as easy. Failure in self-knowledge takes personal forms familiar to us all. We may be blind to our faults of character; we may exaggerate our strengths. These are morally serious matters, but their role in our judgments of ends is secondary to the role of our beliefs concerning what it is to be a self-possessed, free agent. Let us examine the following careful formula: to judge that an end is good for us means first to judge that it is fulfilling *of the kind of agent we are*. That phrase, "the kind of agent we are," presides over a world of disagreements: religious, moral, and political. We have already encountered some of these at the roots of competing models of the firm: an autonomous "interest maximizer" is a very different kind of agent than a conscious participant in the common good.

The fact of disagreement over the kind of agent we are is less important than how we face that fact. It is in this realm that a shiver of apprehension so often greets talk about the distinction between the real and apparent good. For if the distinction is itself real, there are some ends of action which, in themselves and independently of our judgment, are ends that perfect or fulfill human beings. Furthermore, if there are such ends, then with them, the kind of agent we are is given. Moreover, if the distinction is real, then it is possible to judge that a bad end is one that we think should fulfill the kind of agent we *take* human beings to be, yet human beings will be unfulfilled, even harmed, by its achievement. Thus, the distinction between real and apparent goods suggests insistently that our disagreements over the kind of agent we are may not reflect the choices of free and autonomous individuals so much as it suggests a set of correctable mistakes.

How shall we face this suggestion? We could face it by asking: Is it true? Are there ends whose pursuit teaches us "the kind of agent we are," ends whose capacity it is to perfect and enlarge our ability "to be well and to do well in being well"? To pursue the question, we must be willing to risk our beliefs in argument and study (chapter 3, on virtue, will pursue the question). We could also dismiss the suggestion with the culturally approved formula, "Only I know, and only I have the right to say what's good for me." We could also simply turn on the television and ignore the issue.

Those who are moved to dismiss the suggestion may sense something coercive in it. In particular, they may perceive a gathering attack on their freedom of choice. We believe that it is not. For even if the question were decided, it would remain possible for us to judge correctly that an end of action would fulfill or perfect us, and yet choose not to do it; and it would remain possible for us to judge correctly that an end would work to our detriment, yet choose to pursue it. The distinction between real and apparent goods concerns the good as the object of judgment, the good under the scrutiny of truth. Choice concerns the good as the object of active desire, as good and as ours. A world in which the real good is distinguished from the apparent is still a world in which people choose to smoke. If those concerned with freedom of choice have any quarrel with us, it will be with our later discussion of virtue.[45]

In the wake of so much philosophy, we will proceed further into this inquiry of the good *for us* with our feet on the ground, our hearts open, and our heads erect.

First, with our feet on the ground, we can say that the good is an everyday thing. That is because goodness comes to us embodied in ends, we meet it in the particulars of our lives. Marriage and family, the classroom, civic affairs, our leisure and our work are all sources of the good. Our role is, in part, to pay careful attention to the everyday ends we pursue through these sources and to consider our reasons for prizing them. Whatever consoles our spouse, delights our children, and aids a coworker will repay our reflection and attention.

Second, with keeping our hearts open, we can say that the ends that are most fundamental to our good are in harmony with our natural inclinations. For this reason, real joy is a token that we have hit on the good.

Third, with keeping our heads erect, we can say that in everyday human life circumstances will arise in which our end and good are obscured. These circumstances may be a test, but they are not only the test of the steadiness, or the clarity with which we judge our good. The test in the latter respect is our perseverance at the task of enlarging whatever measure of appreciation for the good we have already attained.

Finally, a clear sense that the natural and temporal goods—the goods of this world, however complete in their place—are still not good enough for us should temper our pursuit of them. Prayer, worship, and attention to church teachings are essential to informing our judgment about natural, as well as supernatural, goods.

If this chapter's arguments demonstrate nothing else, they demonstrate that Aristotle is correct when he cautions that a reasoned inquiry into the natural human end and into the good begins with premises that are at best true only "for the most part," and arrives at conclusions that are no better, owing to the "shifting character" of the subject itself.[46] After visiting these uncertainties and paradoxes, we believe that we can best keep our feet on this uncertain ground by looking to the source of all goodness: God.

Aquinas explains that in the Christian faith, God is the universal Common Good, the ultimate good which orders all creation and which provides its complete fulfillment and its final end. Aquinas states that we are made to find our full happiness in God and our existence is complete only in Him. All living beings end in God, but human beings, possessing a rational mind, can contemplate and in some measure know God in this life.[47]

God is our final, lasting, universal Common Good because union with God in heaven is open to all of us equally as we are all drawn into the common, shared love of the Father, Son and Holy Spirit. We see here that both the common and the particular or individual goods are satisfied simultaneously in God, and that the common good is the source of fulfillment for each particular person. In the kingdom of God, there is no longer any danger that the particular good of each person could be submerged in the common good of the community, since the two coexist in God.

Human development and fulfillment come ultimately and completely through union with God. Therefore, we are not meant simply to rest in the goods of the communities in which we participate, "but through virtuous living to attain the possession of God."[48] Furthermore, the full theological reality of the common good cannot be manifested in the family alone, in any organization, or in the state, since none comprises our ultimate end. One must not expect more from temporal communities, including communities of work, than they can give. This is a danger for those who identify their lives totally with their work, even when that work is beneficial in the goods it provides to others. The organization comprises what Aquinas calls a "temporal common good." We read "temporal" here as "temporary" in the sense of "provisional, and due to be replaced," or simply, bounded by time. We would be wrong by reading it to mean "shabby" or "worthy of neglect."[49] Our responsible cultivation of the goods in our care in this temporal world—in the here and now—prepares us to participate in incomparably greater goods hereafter.

PURSUING THE GOODS TOGETHER: DEFINING THE MISSION OF AN ORGANIZATION

We have thus far covered much ground explaining what we mean by the common good, both in principle and in the context of a business organization. We will now combine our three levels of analysis. How should our understanding of the relationships between foundational and excellent goods of the firm, and between common and particular

FIGURE 2.2 The Goods of the Organization organized by the first two levels of analysis of the Common Good Model

	Individual Human Development	Community of Work
Foundational / Excellent Dimension ↑	Integral human development of each member of the firm	Communal development of the members of the firm, or community of work
	Material Conditions	Policy Conditions
	Profits, investments, land, machinery for production . . .	Ownership structures, job design policy, pay policy . . .

Particular/Common Dimension →

goods, influence our understanding of the purposes of business? What does the distinction between real and apparent goods add to our understanding? In this section we examine these relationships between the goods in theory. In chapters 4 through 7, we will examine the implications of this common good model as it relates in practice to job design, wages, ownership structures, communication, and product development.

The above diagram (Fig. 2.2) suggests how one may begin to rethink the organization as a community of work shaped by the pursuit of interrelated ends and goods. The quadrant form represents a fluid and complementary relationship among the chief ends and goods pursued by a firm, rather than a static set of categories or classes. (The quadrants do not suggest that the ends and goods within them are isolated by them.) Since, as we have seen, relationships among the chief ends and goods of the firm serve to produce intricate webs of mean-ends relationships throughout the firm, we can imagine a third axis to the diagram representing those relationships in depth.

In Fig. 2.2, the terms "common" and "particular" signify ends and goods that are achieved by organizational action (as ends in common), and are distributed, respectively, by participation and allocation. The terms "excellent" and "foundational" signify ends and goods that are achieved by organizational action, but that relate to one another as relative ends to means. For example, the ends and goods represented in the upper-right quadrant as "common/excellent" are those ends and goods of organizational action within the work community that are controlling or "final" ends and participated goods. These are the ends of human development that perfect the *firm as a community of work*, and that benefit its members personally by their participation. Thus, they are the ends to which the organization ultimately dedicates itself. Similarly, the ends and goods represented in the lower-left quadrant as "foundational/particular" are those ends and goods of organizational action within the work community that are not "final," but have been achieved as means that will be allocated to other organizational ends. These are the material conditions—earnings, capital, plant, etc.—on which the firm, as a community of goods, rests.

At the upper-left of the diagram, the ends and goods called "excellent/particular" are those ends and goods of individual human development. These are also ends and goods of *organizational* action: the firm is dedicated to the development of its individual members, so in the context of the work community individual human development is a "final" end. We have designated these goods "particular," and thus, allocated goods for reasons that go beyond a consideration of verbal symmetry. Individuals' development through the organization is certainly a participated good: all members of the firm benefit personally from a sound organizational culture. Nevertheless, the firm's role in eliciting the talents or skills of *this* employee requires the allocation of goods: training, equipment, and so on.

Finally, the ends and goods designated "foundational/common" in the lower right-quadrant are those of organizational action, in which the firm's members share by participation, but which also constitute the shared *means* of pursuing further ends. These means include systems of pay, policies governing job design, product development, and the like. These ends and goods representing policy conditions that support the firm's prosperity are of special interest to managers charged with promoting the common good of the firm. They form the nexus through which participated goods govern the allocation of material goods within the firm. They are the glue of the firm as a community of goods. Moreover, through functions such as marketing and product development, they influence the firm's corporate posture in the wider community. The firm is not autonomous; its success *as* a community depends upon the quality of its corporate relations, thus, sound policies might be called "doubly participated goods."

The representation of the true and apparent good does not appear in our diagram, since we presuppose that all goods we try to pursue in the firm are true. Perhaps we should say that judging of ends forms a kind of "universe" in which business decisions are made. If we are given to the pursuit of apparent goods, the universe in which we operate is small, and no longer coincides with the larger universe of the common good. Since God is the guarantor of the common good and since God underpins our understanding of the good, He is the source in which the activities presented in our diagram must rest.

We began our analyses with the relationship between foundational and excellent goods, and it remains crucial. Managers in business usually control no more than the material conditions (the particular, foundational goods of money, plant and so on) and the policy conditions (the common, foundational goods of policies and structures) of their organizations. Management decision making mediates these ends and goods, alternating between considerations of policy and the allocation of resources.[50] For example, in new product development (NPD), managers must be attentive to the particular resources available for dedication to that purpose, and must adjust the goals and business structures devoted to NPD accordingly. Reciprocally, NPD policies in place will affect the use and allocation of organizational resources (particular foundational goods). Thus, the manager's province is ends and goods on the foundational level.

What the common good model requires above all for the manager is that every decision concerning foundational goods must respect excellent goods: excellent goods must *inform* decision making at the foundational level, and decisions made at that level must *promote* the excellent goods of human development in community. Foundational and excellent goods must be considered *simultaneously.* The mistake of the shareholder model is to consider these goods *sequentially;* only after the foundational good of profit has been attained does the shareholder model consider how profits might be used to promote excellent, human goods.

Although the common good model is complex and difficult to apply—no easy, straightforward procedure here—it resembles most managers' experience as decision makers. In particular, the model captures the elements of coherent organizational thinking about *mission*. If mission statements are to give meaning to organizations' efforts to connect with and respond to the human aspirations on which they depend, they must connect to the common good in some way. For example, Cargill's mission statement proclaims that the firm's mission "is to raise living standards around the world by delivering increased value to producers and consumers."[51] By connecting its productive activity to a developmental end and good, Cargill is moving toward the common good, as well as inspiring the imagination, attention and interests of its employees. Cargill accomplishes this with a language that is accessible and personal, without neglecting strategic and financial objectives.

While the language of the common good may be disconcerting to some, it is precisely the language we need in order to reconnect our work to the social and spiritual aspects of our humanity. In its application, the common good model is less developed than the shareholder or stakeholder model for the obvious reason that people have not been applying it explicitly. In some technical respects, therefore, it may appear somewhat crude and undeveloped. Such is the case with any model that has not been widely adopted.

Nevertheless, our research has revealed companies acting on explicit communitarian or Christian views of work and business, and inspired by an understanding of the firm that cannot be described by the shareholder or stakeholder models. Some have incorporated their commitments in a "natural law" manner and others in a more "faith-based" manner, but they all share a desire to create authentic communities of work in which people can develop through and with each other. In later chapters we will introduce these companies and their practices.

The great strength of this model is its *realism:* unlike the shareholder model, it respects the "kind of agent we are," and presents the corporation as part of the fabric of human life and development. We apply the model in subsequent chapters as a starting point for its further development, and we hope this effort will inspire innovative and thoughtful managers to develop its applications in their own situations.

Study Questions

1. Why is organizational purpose so important? Why is the purpose of the shareholder model insufficient to explain the goal or end of a real business?
2. Why is it important to distinguish between particular and common goods? Why does the stakeholder model fail to make this distinction?
3. Why are the three pairs of goods considered in this chapter all essential to the common good model of the business? How would a business person use this model in making decisions?

Video Suggestions

The Culture of Commerce, 1994, coproduced by Hedrick Smith Productions Inc. and Weta/Washington. The documentary examines the different value systems within the U.S., German and Japanese economies. It illustrates some of the implications of the shareholder, stakeholder and common good models of business.

3

The Virtues

Human Development in the
Corporate Community

*The virtues have gone mad because they have been isolated from
each other and are wandering alone. Thus some scientists care for
truth; and their truth is pitiless. Thus some humanitarians only
care for pity; and their pity (I am sorry to say) is often untruthful.*
—G. K. Chesterson[1]

I N THE LAST CHAPTER, WE ARGUED THAT THE PURPOSE OF
a business organization is not fulfilled by maximizing shareholder
wealth, even though we agreed that increasing shareholder
wealth is among the firm's foundational goods, critical to the firm's
survival. Nor, we claimed, does "balancing" the interests of various
stakeholders fulfill an organization's purpose, even though we agreed
that a firm must recognize the claims individuals and groups make on
it in order to pursue its purposes successfully. Rather, we argued that
an organization's highest purpose, the one that organizes and directs
all of its intermediary ends, should be the promotion of the common
good. We defined the term "common good" as *the promotion of all the
goods necessary for integral human development in the organization, in a
way that respects the proper ordering of those goods*, but we did not examine closely what "integral human development" means. Thus far,
we have claimed that in working for the common good, we promote
all the goods of the organization in a way that orders them toward
integral human development, and that the basis for this and the sign

of its success will be a firm constituted as a community of work. Now we address the issue of human development in the context of the firm.

The common good model involves a commitment to definite convictions concerning what constitutes genuine human development. This feature of the model relies upon the distinction between real and apparent goods discussed in the third part of the common good model in the previous chapter. As we noted there, distinguishing between real and apparent goods opens the model to the criticism that it is constricted or doctrinaire when compared to the shareholder and stakeholder models. Yet, the pursuit of the common good is not a pursuit of uniformity. By any account, the most successful community of ends in modern times may be the scientific community. We recognize in it a genuine community of people: bound together by the pursuit of a real, common good, that is, scientific truth. Those in the scientific community share recognized methods and standards of judgment, and are intricately organized into groups, societies, and associations. At the same time, this community is full of opportunity for individual development; it is a stage where personal ambitions may be played out, and its members take sides and debate matters of controversy. It is a community as vital and diverse as its concordance on principles and methods is strong.

Like the actual scientific community, the common good model of the firm makes room for employees' pursuit of their personal ambitions, and welcomes their initiative. It constrains initiative only in the ironic sense that having a clear notion of our destination guides, and so constrains, our choice of route.

The common good model is concerned with the advantages of having a clear grasp of an organization's "destination." Accordingly, then, our first task in this chapter is to clarify what we mean by "human development" in the workplace. The task of *clarification* involves the exploration and organization of an idea that is already relatively familiar to most people. We have therefore assembled a set of distinct dimensions that can help us to promote overall human development at work.

We can consider these dimensions from the point of view of personal or of organizational action. From the point of view of personal action, they represent the sorts of ends that constitute our fulfillment as "the kind of agent we are." They are touchstones for our personal decision making and criteria we should consider when we ask whether we can affirm that in our work—whatever kind of work that may be— we are working *for* ourselves.

From the point of view of organizational action these same dimensions represent criteria for determining whether the firm's pursuit of foundational goods is governed by its pursuit of excellent goods, and whether that pursuit is on target. Here, the dimensions of human development raise broad managerial questions. Are the patterns of organizational action, the policies of the firm, able to promote human development within and outside the firm? Do they support participation in a "culture of development" within the firm, and do individuals participate in it? Do they ensure that the firm's dealings with consumers, suppliers, and surrounding communities extend its concern for human development to these "stakeholders"? In short, do the means of organizational action promote the ends of human development?

In this chapter, we will address these broad questions by linking the dimensions of human development *as* ends to basic principles of personal and organizational action drawn from the Christian social tradition. After considering the constituents of human development and relating them to principles of action, we will turn to the central concern of this chapter, the virtues. In brief, virtues can be defined as acquired, stable dispositions to perform the right actions for the sake of specific goods. Finally, we suggest a simple, three-stage process for ensuring that we keep the goal of integral human development in mind throughout our decision making.

HUMAN DEVELOPMENT AND SOCIAL PRINCIPLES

"Human development" as a term seems such a common and obvious thing that defining it may seem fatuous, yet, like many apparently "obvious" things, when one tries to explain it, it suddenly becomes very elusive. Yet, its elements become most conspicuous to us in their absence. It would require an act of ideological faith to deny that an

FIGURE 3.1 Human Development

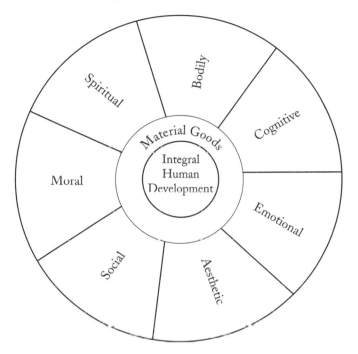

alcoholic, a drop-out, or the man-child who never "grows up" represents failures in human development, whatever the causes of those failures. The very notion of human development, then, implies that there are real human goods, and that having or lacking them, in whatever degree, is a fact as plain as potatoes.

It is important to note that our disagreements over the causes of human failure—and especially over the questions of who or what is to blame—do not extend to the question of what is successful or genuine human development. We may disagree concerning what is effective, but we can agree that it is necessary to develop; and we can also agree on the sorts of ends we must pursue if we are to develop through our actions, including our actions at work.

The chart (Fig. 3.1) represents the various dimensions of the integral development of a human person.[2] Its organization as a wheel suggests that our development involves growth along several axes, each one complementing the others, and that our development involves balanced growth in all areas at once. From the point of view of personal action, we run the constant, serious danger of addressing ourselves to certain dimensions of our development at the expense of others.

We are in touch with the completeness of our own development principally through the experiences of our successes and failures, and these vary in importance and effect throughout our lives: they may be personal or professional, social, educational, and so forth. In the world of work, success and failure can absorb all of our attention. We can easily then become economic giants, but spiritual dwarfs. Let us imagine our professional and technical development in the world as one of our legs, and the other leg to be everything else: the social-familial, spiritual, and moral depth of our lives. When we go through life motivated principally by career success, the one leg puts on muscle, while the other gradually atrophies. Nevertheless, we hobble along, and even convince ourselves that we are walking normally. One day, however, a gust of wind comes along in the form of a major crisis in our lives, and we are shocked as we are blown right over.[3] What we thought was a strong, successful and well-balanced body shows itself to be weak in one leg, and the whole caves in under sudden pressure. One strong leg is not enough. Thus, if it is to be authentic, we must develop along each dimension, integrally, and in depth (See Fig. 3.2).[4]

At the center of the wheel is our goal—*integral human development*—to be whole people. We have represented *material* goods as the hub of the wheel, that which keeps our development from falling apart. Material goods support human development by addressing our basic human needs, such as food and proper shelter. The further dimensions of human development are more complex, and difficult to achieve. Foundational goods are to the organization's more excellent purposes, as material or economic goods are to the further ends of personal development.

The distribution (that is to say, the allocation) of material or economic goods among the members of the human community is the first or foundational act in support of human development. Business organizations play a crucial role at the foundation by producing useful products from the world's resources *and* by distributing them to

FIGURE 3.2 Human Development at Work

Human Development at Work

Bodily development: The physical structure of the workplace and the design of work-processes and equipment are calculated to protect employees' health and to respect their overall, physical well-being.

Cognitive development: Employees' expected contributions to the work-process are made intelligible to them; jobs are kept "smart" to exercise and develop employees' talents and skills; overall, employees' cognitive abilities are matched to proportionately challenging work.

Emotional Development: Through the freedom to take initiative without fear of reprisal, employees exercise responsibility and accept accountability for their work.

Aesthetic development: Craftmanship is encouraged, and within the limits prescribed by their uses, products are designed and manufactured with an eye for beauty, elegance and harmony with nature; services are conceived and delivered in ways that honor the human dignity of both the provider and the receiver.

Social development: Internally, the firm encourages appropriate expressions of collegiality; the firm exhibits a "social conscience," encourages the same in employees, and supports employees' initiatives in the direction of service to the wider community.

Moral development: The firm's managerial practices and work-rules recognize that human acts are as such moral acts; working relationships of every kind should demonstrate respect for the human dignity of each party to them.

Spiritual development: Work is understood as a vocation, and valued as collaboration, in the presence of God, for the good of one's fellow human beings.

meet people's needs. The market is a distributive mechanism. When firms take their goods to market, they act through the market as distributors, and their ability to offer useful products at low prices is an important social benefit, as shareholder theorists rightly argue. In addition, however, firms are organized in themselves for the allocation, as well as production, of material goods. The ways in which they pay executives and employees, the dividends they declare on shares, and the ways in which they structure the ownership of the firm are all among a firm's distributive actions. The question here is what principle guides such acts of distribution?

The shareholder theorist might respond, "Let the markets decide: the costs of labor and executive talent are market prices, whether to declare a dividend and at what rate are market-driven decisions, and shares in the firm are a market commodity; so, pay market rates, declare dividends when earnings per share justify them, and sell shares in the firm's ownership to the highest bidders." As Christians, we must respond that market factors often influence heavily the application of principles of action, but they are not themselves principles of action and cannot substitute for them.[5] The philosophical reason for this is that no art and no form of technical knowledge—even knowledge of markets or of finance—solves any problem of human action. Technical knowledge instructs us in what can be done, never on what *ought* to be done (as is evidenced by the fact that often a mark of technical mastery is knowing when to break the rules).[6] The theological reason for discounting market factors as principles of action is that the Christian belief concerning the gift of creation becomes the principle of action for the distribution of material goods.

The basic principle guiding Christian decision making in regard to the distribution of material goods is that God, the creator, has furnished the earth and everything in it for the benefit of the human race. As recounted in Genesis, the gift of dominion over the earth is offered to our first parents and, thereby, to all humanity. The Genesis narrative implies that human beings' most fundamental relationship to the goods of the earth is communal. God offers them to the human community as a whole, to answer human need. In God's economy, then, human dominion over the goods of the earth is expressly for the sake of their use in meeting human need generally.[7]

We call this principle the "universal destination of material goods." It is, in a sense, the most basic Christian principle of action we discuss in this chapter. This judgment reflects the foundational role material goods play in the order of human development, and the resulting foundational character of the distributive activities that fall under the principle. But its importance is deeper still. The principle suggests that all human agencies alike—persons, organizations, commonwealths—should deal with the elements of wealth solely through means which promote communities of allocated goods. As we have seen, however, any genuine community of allocated goods depends upon a prior community of participated goods: for, we allocate according to desert, which can be measured only by the kind and degree of the recipients' participation in common ends. As far as business organizations are concerned, the principle implies that the resolution of any question concerning how goods should be allocated first requires that the question of participation must be considered.[8] (We will explore this implication in our consideration of just wages and corporate ownership in chapters 5 and 6, respectively.)

However important the universal destination of material goods is, our development as human beings begs for more than mere sustenance. In particular, the promotion of *cognitive, emotional,* and *aesthetic* development plays a critical role in organizational design. Such development presumes that employees will enjoy a certain liberty to go about their work and to exercise initiative as their own best judgment suggests. In Christian social thought, the principle that would guide our thinking about employees' freedom of action is called the principle of subsidiarity.[9] The term is derived from the Latin *subsidium* for "help" or "assistance," and the principle rests on the common-sense truth that people simply do better at tasks they themselves plan and control.

Subsidiarity emerges as a critical organizational principle that responsibility should always be accompanied by commensurate authority, so that people at higher levels of administration or management neither absorb nor supplant the work or responsibility of those in the lower levels. The principle suggests that the role of higher management is to support those "on the ground." It suggests further that organizations should be structured to distribute responsibility, accountability, *and* decision-making authority among those directly concerned with specific tasks.

As a principle of organizational action, subsidiarity allows decision making to seek its proper level, so that the organization as a whole benefits from all employees' talents and experience, and employees reap the benefits of participation in challenging and rewarding tasks. Conversely, the principle of subsidiarity requires that managers avoid exclusively hierarchical or excessively bureaucratic forms of organization, both for the sake of economic success and for the sake of human development. Firms organized subsidiarily stand to benefit more fully from the expertise of those in top management, who are freed to concentrate on long-term or large issues. They stand to benefit from the judgment and initiative of subordinate individuals and groups, who are freed both to undertake tasks within their competence, as well as to enlarge their competence. (Chapter 4 on job design will extend this discussion.)

We describe *social* development as the person's growth into community, that is, of the development of both the person's awareness that human beings are radically interdependent, and of a willingness to act in the light of that awareness. We also describe social development as learning to refer one's personal good to a common good as to an end. The principle guiding both personal and organizational action, in the full awareness of human interdependence, is *solidarity*.

John Paul II has defined solidarity, from the perspective of personal action, as "a *firm and persevering determination* to commit oneself to the *common good*."[10] This definition, linking personal commitment with common ends, implies that solidarity presupposes the "patterns of cooperation" which belong to community, express human interdependence, and are the means of realizing the common good.[11] The task of forging and extending patterns of cooperation, within the firm and between it and other communities, is a key aspect of organizational action. That complex and essential task is a fair definition of management's role in a community of work.

Our *moral* development can be better understood if we make the distinction between actions human beings just happen to perform and properly human action. Properly human acts are, as such, moral acts. The distinction is clear in the difference between the statements

"Harry's beard is growing" and "Harry is growing a beard."[12] In the first sentence, Harry's beard is merely biological; in the second, it is intentional. Human action is purposive action, which is to say that it is rational, that it displays, in the Latin, a *ratio*, a "rule" or "measure." Our actions are "humanized," not merely by the ends we choose, but also by the rule or measure we follow. We eat to satisfy our hunger, but if the "measure" of our eating is an *un*measured appetite for sweets, our eating is objectionable on more than merely nutritional grounds. It is an action performed without thought; because it is unworthy of a rational agent, it is also morally objectionable.

Within the Christian social tradition, the primacy of persons over things, or what is known as the principle of the *priority of labor over capital*[13] should govern the realm of economic activity. As the rule of organizational action, the principle enjoins business decision makers not to treat persons as mere means or instruments for the achievement of economic ends. It implies, therefore, that a business activity should never be considered solely in terms of narrow, technical criteria, but rather should always be evaluated comprehensively as human action, and with regard to its effects on the people who are the employees, suppliers, customers, shareholders, and so on.

Together, the principles of solidarity and of the priority of labor assure that managerial decision making can belong as much to the category of moral leadership as to the category of technical expertise. We will examine the implications of these principles in chapters 5 and 7, in our discussion of just wages and the social implications of product development.

We are told again and again that spirituality is strictly personal, strictly "private," a matter of one's "lifestyle." This view cannot coexist with the belief that our work belongs to our spiritual vocation: we are called to work as collaborators with God for the good of the whole human family. Our work, like our worship, is a public witness to our vocation.[14] Our work is not merely our own, but a calling to change the world, not through our own power or vision, but in cooperation with God's will.[15]

Thus, there is to the *vocation* of management a dimension of spiritual as well as of moral leadership. However, its role at the level of organizational action cannot be expressed in a principle like those we have just considered: the Spirit moves as it will.[16] For our part, we will touch on the question of the spirituality of work throughout this book, but it will be the focus of exclusive attention in chapters 8 and 9.

If applied, the principles we have introduced may serve to keep both personal and organizational action aligned with the ends of human development at work. The overall orientation which these principles establish can be called, in Jacques Maritain's phrase, "integral humanism," a humanism "which is open to the Absolute and is conscious of a vocation which gives human life its true meaning."[17] The principles of solidarity, subsidiarity, the priority of labor over capital, and the universal destination of material goods hint at what a community of fruitful work would be like if we, its human substance, were at our best. Thus, they also reveal our mediocrity.[18]

Principles of action do not instruct us how they may be applied in the real situations of our daily work. They point the direction, but they do not show the way. Nevertheless, we know that if they do not enter into our very marrow, they remain merely high-sounding platitudes.[19] The conversion of principles of action into coherent patterns of actions requires first, a great deal of what Jonathan Boswell calls "middle level thinking"—messy, determined scrabbling for a means to put the principles into practice.[20] Second, we need a history of actual attempts to act according to our principles. Uniting the two elements into a stable disposition to act in a certain well-principled way *is* the conversion of a principle into a pattern of actions. Such a persistent disposition to act well is what we call *virtue*.

THE VIRTUES

Both personal virtues and vices can be understood autobiographically: the patterns formed by our actual deeds over time persist as dispositions to act today in the same way we have acted before. So, too, the paradigms of virtue adopted by historic communities and cultures persist in a kind of ideal cultural biography, sometimes called a narrative account. The Western tradition, for example, holds paradigms of virtue exhibited as idealized lives of the Homeric warrior-hero, of the politically active citizen in the Greek *polis,* and of a Christian saint.

We are currently witnessing a revival of interest in these paradigms of virtue, from Western and other traditions. The field of business ethics has been touched by that revival, and essays resembling narrative accounts of the idealized life of the business person have made their way into the literature. Here, we examine virtue and its role in management from the perspective of the Christian social tradition.

First, we will offer a simple analysis of the nature of virtue, and use this analysis to generate a critique of the belief that management consists of morally "neutral" expertise by examining the teleological—purposive or end-driven—structure behind managerial skills and techniques. Second, we will enlarge on how virtue is developed in community, that is, how it arises as a way of life and becomes the subject of a narrative. Third, we will include all of this in a discussion of the four cardinal virtues of Christian tradition: prudence, justice, temperance, and courage. In the subsequent four chapters, we will examine distinct managerial functions and the virtue particularly important to each.

1. What is Virtue? The Relationship between Means and Ends

A virtue is the *habitual use of effective means toward a good end.* Virtue involves putting the right means in service of the right end *as a habit,* that is, as "second nature" to our action. We may thus define virtue once more (and equivalently) *as a stable disposition to act well, that is, to use the right means in pursuit of good ends.* Virtue involves recognizing means and ends, and forging a stable connection between them in the will of an agent.

We probably all know people who are good at one or the other of these two elements. Some very effective managers or business leaders are described as "ruthless" or as "hatchet-wielders." We might call such people very effective, high-performing or extremely competent, but we would not call them virtuous. Nor would we call them virtuous unless their highly effective pursuit of good ends was something we could count on as a regular feature of their actions, a stable disposition.

On the other hand, there are many people in business organizations who are trying to do their best, but are not very good at what they do. We might say that their "heart is in the right place," but they are not very competent or effective, or they are not *regularly* so. We could call them well-meaning, but we could not call them virtuous in their work. Good intentions are necessary to virtue, but alone are insufficient. Good intentions that are sometimes realized, sometimes not, are evidence, perhaps, that an agent does the best he can or is genuine in his efforts. Good intentions alone, or only intermittently realized, are not equivalent to virtue in the sense we are using it here. Without both of these elements, a good end and good use of techniques, skills, and other means toward those ends, we cannot call someone virtuous. Moreover, unless the connection between the right means and a good end is something we can count on *in the agent*— unless it is intentionally forged in the person's intellect and will— then even though his action may succeed, his success is not due to his virtue (See Fig. 3.3).

The manager of integrity, the virtuous manager, has the difficult job of integrating effective means with good ends—particularly difficult in highly competitive situations. Management demands technical skill, a broad and deep command of means. These skills include such things as reading a balance sheet, calculating the cost of capital, providing statistical analysis, targeting and segmenting markets, managing group dynamics, generating creative thinking, initiating problem-solving techniques, mediating conflicts, to name a few. These are among the things managers must do daily and do well, lest the firm and those who depend upon it suffer.

These technical skills are essential, but any concept of management "that believes itself capable of managing without an ethos mis-

FIGURE 3.3 Means/End Relationships

	Ineffective means	*Effective means*
Good End	Well-intentioned	Virtue
Bad End	Vice	Vice

understands the reality of the person," as well as the reality of work in an organization.[21] While technical skills provide the *matter* of management, they do not provide the *inspiration* that is the driving force behind genuine professionalism. Like an attorney whose forgetfulness of justice makes him merely a mouthpiece or a physician whose forgetfulness of her patient's welfare reduces her to a kind of plumber, a manager who fails to inform his technical performance with consideration for the common good of the organization loses both personal and professional integrity.

To behave with integrity, the manager must always seek to use his skills and techniques not only in the service of his own interests, but also in the service of others. Skills and techniques are not neutral means of getting things done. Their exercise is a human act that demands a deliberate goal and measure if it is to contribute to our development as human beings.

Most introductions to management treat skills and techniques in great detail. Many management textbooks devote most of their pages to the processes and techniques of planning, organizing, leading, and controlling. A few introductory pages may be devoted to how managers must set themselves goals which all these processes will aim to meet, but there will be limited, if any, discussion concerning what these goals ought to be. For example, textbooks will often point out that any organization, however formal or informal it is, must have a goal. The goals will vary from winning a league championship, to entertaining an audience, to selling a product. Without a goal, an organization has no reason to exist. In these textbooks, effectiveness means "doing the right things . . . choosing right goals." A typical example offered in these texts to illustrate a wrong goal is the production of large cars when the current demand is for small cars.

The effect of so narrowly defined goals is to allow us to accept a superficial understanding of our aims in business. When our goal is simply to win a league championship, we are prone to lose our sportsmanship; when our goal is merely to evoke an audience's laughter, we may slip into vulgarity; and when our goal is solely to maximize market share, we may not hesitate to instrumentalize people to achieve that end. If the goals of winning, entertaining, and selling are not to corrupt those who pursue them, they must be embedded in much larger purposes which invite a comprehensive, moral evaluation of the means we employ. Such purposes include the service of others and the promotion of the good of all, the common good.

As we mentioned in chapter 2, this is why, the end we seek is of such critical importance. For example, one will often hear in business circles that good ethics is good business. What is meant by this is that the purpose of business is to make as much money as possible (good business), but in order to do this management has to be nice to employees, serve customers well, relate well to the community, etc. (good ethics). Dennis Bakke, CEO of AES, argues that this sort of reasoning is problematic for three reasons:

> One, it's simply not true. Those of you who are believers know that the rain falls on the good and evil alike. In fact, there is an article that came out in the *Harvard Business Review* not too long ago that says something like, if honesty doesn't pay, why be honest? It's a whimsical article. I recommend it to all of you. It talks about this business, just exactly the problem that the good guys don't always win and the bad do win. I think that in fact God created the world to be a place where these kinds of values will probably produce better results, so it isn't surprising if good things happen. But we all know that we are in rebellion and that the world is not like that, and in fact often people who do not follow these values will do equally well or better.
>
> The second problem with the "values equal profits" mentality is this. In fact people start relying on this linkage and saying if I follow these values I'm going to get the Holy Grail, then what happens when they don't? What happens to their behavior? That is the second problem. If, in fact, profits are the main objective and it doesn't happen, people are going to go back and change their values. They'll say, This technique is no good; let's throw it out. And that's very dangerous.
>
> The third problem is that it's filled with hypocrisy. In effect we're doing something for someone else with an ulterior motive, in order to get something, and we're not being up front about it. There can be no integrity in a company with that kind of hypocrisy built into its value system. It looks a great deal to me

like the health and wealth gospel of some of our evangelists on television. This kind of mentality is very prevalent in business circles and is being taught in business schools today. I want to encourage you to take your biblical values into business because they are right, not because they work, and to let the economic consequences fall where they might.[22]

2. Virtues Develop in Community

The development of virtue, which is learning to use good means toward good ends, does not come about automatically, nor does it develop through solitary introspection. Neither does practical intelligence, our ability to recognize ends *as* ends and to connect them with means *as* means, reach the realm of virtue. There remains the task of realizing the connection in ourselves, and developing that realization into a stable tendency to act in one way rather than any other. As anyone who has tried to break a bad habit or acquire a good one knows, we do this by deliberately repeating actions of the kind we wish to establish in ourselves.

At the same time, common human experience teaches that our present actions, however deliberate, are deeply colored by our existing tendencies or dispositions, for we deliberate as we act, in *characteristic* ways which are themselves patterns established by our past actions and deliberations. So far as our life of thought and action goes, the claim that we *are* our history requires just two qualifications: first, the history-we-are is a history-we-are-making; we are always in the midst of our moral lives, and can never stand outside them. Second, we make our history largely with, through, and for others who have the advantage of seeing our actions from the outside.

An African proverb states: "A person becomes a person through other persons." To this we might add: "A person becomes virtuous through the virtue of others." Our first and most enduring dispositions are typically the result of our actions in response to demands of parents and teachers. Our latest dispositions result from actions prescribed for us by our work. In these and in countless other connections, the actions we have taken that have formed us have been proposed to us by others, through community life. If the majority of our dispositions are for our good, are in fact virtues, we can thank family, school, church, and the other communities in whose common ends and goods we have participated through our actions.

The Christian tradition is consistently realistic because its understanding of the human is fundamentally social. Our common-sense experience of being educated by others, and of cultivating our own lives as mature adults in the company of friends, coworkers, co-religionists and fellow citizens, teaches us that we need other people to come into our own. More than that, however, in God's scriptural revelation, we learn that we are each made in the image and likeness of God, who exists in a mysterious way that we describe as "being in three persons." Our image of God tells us that we are each whole in ourselves, yet we are made for, in, and through relationships. We cannot separate our identity from our relationships with others. The two are inextricably linked.

The recognition that virtues are formed in community through a constant dynamic process is often missed by modern writers on virtue. For example, one of the most influential contemporary writers on "habits," Stephen Covey, takes as his starting point the dilemma experienced by many people who are outwardly successful in business, but who are "struggling with an inner hunger, a deep need for personal congruency."[23] Covey rightly advises these people to focus on a "character ethic," rather than a "personality ethic," because, he argues, deeply established character traits engender coherent behavior in themselves, while a superficial, public persona may produce only knee-jerk responses.

However, throughout *The Seven Habits of Highly Effective People*, Covey's approach to the development of character suffers from a strongly individualist tenor. He insists that we can make ourselves into what we want to be: "start first with the self; even more fundamentally, . . . start with the most inside part of self—with your paradigms, your character, and your motives." It does not occur to Covey to wonder whether we even *have* a self that is ours to mold. Nor does he deal with friends, upbringing or social environment as influences that shape us as we both cooperate and contend with them.[24]

Covey's aim is unobjectionable: he encourages his readers to forsake a defeatist and determinist view of themselves. Unfortunately, he does not distinguish such encouragement from the claim that personal growth depends upon the ability to somehow overcome our social environment. The most telling indication of this attitude is Covey's decision to combine the first three habits he considers under the heading "Private Victory." Covey's approach, while alive to social relations as matters of personal choice, ignores the role of social support—often subtle and not wholly chosen—in the molding of a good character.

As we have already observed, managerial virtue unites technical expertise with moral and even spiritual leadership. The union is vital: no manager with questionable technical competence can or should expect to be charged with matters involving moral leadership, for technical competence is one of a manager's moral obligations. Similarly, no manager with questionable moral competence can or should expect his technical directions to be accepted at face value, for employees will assess the moral implications of those directions even if the manager has not. But while deficiencies in a manager's technical competency can be more or less easily remedied through further training, deficiencies in a manager's moral makeup present a different kind of problem altogether.

Moral virtue is neither an art nor a technique, and it cannot be taught as an art or a technique. Nor, as we have seen, is virtue a matter of heroic self-improvement, an inner discipline issuing in "private victory." We come to know what it is to be virtuous above all by following the example and admonition of those who already know, who do easily and naturally what we only imagine we might do. As our personal dispositions come to us through our actions, they can be curbed or deepened only by calculated action. To make the right calculation, we ordinarily need help. We can find it in the advice and example of friends, in biography, and in hagiography, and above all in the figure of Christ: "I have given you a model to follow, so that as I have done for you, you should also do."[25] We can also find it by volunteering in organizations—civic, charitable, fraternal—in whose ends we recognize the good; our participation will shape and reshape our actions, and will return to us as virtue.

Managerial virtue also comes by imitating virtuous management. Contrary to appearances, this claim is not a circular argument. The resources of advice, example, and apprenticeship in a real community of work are available to managers *as managers*, just as they are available to managers as persons seeking their fulfillment. Within the firm as well as outside it, we learn to be virtuous by living and working with virtuous people; from their example and in discussion with them, we are able to discern the elements of virtue that our shared circumstances reveal and require.[26] In chapters 4 through 7 we introduce some of these virtuous managers.

3. The Four Cardinal Virtues

The present revival of interest in virtue has generated a number of attempts to catalogue the virtues. Robert Solomon, for example, includes in his list of virtues for corporate managers: Toughness, Caring, Compassion, Honesty, Fairness and Trust. He places Justice as the crowning virtue, the "ultimate virtue of corporate life."[27] Yet, there is something disquieting in this approach, which suggests that one might apply or discount virtues according to one's needs in life as one might put on or take off a coat or tie.

Thomas Aquinas, and those following him, take a rather different approach.[28] Aquinas asks: What are the dispositions that make *action itself* good for us, so that to act through them makes us good as agents, even if by some circumstance our particular action fails to achieve the particular end we desire aiming? He identifies four such dispositions, and names them *cardinal* (from the Latin for *hinge*) virtues. To act well "hinges" on these four virtues in the sense that no matter what end we are seeking or what means we employ, if we are to do *well*, we must perform every action prudently, justly, temperately, courageously.

First of all, Aquinas considers our *practical thinking:* the use of our intelligence to identify what is to our good. *Prudence* or *practical wisdom,* for Aquinas, is sound reasoning concerning what is to be done: the end to be pursued and the means appropriate to it. He sees this as the center of our active lives and the condition of our growth in other virtues. The ability to act in any way for the good hinges upon our ability to perceive it in its relation to us, and that developed ability is called prudence.

Second, Aquinas considers our *willing*, which is the faculty through which we seek to make the good we see manifest and real, by ordering our relationships to other persons according to it. In this connection, virtue is concerned with how we relate to others: giving them their due, treating them as their nature and our relationship to them require. To act out of this disposition is *justice*.

Third, Thomas turns to our *feelings*, which are the emotions that drive us in the life of action. He identifies two kinds of emotions: the first are affective emotions, which are our strong, premoral attraction to pleasurable things. The problem with our affective emotions is that in themselves they are unruly: there is nothing inherent to our capacity for pleasures that announces "too much" or "enough." *Temperance* is the ingrained disposition to listen to practical reason—the judgment of what is good for us—when we feel the tug of promised pleasure.

The second kind of emotions are our "spirited" ones, such as anger, which we feel when we encounter difficulty in the pursuit of the good. *Courage*, which Thomas also calls *fortitude*, is a virtue similar to temperance in that it directs our reason to control these emotions in pursuit of our overall good.[29]

Given this framework for our development as rational agents, Aquinas also shows how more specific virtues, applicable in narrower circumstances, fit into this scheme. Thus, he sees *enterprise* as a particular form of courage, since it requires the application of courage in a particular environment and set of circumstances. *Perseverance* and *patience* he also sees as part of courage, since they require us to remain firm in the presence of adversity. *Honesty* is a form of justice, since to tell others the truth is to treat them with the respect they deserve.

Aquinas also makes two overarching observations. The cardinal virtues represent our perfection as *human agents;* they address our fundamental capacities for action. The more specific virtues, those that would figure prominently in special human undertakings—honesty for the clerk, patience for the schoolteacher—arise from the cardinal virtues. For Aquinas, then, we are human agents before we are human agents who manage bank assets, or fight fires, and so on. The development of our human capacity for virtuous action precedes and informs our capacity to do this or that job well. This concern for the integrally developed human character cannot be matched by the "shopping list" approach to virtue. If we are to grow integrally, with integrity, we need to take seriously the difficult pursuit of the unity of the virtues, namely that the virtues stand or fall together, to fail in one is to fail in all.[30]

Developing the cardinal virtues of prudence, justice, temperance and courage is indispensable to our general human development and to our specific development as agents in the work we do. These virtues illuminate the four management issues we address in the next four chapters: job design, wages, ownership, and product marketing and development.

Prudence (Practical Wisdom): Effectiveness for Humanity

Prudence concerns something familiar to all managers: good decision making. Its Latin root (*prudens*) means "looking ahead," but prudence also involves planning one's actions with regard to past events and to the particular circumstances of one's environment, while looking ahead to one's aims. A prudent manager can see the big picture in all its aspects and constraints, and knows how to apply the rules in each specific situation.

Nevertheless, the virtue of prudence cannot be reduced to a cautionary checklist. Prudence involves engaging our whole capacity for action, emotion, and will alike, toward the common good as the controlling end in our decision making. Accordingly, we can equate part of the virtue of prudence with following sound decision-making guidelines. A fuller, more mature prudence, however, will involve the complex of the whole person who makes decisions, including personal, political and social factors.

A prudent manager always keeps in view the good of each person in the organization, and of the organization as a whole, whenever a decision must be made. As we argued in the chapter on the common good, all decisions on the "foundational plane" (policies, products, forms of communication, etc.) must be influenced by attention to the goods of the "excellent plane." Because the common good requires that the organization's resources be used effectively, but cannot be limited to that end, the prudent manager must consider how the organization can be run most efficiently, but without making efficiency the sole criterion (see chapter 4).

Sometimes, such as in the start-up phase of an organization, it may be essential to focus exclusively on some aspect, such as the efficient use of resources, or on increasing earnings, to ensure that the organization continues to exist at all. In such a case, decisions promoting the survival of the firm are decisions in pursuit of the common good, and do not constitute a surrender to the principles of shareholder theory. The prudent manager's return to a more direct pursuit of the personal and social ends of the organization as soon as conditions permit will testify to that fact.[31]

Justice: Right Relationships

Within the Christian social tradition, justice is considered the highest among the cardinal virtues, precisely because it is oriented toward others. Justice has always played a central role in the social teaching of the Christian churches. Solomon is certainly correct in calling it corporate life's crowning virtue.

"Justice" comes from the Latin *ius*, which means "right"; that is, the just person is in right relationship with others, or (in Aquinas' words) is "well disposed towards another."[32] It is precisely this "rightness" in relationships that serves one's own development. Managers need to be "entirely possessed by justice," so that their intentions are in accord with the common good (see chapter 5).[33] Justice is "the constant will to give all their due."[34] Without the fundamental solidarity that right relationships with others inspire among all the members of an organization, managers and employees shrivel into small-minded wealth- or interest-maximizers, incapable of fruitful participation in the common good.[35]

Temperance: The Rational Pursuit of Wealth

To discount the virtue of temperance in the modern corporation is to adopt a naïve attitude toward the corrupting effects of wealth and power.[36] While there is nothing wrong with the desire for wealth for the sake of living well, all of us face the temptation, especially in a consumer society, to exchange reason for an anxious desire for wealth.

This is why temperance (or moderation), the rational discipline of desire, is so important to economic life.

The loss of temperance may be the most conspicuous feature of our consumer culture. Hostile takeovers, environmental exploitation, pornography, drug abuse, and overworked two-earner households, all point to an anxious and pervasive culture of excess. Everywhere we are pressed to choose what we shall *have*, while what we shall *be* should be the more urgent question. Ownership structures, for example, too often do not express moral choices directed toward the good of the community, but express, rather, financial options for increasing personal equity (see chapter 6). Peter Maurin, cofounder with Dorothy Day of the Catholic Worker Movement, captures the core of temperance in one of his "Easy Essays":

> The world would be better off
> if people tried to become better.
> And people would become better
> if they stopped trying to become better off.
> For when everybody tries to become
> better off,
> nobody is better off.
> But when everybody tries to become better,
> everybody is better off.
> Everybody would be rich
> if nobody tried to become richer.
> And nobody would be poor
> if everybody tried to be the poorest.
> And everybody would be what he ought
> to be
> if everybody tried to be
> what he wants the other fellow to be.[37]

Unless we can manage a return to the rational, temperate desire for wealth—which, to paraphrase Aquinas, would refer it to the common as to an end—every attempt to build authentic communities of work will stall.

Courage: The Virtuous Face of Competition
Like the other cardinal virtues, courage is, as Aristotle said, the mean
between possibilities for excess and defect. As we observed previously, Aquinas establishes courage as the virtue that channels our aggressive powers for use to our good. We can misuse these powers by
way of excess: take too many risks, fight battles that do not need to
be fought, and damage others and ourselves unnecessarily. We can
also misuse them by way of defect: we may accommodate ourselves
too easily to difficulties, shrug off persistent evils, or fail to take up the
opportunities for good that present themselves to us.[38]

To avoid excess, we can act to soften whatever pricks our aggres-
sion. Aquinas uses the Latin descriptor "irascible"—*easily aroused*—
to describe "spirited" emotions: our pride, presumption, ambition. To
avoid the defect, we need to exercise what Aquinas calls "magnificence," the ability to do great works within the means available.[39] We
need to be willing to take on projects for the common good that involve risk, though not an irrational, reckless level of risk, and to insist on seeing them through. Often, courage needs to be exercised
over an extended period of time, when we face persistent difficulties,
or when a new project seems to expand endlessly.

Throughout the whole life cycle of a product, courage is needed
to make the right, frequently difficult, decisions. Courage figures as
much in dealings with colleagues as it does in decisions over finance
or production (as we will see in chapter 7). How often do we avoid
challenging someone in a business situation just for the sake of maintaining a quiet life? The problem can often be that we do not know
how to voice the challenge without causing more harm than good, so
we say nothing. Here we are reminded again of the importance of
the "How?" question to virtuous behavior, and of the fact that we
need real skills—and not merely technical skills—if we are to work
effectively toward good ends.

The renewed emphasis upon communication and listening skills
in business is a welcome development, since listening skills can be as
crucial to managing well as skill in financial analysis. We often hear
today that information is the basis of business, and research on managers' behavior shows that most of the time they are gathering data

or thinking about it. Skilled communication is of central importance. Nevertheless, no single technique can solve any problem of human action. A courageous attitude to one's relationships in the firm puts communication techniques to proper use.

Decision Making

How do we make decisions that promote the common good and the growth of virtue in our corporations? We have no easy method to suggest, and no method at all beyond learning through practice. Learning through practice is more than just learning by experience. Experience is a good teacher only if it is coupled with reflection and contemplation, and only if the fruits of this reflection and contemplation are put into practice.

We have found that prescribed decision-making methods are often either too complex to use or too simplistic to take seriously. In general, simple aids to serious reflection are best. They do not pretend to absolve us from the necessity of growing as persons, nor do they give the impression that our decision making can be reduced to a technical routine. We therefore offer a very simple pattern of reflection, which will aid our examination of particular areas of management through the next four chapters.

Within the Christian moral tradition, an action can be good if it satisfies three basic conditions, which we present as three questions:

1.   End: What are you doing it for?
2.   Acts: What are you doing?
3.   Circumstances: What are the particular circumstances?

Asking ourselves these questions each time we must make a decision will at the least keep us mindful of the place the common good claims in sound decision making, and will invite us to recollect, as we deliberate on the principles we have examined through the last two chapters.

1. *End: What are you doing it for?* As we mentioned in chapter 2, human beings move toward ends or goals. We are seekers of ends.

Often we pursue several ends at once, but in our actions, certain ends supercede others. When we anticipate doing a particular thing, we need to be painfully honest about our motive and purposes. For example, are we searching merely for career advancement? We need to develop the habit of considering closely whether our actions are ultimately directed to the common good. Developing this habit of mind involves sorting through and prioritizing our mixed motives: personal career success, the good of our family, the applause of coworkers, and the good of the firm or of society. As we stressed in chapter 2, the common good is not something we promote automatically without intentionally thinking about it; we must actively pursue it and deliberately further it.

2. *Acts: What are you doing?* We achieve our ends through the patterns of our actions. The actions we plan need to be proportionate to the ends we seek and must respect the richness of human development, even when we need to focus only on a particular element of it. Our actions need to be good both in ends and in means. Furthermore, the repetition of particular acts forms our personality and creates the virtues or vices within us. Our virtue forms our actions, but actions also form our virtues—and our vices—in the long run.

3. *Circumstances: What are the particular circumstances?* To act well entails not only the right intention and right action, but also an understanding of the circumstances that surround the situation: What is the history of the situation in which we propose to act? What is the current situation? What are the possible future consequences of the action we propose? This will be clearer in the following chapters, as we discuss particular situations in the firm.

Through the next four chapters, we will examine the organizational issues of job design, wages, ownership and product development through the questions of *end*, *act*, and *circumstance*. The study questions at the end of each chapter also follow this structure.

STUDY QUESTIONS

1. Why is an explanation of human development so critical to the common good?

2.   Define virtue. Explain how virtues complete management techniques and skills.

3.   Why are the cardinal virtues called "hinge" virtues?

Video Suggestion

Robert Bolt's, *A Man for All Seasons*.

Making
the
Engagement

4

Job Design

Prudence and Subsidiarity in Operations

If engineers could think of people as if they were robots, they would give them more human work to do.

Howard Rosenbrock, Emeritus Professor of Control Engineering, University of Manchester Institute of Science and Technology (UMIST)

I N HIS ARTICLE, "ENGINEERS AND THE WORK PEOPLE DO," Howard Rosenbrock describes a possible design problem connected with mechanizing a task in a real light-bulb factory.[1] The task involves picking up a short piece of wire and placing it within a coil. To mechanize this task, an engineer might first try to design a specialized device, but since the design and manufacture of such a machine is relatively expensive, another engineer might suggest instead the use of a relatively cheap robot. If they were to decide to use the robot, the engineers would try to reorganize the production process so as to use it more effectively and extensively, by allocating other tasks in the production process for it to do. It would offend their sense of good design practice if the capacities of a highly advanced device were not utilized as fully as possible.

The sting in this story is that, prior to its mechanization, the simple task under discussion was being carried out by a human being. Every four and a half seconds, using tweezers, a woman selected a piece of wire from a box of precut lengths and placed it in the coil of a light bulb. The paradox here is striking: the engineers are concerned to maximize the use of the robot when they try to mechanize this task, but they feel no such need to make better use of the available talents, skills and abilities of the human worker. As Rosenbrock says above, in a phrase full of irony: "If the engineers could think of people as if they were robots, they would give them more human work to do."

This chapter considers why jobs are often designed in this strange and wasteful way, and what we can do about it. First of all, we need to realize the importance of job design. Many people are surprised by the idea that jobs are *designed*. We all know that machines are designed—cars, production lines, computers, aircraft—but don't people just "do" jobs? In reality, the design of jobs, especially in manufacturing, has been a crucial factor in the development of the modern economy, and is a crucial factor in the success of any business. Yet, despite its great importance, job design remains an understudied topic. More often than not, questions of job design arise explicitly only at the level of ergonomics, that is, the design of a workplace to prevent body strain and to promote safety.

In business economics we often come nearest to discussing job design when we consider what goes under the abstract term "division of labor," coined by Adam Smith to describe the way work is organized in a market economy. All economists from Smith onwards, including even Marx, have talked about the division of labor rather than job design. This term, however useful from an economic point of view, is limited: it creates the impression that there is a certain amount of predefined labor to carry out, and that all we have to do is to divide it up among workers. In contrast, the term "job design" suggests the creativity that can characterize organizing and allocating work, as well as managing the work process. The general ignorance of the whole issue of job design prompts us to treat this issue's conceptual and historical fundamentals more extensively in this chapter than we treat the fundamentals of marketing, finance, and human resources in other chapters.

The importance of job design from the perspective of the Christian social tradition is tied directly to the conclusions of our discussion of human development in chapter 3. One of the tradition's central tenets mentioned in chapter 3 is the priority of labor over capital.

Human labor is prior to, or more basic than, capital in the production of goods and services, so that it ought not be treated merely as one more factor of production alongside capital.[2] Logically, human activity comes before capital, since without it, capital could not be applied to productive effort (capital without human agency is inert). Putting this into the practical terms of job design means, for example, that the technical equipment of a production process needs to be designed around the workers who will use it, and not the other way around. In business practice, however, we frequently see things working in the opposite direction—people are simply assigned to fill procedural gaps between machines, as in our light bulb example. Such a practice is clearly based upon the goal of maximization of shareholder wealth, as we discussed in chapter 2, rather than on the promotion of the common good through human development.

Furthermore, from a Christian perspective, work is a "fundamental dimension of (our) life on earth,"[3] because we are made in the image of God, who also "worked" in creating the world. We are "called" to work,[4] and in a sense, define ourselves through our work.[5] We express and develop part of what it means to be in the image of God through working *creatively* and responsibly, in a "God-like" way, using our talents and abilities in a fully human way. A further consequence of understanding work as a calling is that it implies the presence of "the other," and service to that person, as part of what it means to work.[6] If we are called to do something, someone other than ourselves must be calling us. In the Christian tradition, it is primarily God who calls, but since each person is made in God's image, and because Jesus said, "As you did it to one of the least of these my brethren, you did it me,"[7] this inevitably involves our service to the human community around us. The communal and service aspects of our work can be considered as part of the *solidarity* that we should be promoting among all the members of the business. Translating this into practical job design terms, we could say that in the Christian tradition, the possibility to serve others in our work, and, more generally, the kinds of relationships we have with others through our work are important considerations for job designers to keep in mind.

All this can be summarized by saying that the subjective dimension of work needs to be included, and even considered as the central factor in the design and organization of work. In doing so, we include the moral and spiritual needs of the person, along with a consideration of the kinds of relationships our job design permits, which should be those of service informed by mutual love and respect within work. Work must be an activity in which the person is the subject, that is, the active agent who both accomplishes an external task through working on objects, and accomplishes her own internal development by deploying and developing her own human powers. Thus, in John Paul II's words, "the (primary) purpose of any kind of work that man does is always man himself," so that "man does not serve work, but work serves man."[8] Job design in the Christian social tradition implies an insistence on the primacy of the person throughout the work process, so that at no point is human development simply made an instrument of economic gain.

The writings of Pope John Paul II before he became pope (when he was known by his given name of Karol Wojtyla), provide a particularly rich resource within the Christian social tradition for the subject of job design. In one of his main texts, *The Acting Person*, written while he was teaching philosophy at Lublin in Poland, Wojtyla supposes that human persons find and develop themselves through their actions and that persons both reveal and form themselves as agents. In this sense of personal agency, "human action" excludes those acts that are, for example, carried out only because they are orders. For in the latter case, however busy or engaged a person appears, the cause of the activity of following orders is not within the person, but introduced from outside.[9] In contrast, when acting as a fully human person,[10] one experiences oneself both subjectively and objectively: one is the subject of the actions performed on external objects, but also one forms oneself as a kind of object at the same time.[11] Thus, we can be said to transcend ourselves in acting, in order to become more fully what we desire to be, or feel called to be.[12]

The aspect of self-determination is crucial to true human action, and is linked to the person's potential for self-governance. In acting, one experiences a moment of efficacy, of "making a difference," whereas in experiencing something happening to oneself, one experiences one's passivity. The experience of passivity is genuinely human, and is certainly not purely negative, but what must be emphasized regarding work is the importance, for the development of that person who is the worker, that she is able to act purposefully. In acting, a person exercises her will, which is both motivated by external objects and directed by her knowledge of practical truths. That is, a person responds to motives according to her sense of what is morally right and to her sense of what is technically or artistically correct. We are not "determined" by external motivation.[13]

In the light bulb example, by contrast, the woman doing the job had neither reason nor opportunity to act as described above. She was being "acted in," used as an instrument, by those who set up the production system of which she was a part. Her whole working activity was determined for her from outside. The organization of work in this system did not respect her human nature. It treated her, rather, as part of the plant's machinery. By means of this technical system, her employers demeaned and dehumanized her: they treated only her objective output as valuable.

In order to allow people to take charge of their own work and to act on their own initiative, an important organizational principle must be applied—the principle of *subsidiarity*. The word comes from the Latin *subsidium*, meaning *help*. According to this principle, higher management levels need to support workgroups involved directly in production when the latter need help. Responsibility for the control of their work, however, rests with the workgroup or working person. In other words, the operation of the principle of subsidiarity requires that power rest at the most basic level of production, so that those working at this level can call on higher levels of management to aid them in their contribution to the common effort. Subsidiarity suggests that responsibility and commensurate authority should never be separated.

In all this, technology clearly plays a key role, and the way technology is designed and used allows the possibility for truly human job design in the workplace. Technology should be an ally in making the personal, subjective side of work central to its organization, because technology is "a set of instruments which man uses in . . . work" to make work more effective and productive, and because it is a link to those who have enriched the human capacity for work before us.[14] However, as we can see in the example above from the light bulb factory, another dynamic can inspire technological advance. The person can be reduced to dependency on technology and deprived of the opportunity to act as a person in work. That is, the worker can be forced to become the passive thing that is "acted on." Such "instrumentaliza-tion" suppresses the development of the worker's human potential.[15] It is analogous to the instrumentalization that can take place as a result of a purely strategic pay policy, as we will discuss in chapter 5.

THE CLASSIC APPROACH TO JOB DESIGN
AND ITS DEVELOPMENTS[16]

The classic approach to the design of jobs is the "scientific manage-ment" system of Frederick Winslow Taylor (1885–1917). Although de-vised at the turn of the century, this approach to job design is still sur-prisingly influential today. Indeed, Taylor's system for the "scientific management" of work plays a role in the world of operations and pro-duction engineering similar to that which the principle of "maxi-mization of shareholder wealth" (MSW) plays in finance circles. Al-though many managers and production engineers would not want to subscribe to the assumptions behind Taylor's theory, in their practice many firms still use Taylor's basic ideas when they organize and design their jobs. These ideas have been modified and reformulated so that some of their harsher aspects no longer exist, but the basic system is maintained. The Japanese, in particular, have taken up Taylor's ideas and applied them very effectively, though they have transformed them in the process. It would not be an exaggeration to say that most manu-facturing jobs in the world, and perhaps even most paid jobs in all forms of business, exhibit a modified "Taylorism."

As a young man, Taylor worked for a short time as a machinist on the shop floor at the Midvale Steel Works. During this period, he controlled his output because of the way the piecework payment sys-tem operated. He realized that management had no idea how long jobs should take, or any idea of the rationale behind employees' re-striction of their output, or of the way the payment system rein-forced that practice. When he became a gang boss, he determined he would put a stop to the restriction of output, fighting a battle over it for three years. Thereafter, he was determined to find another way of overcoming this problem. He was convinced that there must be an objective or "scientific" way of determining how much time each job required. Taylor realized that one had to analyze every aspect involved in a task, and understand it completely. After doing so, one could wrest control of it from the workers.[17]

The novelty in Taylor's thought was this: he aimed to raise productivity to *possible* levels, as measured by "objective" and "scientific" data, rather than by relating present production to past levels. Increased production, he reasoned, would translate into a greater surplus for everyone: employees could be paid more, and employers would have lower wage costs. Taylor wanted to fix the eyes of all those in the firm on increasing their total surplus. Hence, Taylor proposed the application of scientific method to the question of how long a job should take in order to discover an objective standard by which to measure work. Taylor's method was twofold: a breakdown of the job into its constituent parts, and then a timing of these at the quickest speed they could be carried out "without harm or injury to the workmen." This task was to be carried out by a group called the Rate Fixing Department, who were also to be in charge of organizing pay so that these new levels of production could be attained. Taylor integrated detailed studies of machinery and its performance characteristics into his approach, since he was well aware that machine failure could have a great effect on production levels.[18]

Taylor followed existing trends, and made no attempt to innovate in working practices. He did not slavishly advocate the division of labor at all costs. In fact, in his 1903 text he promotes the combining of tasks to make a "large day's work" for above-average pay. Taylor did add legitimacy to the division of labor by associating it with science and, hence, with objectivity. Further, although Taylor did not advocate the actual division of tasks in all cases, he did favor the separation of thinking and doing. He thought the managers should be "thinking" and the workers "doing," and that this division would be efficient. He saw himself calling on managers to take on more responsibility than they had traditionally accepted. They had previously relied on the knowledge of shop floor workers rather than on a systematic management system for the organization of production.

In general, Taylor conceived of subdivision as a means rather than an end. He was not unaware of the need for markets and of the way markets could limit labor division, as Smith had also realized before him. The payment of high wages was understood to be the generator of those large markets, and those markets could, in their turn, support a highly divisional labor organization

More modern approaches, such as the "reengineering" process, do not differ much from Taylor's in their attitude toward the human person. Much is made in "reengineering" literature of creating integrated jobs, of devolving responsibility, of teamwork, and the like.[19] These are certainly very helpful as techniques in creating the possibility for more human development in work. However, it is clear from their proponents' presentations that they are perceived as means to the end of increasing shareholder wealth. Again and again in Hammer and Champy's standard text, *Reengineering the Corporation,* one encounters the assertion that the goal of a reengineering process was "to reduce costs by 30%," or something similar.

"Reengineered" workers are still instrumentalized, whatever the appearance to the contrary. Were a ruthlessly divisionalized and fragmented set of jobs the fashion in today's strategic management, Hammer and Champy would be advocating divisionalization and fragmentation. Instead, they are lucky enough to live at a time when more humane working practices are considered to be the best way to maximize shareholder wealth. A critique of Taylor's fundamental principles can be extended to a critical examination of most methods of job design used today.

A Critique of the Classic Approach and Its Developments: Prudence in Job Design

Taylor was quite open about the goal of his system: increase the general "pool of wealth" generated by the firm. He thought that the firm was wholly described as a generator of wealth, and that his systematic reorganization of its functions would enable the firm and its members to generate greater wealth, and thus achieve their purpose more completely. Initially, Taylor thought he could show this scientifically. By the end of his career, he was preaching it as a kind of economic virtue to which all members of the firm should aspire. Either way, we can see that his idea of the firm was limited merely to its foundational, economic element. As a result, Taylor's system offends the dignity of the human person, since it reduces some people merely to a "pair of hands" and others merely to controls for those human "machines." Interestingly, however, Taylor strongly emphasized the communal dimension of moneymaking—the shared activities of the business—while regarding the distribution of wealth among the organization's members as secondary. Thus, Taylor did have some understanding of the common, foundational goods of the business.

Taylor himself can be forgiven for his narrow focus limited to purely economic gain, for he lived through a period of U.S. history marked by exaggerated business cycles. Rates of bankruptcy among firms were high. Booms followed slumps, aggravated by the effects of rampant stock market speculation. Stability was the great economic prize. We have already suggested that firms, like the persons who make them up, can be subjected to circumstances that compel them to subordinate all else to the achievement of foundational goods for the sake of their survival. People involved in new start-ups or in firms struggling in the midst of economic recession could certainly experience circumstances that would dictate they temporarily elevate increased earnings above every other goal.

"Temporarily" is, of course, the crucial qualification. A firm's deliberate reordering of foundational and excellent goods is justified only as long as adverse circumstances persist, and only if the reordering itself is calculated to help limit and overcome those circumstances. Taylor, like most other business theorists, did not see the elevation of wealth-creation above every other end as a temporary expedient, but as the very norm and principle of business rationality. Nor did Taylor seem to realize that as a result of the pursuit of wealth above all else, his system was predicated on the instrumentalization of workers, and therefore promoted the bitter, strife-ridden workplace he professed to abhor.

It may seem that those forms of work organization discussed above are very distant from modern forms of job design—until one begins to examine modern forms and realizes how close to Taylor's ideas they remain. We are told, for instance, that reengineering "posits a radical new principle: that the design of work must be based not on hierarchical management and the specialization of labor but on end-to-end processes and the creation of value for the customer."[20] Unfortunately, this principle is not radical enough. It might reject unnecessary, excessive specialization (although, recall, Taylor never recommended specialization at all costs), but it still makes no reference to the basic tenet of work: persons at work need to be respected as ends in themselves and not merely as means for the "creation of value for the customer." Reengineering may appear to offer human gains for the time being, but its basic deficiency will eventually undo it, as it has undone other similarly grandiose and limited schemes.

The critique of Taylor and similar, subsequent theorists can be taken further. Taylor and his technically minded heirs neglect—and teach others to neglect—*prudence* in their approach to the organization of work. As we discussed before, prudence is at once a virtue, that is, a mode of human effectiveness, and the condition for our acquisition and exercise of other virtues. Prudence is our power to recognize and direct our thinking and decision making to the good here and now. Without the ability to make good decisions, we cannot hope to deal fairly with others (justice) or to use wisely our affective and aggressive drives (temperance and courage).

As Adam Smith, the father of economics, knew, job design is central to the generation of wealth, and so it is not surprising that it is also central to the development of the moral character of an organization. When we directly instrumentalize others with whom we work everyday by assigning them jobs that will make them, as Smith recognized, "as stupid as it is possible for a human creature to become," it becomes much easier to pay them unjust wages or to deny them any stake in the ownership of the company.[21] These forms of mistreatment go together, and they are consistent with treating workers as if they were less than machines (recall Rosenbrock's moral, from the beginning of this chapter).

Even a more insidious form of vice is possible here. It resembles Smith's suggestion that workers who have been stupefied by hours of repetitive toil might somehow be restored through access to education apart from their work. A firm might choose to pay workers very well (as Henry Ford did with his revolutionary $5 a day), and might even offer employees a stake in the company, but if its working conditions or its operating policies are an insult to its employees' very humanity, the monetary benefits could hardly be considered just compensation. The loss or frustration of excellent goods cannot be repaid in the coin of foundational goods.[22]

Prudence does not mean skill in calculating what employees will tolerate in exchange for this or that inducement; it does not mean juggling outcomes or shrewdly playing competing interests against one another. It means decision making enlightened by a clear view of the ends of the organization taken in their proper order, and by a sober estimate of how the goods achieved as common ends are best distributed. In no business connection is this virtue more necessary, because in no connection is the wise decision more beneficial or the unwise one more destructive than in connection to job design.

Let the firm pay just and living wages; let the firm's husbanding of its resources breathe temperance; let the firm's spirit of enterprise teach why enterprise is a form of courage. But if the central and organizing excellence represented by jobs that promote the development and preserve the humanity of those who do them is lacking, then no other excellence of the firm is secure. Humane job design is the acid test of the organization's pursuit of the common good, and a basic necessity for the development of the employees' virtues necessary to sustain the pursuit of the common good. As the Christian social tradition states constantly, any business enterprise must be built on the basic principle that the organization of human work must reflect the nature and dignity of the human beings who do it.

Prudence, which we would call practical wisdom, is also crucial to job design in another sense. The reorganization of jobs in patterns that are conducive to human development is dauntingly, achingly difficult. Those business leaders who combine business acumen with deep practical wisdom will have to show the way out of the Taylorism which, in one or another contemporary version, dominates the practices of our organizations, colors the thinking of management and labor, and diminishes our expectations of working life. Only with a real commitment to the promotion of the common good and to the development of employees as human beings can we hope to rethink and rehumanize our workplaces.

PRACTICAL ALTERNATIVES

We will consider here a case in which cellular manufacturing (CM) is implemented in an aerospace company. CM involves the reorganization of jobs so that groups or "cells" of people work on particular parts of the production process together. Ideally, the group will not only handle practical production, but also manage stock and improve their performance toward agreed upon performance targets. CM offers advantages over "Taylorized" systems of separated thinking and doing, even though limitations to the concept remain, and the application of the program is not uniformly successful. Next, we consider a development noteworthy because of its explicit stand against the Taylorist principle of the division of labor and the degradation of the worker it promotes—an idea still operative in many contemporary business organizations. This development is the *human-centered* approach to job design. It is a design approach that actively aims to put the human person at the center of the design framework.

1. The Hatfield Site in Crisis: A Case Study of CM[23]

At the end of 1988, the managers of the Hatfield site of British Aerospace (BAe plc) knew that they faced a life or death situation.[24] Sales forecasts showed that the market for their product, civil aircraft, was about to drop alarmingly, while benchmark data showed them trailing their competitors. After much investigation, visits to sites in Britain and abroad, site management decided that cellular manufacturing (CM) was to be a key element in their reform program. CM would be complemented by Total Quality Management (TQM) and Just-in-Time (JIT) initiatives. After hammering out a strategy for the program, management decided that their mission statement should be: "to have the highest sales per employee of any Commercial Aircraft site."

Cellular Manufacturing as Viewed at Hatfield
Cells were to be set up in the component manufacturing and assembly areas, with a Manufacturing Centre Manager (MCM) running several cells in an area. The cell was defined as "a multi-skilled,

multi-process production unit with a defined physical boundary . . . small enough to be managed by one person who is responsible for inputs, outputs and all internal activities." There was to be a support team working for the MCM and serving the cells, covering production control, quality control, and production engineering support.

All these changes were designed to achieve low inventory, high quality and faster response to customers, with simple performance measures controlling the new system. Many changes in jobs were envisaged: moving to a new part of the site, changing shift patterns, retraining or working in new teams; but the company promised, "[E]veryone who wants a job will have one."[25] The means of the change was also discussed, and a promise was given that people would be informed and involved as the changes progressed. Management had already decided to set up an experimental pilot cell in the doors subassembly area because, as the support manager later put it, "nobody really knew what the full implications of cellular manufacturing would be."[26]

In order for the change to work, good communication was essential. Team briefings were established and a "control room" was set up, full of progress charts and housing a model of the reorganized factory. This room was used for meetings, but most of the day it was open for people to visit. A series of visits to other sites was organized, involving a broad cross section of the workforce. One of the most important aspects of these communications exercises was to convince workers that the problems management was addressing were real and that the disruption of existing systems (with the concomitant threat of loss of status and even of jobs), would actually help both the company and the workers. There had been a history of too many "flash in the pan" initiatives that had left people cynical; management had to address that cynicism.

The experimental pilot cell was started in October. Conditions were not ideal from the point of view of management: they had to ask for volunteers, but the unions nominated the cell leader. After initial training and floor layout, production began. For workers on the shop floor, technical tasks were as they had been, except that the workers could call on members of the support team as they needed. Trust and honesty were required in this new situation. For example, if a fitter were to make a mistake and needed to scrap a part, the support engineer would need to know about it to be able to pass an order back to component manufacture.

Symbolically, the office doors to the manager and the support team leader remained open, so that those out on the shop floor could come straight in. As planned, supplies were controlled by the cell leader working with the MCM, who later claimed that this was the most important change to his job, as it allowed him to accept much more responsibility for what went on than before, when material control was located elsewhere. Under the pilot cell regime, the aircraft doors were delivered in specially designed boxes to hold the kits, so that it was easy for Hatfield dispatchers to see if all the pieces were included. Production meetings were held each morning for a few minutes, with the whole team involved. It took some time to devise and implement performance measures that were helpful to the team, but once created, these measures allowed the meetings to be more effective.

Some small incidents that revealed the emerging social system within the cell were recorded by the operations development manager. One member of the cell team used to sit in his car until the 8:00 A.M. bell and then get into the cell a few minutes late. This irritated the other members, who encouraged him to come in and talk to the rest of them if he arrived early. He agreed, and the difficulty was resolved without management's intervention. Similarly, someone who was a slow worker, and who some of the others initially wanted moved out of the cell, instead became a focus for their attention and help, and his work improved considerably.[27]

The four members of the pilot cell's support team were located together in an office next to the shop. When production began, the operators began to experience the benefits of the support team concept. They had particular people to whom they could go; they knew these people, worked with them day by day, and more important, the power bases in the relationship had officially shifted. Instead of having to request help from the experts, as they had had to do in the past, the MCM and the shop-floor employees, rather than department managers, had authority over the support team. The support team had official responsibility for dealing with the technical problems of the shop-floor workers.

The MCM and the shop-floor workers were persuaded that the members of the support team had to be as committed as they were to the work on the shop floor: their careers and self-respect in their jobs depended on the success of production. Similarly, the support personnel knew both the people and the product they were "supporting." Communication was developing; everyone was learning. In the past, the shop-floor connection to support would have been through a "faceless paperwork system," as they called it, with delays in responses to their queries blamed on its processing.[28] The immediate contact between shop-floor and support made that dysfunction disappear.

Critique of the Hatfield CM Program

At Hatfield, economic survival was the driving force behind the program. Even the "mission statement" was limited in its scope, describing management's target in purely monetary terms. We have seen, however, that focusing on the foundational good of making money can be necessary for firms in crisis. The key point to remember is that such a focus should be seen as a *temporary* measure to ensure getting out of the crisis and into a healthier situation that permits the pursuit of wider goals. At Hatfield, the assumptions concerning the human person and human work within the CM program were motivated by the need to survive.

How would the program rate in its promotion of the common good? Participation was clearly evident in the cell members' new jobs. Crucially, they were involved in their own control; the cell leader was trained to be a "facilitator" rather than a controller. Each morning, the production meeting involved them all, and they all shared in gathering the data for the performance statistics on which the morning's meeting focused. Symbolically, participation was encouraged between the cell members and the support staff through an "open door" connecting the support office and the shop floor. In physically laying out the cell, the members had been able to suggest improvements, which were incorporated before the cell was set up. Several of the pilot cell members later described this phase as "wonderful."[29]

Evidence of an expanded sense of subsidiarity, as compared to the more centralized decision-making structures of the past, also emerged, as the cell could make decisions and run itself to an extent because of its direct access to resources. Measuring itself against its own performance standards, controlling its own material supply, having the authority to call on members of a support team when needed: all these things allowed genuine control to be exercised by the cell. The implementation of Total Quality and Just-in-Time programs underpins this devolved responsibility, without loss of connection to higher levels of management. Managers liked to talk of the cell as a small business with customers and suppliers within the firm, because they felt it captured the new sense of localized control within the cell. The danger with this analogy, however, is that it makes the contacts with higher management seem an intrusion into the cell. If managers had been able to think of authority within the cell in terms of subsidiarity rather than customer chains, a clearer concept of how authority worked within the firm would have been possible.

Solidarity was also operating within the cell. The ways in which the group tried to integrate the tardy and slow workers indicated a greater awareness of, and commitment to, participation in common ends and achievements. Between cells, however, relationships were not quite so easy. The pilot cell had considerable difficulty in dealing with its "customer," the final assembly line. Since the latter was designated as a "customer," it was difficult for the cell to apply any pressure to receive clearer schedules. Since the model of the relationship between the supplier and the customer is that the supplier "serves" the customer, who is "always right," it was difficult to make a case that persuading the customer to be more organized and predictable was a responsibility of the cell.

The lack of development of subsidiary relationships was felt here too: if the cell had felt more able to draw on the assistance of higher management in dealing with this problem, there would have been a potential for a better relationship between the cell and the final assembly line. The problem, which the management program had not addressed, was disagreement and even conflict between cells or MCMs. The egalitarian structure coupled with the dominance of the customer-supplier model made this problem very difficult to handle.

Either of two very different courses could develop as an effect of "intercellular friction." There could be a regression to more centralized management, that is, a return to the way problems were dealt with before. Or a more ample subsidiary relationship could develop, which would allow the initiative for dealing with these problems to remain with the shop-floor, while shop-floor personnel felt more inclined to call on higher management to assist them in a "subsidiary" way. When this study was conducted, cell members were able to call on support teams for technical support. It would have been a new and beneficial development had higher management become responsive to their needs in an analogous way. This kind of relationship would certainly facilitate a greater degree of solidarity between cells, something impeded by the original design of the reorganization. Too much concentration on the small business model for the cells meant that the possibilities for deeper cooperation, based on cells' shared employment contract and shared production goals, had not been reached.

The Human Person and the CM Program
What assumptions about the human person were made in the Hatfield cellular manufacturing program? Certainly, the key assumption is that employees can be allowed to act on their own initiative, as responsible agents, even on the shop floor. With this assumption, we see a shift away from one of the basic premises of Taylorism, which favored the separation of planning and execution—thinking and doing—into managerial and employee functions. CM proposes that workers on the shop floor perform better when they integrate the planning and execution of their own tasks.

Workers' resulting ownership of their tasks is balanced by the introduction of performance standards. These serve a dual purpose, providing the cell's members with information about their own performance, so they learn where improvement is most needed, and also providing information to higher management so that those on the shop-floor can be held accountable to them for what they do. The assumption that employees work better when they are treated as responsible agents is a good place to begin if one is concerned about human development in the workplace.

A second, related assumption is that Hatfield's employees should be agents of the changes required for the firm's survival. The great emphasis placed on agency in this area stemmed from the importance management placed on its employees. As the development manager put it, "[the] most important issue in the whole change program was our people."[30]

However, change was such an imperative that there seemed no way for older "traditions" of working within the firm to remain valuable. This is a problematic situation in the area of view of human development. As we will see later in this chapter, one of the most important human-centered design principles is "compatibility."[31] Compatibility here means that new work systems should relate to the old, allowing workers to transfer their skills and understandings from one work situation to the next. Since no technical changes were planned in the transition to cellular manufacturing, compatibility was virtually assured at the technical level. Where compatibility became problematic was at the level of organization and management. In practice, there was considerable overlap between the way the cells worked and the way employees had worked in the past, but this occurred despite, rather than because of, the declared aims of the cellular manufacturing project.

A strong argument might well be made that were it not for the strong rhetoric of change associated with the cellular manufacturing plan, and the fact that the changes made were more organizational than technical, Hatfield's reorganization would have failed. Certainly, managers were aware of the fragility of the program during the transition period, and fears that the project would not have the substance and momentum necessary to bring about a real and lasting change ran high.

To assume that change is good and tradition is bad, without weighing the value of existing practices and of the practical wisdom embodied in the workforce denies both human-centered criteria and the understanding of human development in the Christian tradition. Hatfield's focus on change alone caused the employees no little anxiety. It motivated them to raise questions concerning continuity: demarcation, job security, and status. The transition was slowed down by this questioning.

In hindsight, it seems that management was wrong not to have recognized the value of some of the traditional patterns of the firm's social system, and not to have tried to harmonize the old with the new system. Since management saw the existing ways of doing things as simply "wrong," they did not consider how the old could somehow link to the new in a way that used them both; they preferred to think of the old as something to be replaced or destroyed by the new. An understanding of the principle of compatibility could have helped them avoid the problems this caused. It would have contributed to discovering a more humane way of introducing change.

The data in the Hatfield case suggest that management's design for the reorganization makes assumptions that are at least compatible with the principles of human agency familiar to Christian social thought. It is possible, therefore, to conclude that under pressure of an economic crisis, Hatfield's management was turned toward consideration of the subjective dimension of work. Although the data will support hopeful interpretation, there could be a number of reasons behind any particular change. We cannot be confident that management's actual reasons were the best in every case. An operator training plan, for instance, could well be based on the assumption that "enhancement of human skill" is a good thing, but it could also be based upon the anticipated pure economic benefits of a more flexible workforce. Indeed, the plan in itself is a good thing for the employees, but if its justification is purely economic, changing economic forecasts could lead to its removal, regardless of its human benefits.

The need for an approach to those issues that rely upon virtue becomes clear at this point. True development at the workplace comes about not only through good—that is, sound and successful—techniques, but also through the deliberate enlistment of these techniques in the service of good ends. The active exercise of prudence in job design would ensure that both good techniques and good ends are involved in the redesign of a workplace.

However, the cell system as arranged and practiced at Hatfield does seem compatible with our understanding of the person, at least when compared to the previous work system. People had a greater degree of choice over operating strategy. Monitoring focused on performance standards, leaving the cell with the responsibility and freedom to work toward them. Yet, while it was good that the firm was organized so that all those within it could act responsibly, there was no sense that the employees were there to work primarily for their own development, and should not be treated as instruments for the economic gain of the whole group.

We could argue that even if the system is not solidly founded on the kinds of assumptions that we would like to see, if it allows scope for these assumptions to operate—and at least does not declare them "unscientific," or otherwise irrelevant—we open the possibility for the gradual movement of the system in a humane direction. That possibility depends entirely on the way the managers and employees act day by day. Through their patterns of behavior, they may "reshape" the social system within the firm around the cell form of organization. No doubt, they are heavily influenced by the external environment, but they may also exercise influence over it, especially because they belong to one of the leading manufacturing companies in the country.

Overall, the case shows that there were improvements made in the working practices of the firm from the Christian perspective. There were drawbacks, too, but these are, to a great extent, inherent in the present economic system. The common good as defined here was promoted and the human person empowered to develop in the new working environment. In general, cellular manufacturing seems to include a form of job design that can be tentatively encouraged by those with a Christian viewpoint.

2. The Human-Centered Approach

The human-centered approach to workplace design emerged in the mid-1980s. The basic idea behind it is that both human needs and technical possibilities must be included in the design process. The aim is to foster skill and human development, partly through allowing a choice of operating strategies, so that the worker really controls the technology, and not the other way around. Opportunities for communication between workers are maximized, as is the integration of planning and thinking with the process of work, so that the human dignity of the worker is reflected in the way work is organized.[32]

The basic tenets of the human-centered approach were hammered out as part of an ESPRIT project (European Strategic Project of Research in Information Technology), organized to design a "human-centered Computer-Integrated Manufacturing (CIM) cell."[33] In this context, a cell is a small, defined production unit, usu-

ally a combination of workers organized as a group and certain production equipment dedicated to their use. Cells of this kind are preferred by human-centered designers because they allow some local
autonomy and accountability to the workers in the group, as we saw
to some extent in the Hatfield case.[34] Three partners from the UK,
Germany, and Denmark were involved in the ESPRIT project. The
project teams involved psychologists and sociologists, as well as production engineers and other designers. The lead partner was the
Greater London Enterprise Board, which had an interest in promoting the possible results among small businesses in London.

In the course of the project, its members created a number of devices to aid the designers in thinking and working in a human-
centered way. A scenario was created to provide an image of the way
that the factory's functioning could be made more human, and the
designers were also exposed to the comments and criticism of those
who would be using the systems.[35] The interdisciplinary nature of the
teams was important. The engineers and managers had to remind
themselves continually of the importance of criteria other than the
generation of wealth in the design of a system. Furthermore, the
project groups devised two tools that were particularly effective in
promoting a human-centered design

The first tool, the "dimensions of work," provides a checklist for
the designers at the organizational level of a design. Each dimension
presents two poles, "restrictiveness or flexibility," and thus each is
characterized in two ways. It is important to see these dimensions in
an interrelated way, even though the project designers found this
difficult to implement.[36] In any case, the dimensions represent an important tool for drawing attention to critical aspects of the design in
a system that aims to be human-centered.

The seven dimensions are presented in the table that follows
(Fig. 4.1). *Time Structure* alerts the designer to look at the time pressures imposed on the worker from outside, and also to look to the
worker's control over allocation of his or her time. *Space for Movement*
draws attention to the possible movement of workers from one place
to another, and to restrictions in this regard. *Social Relations* covers
the explicit formalization of interaction between workers and draws
attention as well to design factors that should permit spontaneous

FIGURE 4.1 Dimensions of Work in Human-Centered Design

1. Time Structure	external time-pressure deadlines
	degree to which operator can plan use of time
2. Space for Movement	movement required to satisfy job tasks
	degree of freedom of movement not required by tasks
3. Social Relations	degree of required communication (to whom and when)
	degree of freedom of communication not directly task related
4. Responsibility and Control Flexibility	degree of responsibility placed on operator
	degree of management of responsibility available to operator
5. Qualification	required level of ability for task
	degree to which operator can learn from task
6. Stress Control	degree to which operator is able to control physical and mental pressure

interaction. *Responsibility and Control Flexibility* stimulates thought about the scope and degree of responsibility available to workers. *Qualification* covers consideration of the abilities that the tasks require, as well as the "more comprehensive aspects of personality development and learning as essential human abilities."[37] Finally, *Stress Control* includes the control the worker has over stress-inducing factors, both at the level of human-machine interaction and at the level of work organization.

At a more detailed level, the second tool proposed was a set of psychological criteria for dealing with the design of the human-machine interface. These have been used in conjunction with the dimensions of work in order to bring human-centered thinking to bear on the design choices made at the detail level of the human-computer or human-equipment interface. They are used in conjunction with the usual technical and economic guidelines to evaluate design options. The human-centered approach to technical design may thus provide us with a set of general assumptions on which to base evaluation of a technical system from the human point of view. It also provides a number of more operational criteria for guiding the assessment. However, at the same time, we need to be aware of some of the limitations of the human-centered approach.

Limitations of the Human-Centered Approach
Human-centered theory suffers from difficulties of application within the design process and also embodies an understanding of the human person that differs from the concept we presented thus far. Throughout the human-centered CIM project, the designers found it difficult to apply the dimensions of work, the criteria, and the other design tools to their work.[38] The holistic methods of the scenario, the interdisciplinary team, and the user involvement were intended to counteract this problem, which is common to criteria-based approaches. However, the engineers were unfamiliar with such new synthetic design aids and found the solutions only partially satisfactory. Other problems afflict these approaches, too, and often concern widely differing experiences, as well as language problems and incompatible sets of technical terms used by the users and nonengineers on the design team, and by the engineers themselves. These problems were not clearly resolved during the project and needed further work.

In their concept of the human person, the human-centered school can be criticized for not taking the social, communal, and moral aspects of the human being seriously enough. While they certainly recognize these levels of the human personality, they do not pursue the implications much beyond the level of individual human psychology.[39] For instance, human-centered theory does not give adequate consideration to the interplay between personal satisfaction and the needs of others. Human-centered theorists would agree that work is not exclusively about the pursuit of personal satisfaction, since other people in the work situation should not be seen as a means to one's own ends, but this critical question is set aside in the hope that consultative and democratic processes within the group will

FIGURE 4.2 Dimensions of Work in Human-Centered Design[40]

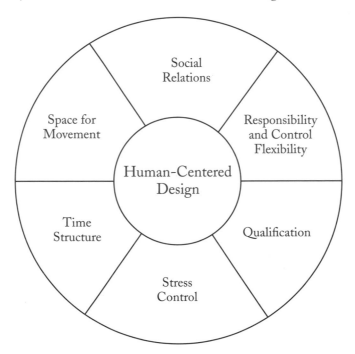

deal with it spontaneously. This deficiency from a group of theorists well-acquainted with the political aspect of organization should be considered a serious flaw.

These theorists lack an adequate theory of the common good and of the transcendent dimension of work. In particular, the notion of "self-giving" must be considered a part of the way any group works. Giving of oneself is needed in the group, if it is to work at all. Where self-giving is not explicitly recognized as an element of a human-centered work system, it will tend to be expected of, or even gently forced upon, the more vulnerable members of the group, often without those responsible for doing so being aware that this is happening. A less skilled person, for instance, could get put into a position where he is constantly occupied with unskilled but necessary tasks, thus making it difficult for him to develop. It might just be necessary for the good of the group as a whole that this happens for a while, but unless the self-giving and personal sacrifice of that person is recognized, the resulting tensions will not be easily articulated or addressed. The appropriate language for doing so is not part of the group's vocabulary for its self-description.

We have, then, a case in which the workgroup has set itself up explicitly for the sake of its members' development through their work. Criticisms from people who do not find this satisfaction within the group can easily be taken as personal attacks on other members. There may be some form of manipulation taking place, but it may not be easily recognized in a group that does not identify itself as a locus of communal self-giving. In fact, *membership* in a group, a felt bond analogous to friendship, requires that one regularly give something up or do something more than necessary for the good of the group altogether. Self-giving of this kind is a necessary part of personal self-fulfillment, though it contradicts the simplistic notion in which "self" effectively consumes "fulfillment." Human-centered theory has yet to incorporate these deeper insights into its concept of the human person, and thus has yet to develop a real understanding of the common good.

Conclusions

We have traced the development of job design approaches from Taylor, whose "scientific" system reduced workers to objective factors in the work process, to an example and to techniques that are much friendlier to the common good and to virtue. More work needs to be done on these latter approaches to make them more truly "human-centered" in our view. Nevertheless, they represent approaches that are moving in the right direction. We can encourage engineering and operations faculties in Christian universities to take up the cellular manufacturing and human-centered approaches to design, and to develop them in a more fully Christian way through teaching and research. At the same time, Christian business people could implement similar design proposals in the workplaces they manage. This would be a real service in the spirit of Christian social teaching, and a real benefit to the wider business community.

STUDY QUESTIONS

1. What is the end that we try to achieve in Job Design?
2. Discuss the means to achieving good job design that are considered in this chapter (cellular manufacturing and human-centered design). What are their strengths and weaknesses? What other means to good job design could you suggest from your own experience? What would be the strengths and weaknesses of these methods?
3. Using the particular case of the Hatfield cellular manufacturing project as a starting point, discuss some of the specific circumstances that can have an impact on job design. How does developing the virtue of prudence help us in dealing with these circumstances?

VIDEO SUGGESTIONS

BBC video: *Will Tomorrow Work?* This video discusses the way jobs are designed and the principles and practices of human-centered technology in the context of modern technological changes. Although somewhat dated (1980s), the demonstration of principles remains valid and useful.

Open University/BBC (1991), Open Business School video on the cellular manufacturing project at BAe Hatfield, for the course B884.

5

Just Wages

Justice and the Subjective Dimension of Work in Human Resources

Our incomes are like our shoes; if too small, they gall and pinch us;
but if too large they cause us to stumble and trip.
—Charles C. Colton, English clergyman, 1822

IN 1995, COMPENSATION FOR THE CEO OF GREEN TREE Financial, Lawrence Coss, totaled $65.5 million; for the same year, a credit manager for the same company, Rob Albin, received $21,000 and worked another job to make ends meet. In this case, the shoes, in Charles Colton's terms, did not fit.[1] Colton's shoe metaphor captures a basic insight into pay: a good fit between employees' pay and their dignity as human beings is a vital organizational condition for human development and community. When large numbers of employees see their pay stagnate or decline, we see massive "galling" and "pinching"; when executives are paid exorbitant salaries and bonuses, we sense personal "stumbling" and "tripping." When both "galling" and "stumbling" occur in the same organization, we have a recipe for cynicism, disillusionment and animosity.

This is not to suggest that Coss and Albin should be paid the same amounts; it is simply to note that in determining pay, as in most human activities, we can err either through excess or deficiency—we can pay too little or too much. Just as a shoe needs to fit the physical dimensions of a foot to serve its function, so systems of pay must fit the moral dimensions of the human organization. The employee who is asked, "Are you paid fairly?" never responds with a relativistic shrug. Since pay is a foundational element of everyone's standard and quality of living, dubious compensation incites even the most confirmed relativist to a rhetoric of justice. Just as there are no atheists in foxholes, so there are no relativists when it comes to salaries.

In the Christian tradition, the standard for determining wages has been a moral one.[2] In the Old Testament, Jeremiah condemns those who cheat workers from their wages: "Woe to him . . . who works his neighbor without pay, and gives him no wages."[3] In the New Testament, St. James continues the prophetic tradition: "Here crying aloud are the wages you withheld from the farm hands who harvested your fields. The shouts of the harvesters have reached the ears of the Lord of hosts"[4] and the Lord's "justice will not sleep forever." So, too, in Islam, the worker must be justly compensated before "his sweat dries."[5] Recently, John Paul II stated that a family wage indicates "the justice of the whole socioeconomic system"—a litmus test of the fairness in society's economic system.[6] The Christian tradition has emphasized the moral implications of compensation policies by asking: "Do employees receive what they need?" "Do they earn what they contribute?" and "Can employers compete while paying just wages?"

Unfortunately, this tradition of justice concerning wages has been virtually lost in the modern business's understanding of pay, both in theory and practice.[7] The issue of pay is conventionally handled by an organization's human resource (HR) department. Increasingly, HR departments describe pay primarily in strategic terms: *the purpose of pay is to attract, reward, retain, and motivate employees who best achieve the strategic goals of the organization.* These strategic goals tend to be exclusively economic in nature: beating the competition, increasing market share, enhancing quality, raising customer satisfaction and retention, increasing efficiency, motivating performance, and maximizing shareholder wealth.

From a strategic point of view, compensation is an instrument for increasing the economic value of the organization. If paying executives 200 to 400 times more than the lowest paid employee, or paying subliving wages to employees in developing countries, or reducing health benefits and pensions for the less skilled in the company promotes an organization's economic goals, then such actions are considered strategically justified. By the same token, if paying executives only five times more than the lowest paid employee, or paying above market wages, or increasing employees' benefits promotes the organization's economic goals, then these make equal strategic sense. When pay is considered simply as a part of a strategy to meet the firm's goals, employees "happen" to be treated justly, that treatment owes nothing to their inherent dignity or to management's commitment to just dealing as an end of the firm. Rather, they are treated justly because a business strategy that resembles justice *currently* makes sense, but as business conditions change, policy may be altered at any time by a fresh appeal to strategic advantage.

As we might expect, a business's strategic and "instrumentalized" use of compensation stems from its understanding of the ends and goods in the pay relationship between employers and employees. The strategic use of pay is based on the premise that one's labor is fully compensated by the pay one accepts. It does so because it limits measure of the wage exchange to the *objective dimensions* of work. That is, it is only interested in answers to questions like: How does pay affect profits, productivity, and quality? What motivates employees to add economic value? What techniques—such as market-based comparisons, gainsharing, profit sharing, stock options—can advance the economic goals of the organization? As we will see, many of these "objective dimensions" of pay are critical to a just compensation system, but the strategic mind limits itself to them.

To consider only an "objective" dimension of pay is a drastic mistake, we believe, because it fails to regard the whole reality of pay and this limited perception makes managers incapable of taking a truly prudent view of the ends and means in question. In contrast to this strategic view of pay, the fundamental premise of a Christian view of just wages is that *pay can never exhaust human labor*, that is, the wage given can never fully account for the labor done, precisely because work participates in the ongoing work of the Creator. It is because of this transcendent reality that monetary pay can never be equivalent to the value of work.

From the perspective of the Christian social tradition, the root problem with the strategic view of compensation is that it is based upon a *deficient* description of the actual exchange. Strategic thought misses the aspect of pay determination that follows from the *subjective dimension* of work.[8] Work is not simply an activity that terminates in an object. As a self-reflexive activity, work reflects right back into the person—it changes *me*, the employee or manager. This subjective dimension of work should persuade us that human work can neither be understood nor regulated through strategic goals alone, however important those goals are. Every person must ask, "What is work doing *to* me as well as *for* me, and *for* others?" Work is a self-transforming activity, and therefore, an inherently moral and spiritual one. Indeed, because work is other-transforming, it is self-transforming.[9] The failure to take into account the subjective dimension of work does not place one in a merely neutral position; rather, it leads inevitably to a commitment to a wholly materialistic view of the organization, based exclusively on the objective dimensions of work.

An exclusive focus on the objective dimensions of the organization as they relate to pay displaces and marginalizes the subjective or human meaning of work and of the organization. There is something more profound going on between employee and employer in their pay relationship than the pursuit of strategic goals. Recognition of the subjective dimension of work redirects the discussion of human work and pay from an exclusive focus on the kind of work being done "to the fact that the one who is doing it is a person."[10] When people work they leave an unrepeatable imprint on the world, through their products and services, and through virtue of who they become—that is, a unique, unrepeatable image of the creative activity of God in them. No salary can adequately compensate the act of human labor. No exchangeable item, whether in the form of a wage, salary, perk, or benefit can define the meaning of this human activity. Hence, it is better to avoid speaking of pay as primarily an *exchange*, and to speak of pay instead as part of a work *relationship* between employer and employee, a relationship that is, at its core, a moral and spiritual one. Jeremiah and James condemn the employer not simply because an economic exchange has been made unfairly, but because the employer has elevated capital income over the dignity of labor. Consequently, he has violated a moral and spiritual relationship. The employer here has chosen to serve Mammon rather than God—a sin against God's covenant.

Integrating the subjective and objective dimensions of work within an enterprise that is both just and profitable is one of the greatest challenges to modern managers and entrepreneurs. If they were to reform organizations without consideration of the objective dimensions of work, chaos would reign as a prelude to bankruptcy. Conversely, if they were to reform organizations without recognizing the subjective dimension of work, chaos of a different order would reign, namely, the moral and spiritual stagnation of people. It is in response to this challenge of integration that the Christian social tradition proposes the virtue of *justice* as the central habit in a wage relationship. In order to honor the subjective value of employees' work through their wages (following the principle of the priority of labor over capital), managers create right relationships with their employees through the virtue of justice.

Throughout this chapter our argument for just wages does not involve rejecting the effective techniques of a strategic view of pay with its stress on the objective dimensions of work. On the contrary, in this chapter we are most concerned with integrating the subjective and objective dimensions of work, which includes incorporating the insights and the existing programs of the strategic view of pay. Under the influence of strategic theory, those working in the field of human resource management have developed effective pay systems that are necessary to any just compensation system. As we pointed out in chapter 3, any virtue, such as justice, must include not only good ends, but also effective means. A "right heart" without technically sound programs degenerates into sentimentality and hollow moralisms; to attempt a "moral" account of pay without regard for strategic concerns would be to court empty abstractions and feed frustrations; that in itself would be unjust.

We do object, however, to the economistic logic underlying the strategic view of pay. Justice comes from the Latin *ius* which means "right," that is, the just person is in *right relation* to others, or, in the words of Aquinas, is "well disposed toward another."[11] Moreover, this right relationship is a condition of one's own moral and spiritual development; that is, we do not become fully human unless we participate, in both our acts and in our intentions, in these "right" or just relationships.[12] By failing to acknowledge both the subjective dimension of work and the notion of human development as the end of pay, the strategic view misses a major element in the complete and fully human understanding of pay.

Thus, compensation is no mere exchange, but an opportunity for employees and employers in organizational life to grow in virtue, an opportunity too often lost in our desire to maximize our own particular interests.[13] The work of entrepreneurs and human resource managers is not only to execute strategy. Their vocation and profession should not be so narrowly defined. One might consider, rather, that they are charged with promoting the excellent as well as the foundational goods, thereby creating the organizational conditions for human development (the common good). This idea places a great responsibility on them, at the same time it greatly elevates their work. But to ask anything less of them is to settle in advance for less than the management profession can and should achieve. It is to ignore the reality of business in which right relationships between employer and employee are central and essential.

DISTRIBUTION OF PAY AND RIGHT RELATIONSHIPS: THE FORGOTTEN CRITERIA

In this chapter we present an integrated set of practical illustrations showing how managers can take seriously the strategic insights of contemporary human resource management, and embed those insights in the virtue of justice in order to create right relationships in work organizations. We do this by asking three essential questions that cover the three basic tests of a just wage in the Christian social tradition:

"Is it a *living* wage?" (the test based on the principle of need)
"Is it an *equitable* wage?" (the test based on the principle of contribution)
"Is it a *sustainable* wage?" (the test based on the principle of economic order)[14]

For a business to be able to offer an affirmative answer to all three questions within a competitive marketplace is not as easy as it may appear. Determining together a just wage is a complex and difficult

FIGURE 5.1 Our understanding of pay is based on a moral and spiritual relationship that highlights the subjective dimension of work and requires the relationship to be handled according to the virtue of justice. It is this virtue of justice that should animate the whole compensation project. Three essential principles of this right relationship are need, contribution, and order. If justice is to take root in an organization, it must be nurtured in an organizational culture that supports these principles through pay programs such as skill-based pay, gainsharing, and employee ownership programs.[15]

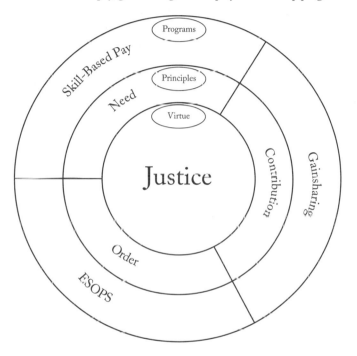

task combining tremendous insight, sensitivity, competence, and balance in the face of varied and conflicting organizational and societal contingencies. Yet, a just wage is a critical organizational condition essential to human development because it can

> meet employees' needs (*a living wage*);
> tap their contributions (*an equitable wage*);
> sustain a viable economic order (*a sustainable wage*).

These three vital elements comprise a just wage—to which we now turn our attention.

1. A Living Wage

The Principle of Need

When employers or entrepreneurs receive work from an employee, they benefit not merely from economic activity, but also from *human* activity. Because this work relationship depends on human activity, wages must be paid on the basis of one's being human, or as we explained above, in consideration of the subjective dimension of work. Because of this human relationship, the Christian tradition and various other moral traditions insist that employees are entitled to receive sufficient compensation to lead a human life with dignity; sufficient, that is, to allow the development of the very humanity they have expressed in their work for their employer. Employees surrender their time and energy to an employer, and so cannot use it for another purpose.[16] The wage is a way, and for many the *only* way, of filling the human needs that include food, clothing, housing, transportation, insurance, education, leisure, and pension income.

A living wage, then, is *the minimum amount due to every independent wage earner that takes into account the fact that she is a human being with a life to maintain and a personality to develop.*[17]

Problems

In the West, many workers do not receive a living wage, even though many others do very well. For example, the U.S. has one of the highest standards of living in the world, with some of the highest wages in the world. In many cases, the market wage in the U.S. has proven to be an efficient instrument for providing living wages. This is especially true for highly educated or highly skilled employees. They work at wage levels that more than adequately meet their basic needs. However, unskilled workers have not done as well. For example, "real hourly wages of young men with twelve or fewer years of schooling dropped by some 20 percent from 1979–1989."[18] The displacement of unskilled work by technology, competition from lower-wage foreign workers, and the decline of wage supports from unions and government have combined to produce a supply of unskilled workers greater than the demand for them. As a result, wages have declined,[19] leaving unskilled workers not only lower paid, but also less secure in the jobs they currently have.[20]

It is clear that skill and education are critical elements in achieving a living wage. Education is a complex topic, tied to the foundational institutions of society—family, schools, and government. Our concern here focuses only on how organizations have dealt with the issue of training and ongoing education; we are particularly concerned with the distribution of training in organizations.

The availability of training for employees in U.S. organizations seriously affects workers' prospects for earning a living wage. Company resources go disproportionately to managerial or professional employees with university or college degrees.[21] One study found that "while 17% of executive, administrative, and managerial personnel re ceived training provided by their employers in a given year, the comparable figure for machine operators was 4%."[22] A Hay Group report revealed that more than 60% of employees felt their company did not provide them with the training necessary to advance.[23] To this injury is added the insult of executives going off to exotic locales and enjoying luxurious accommodation for training.

When they are compared with German and Japanese corporate training programs, U.S. efforts look elitist.[24] German firms' yearly investment in worker training is more than double the amount U.S. firms invest. German firms also invest approximately 17 times the amount U.S. firms spend on training per apprentice. Consequently, the German workforce is one of the most productive, most disciplined, and most highly skilled workforces in the world, as well as the highest paid. They are worth more as employees because they have become educated workers whose economic value to their firms has increased. In Japan, new workers in certain industries receive "approximately 300 hours of training, while their U.S. counterparts receive only 48 hours of training."[25] Although there are changes in U.S. companies, the current training patterns have made it difficult for more U.S. workers, particularly younger and less skilled workers, to earn living wages.[26]

This brief description of patterns in corporate training suggests that one of the chief economic problems for many workers is their lack of access to the skills or knowledge they need to benefit from the market economy. Many workers today are crippled participants in the market and production process because they lack skill or knowledge.[27] The root cause of subliving wages is often submarketable knowledge or skill.[28]

Some Facts about Diverging Incomes in the U.S.[29]

- Highly skilled and educated groups have obtained greater pay increases than less skilled and less educated groups. Women (still paid less than men) are the only low-paid group to advance in the earning distribution.
- Divergence in the provision of fringe benefits has increased; fewer low-paid men and women receive pensions or employer-paid health insurance.
- Americans work more hours than Europeans and roughly as many hours as the Japanese, so that Americans' higher level of GDP per capita exaggerates the U.S. advantage in living standards.
- Real hourly pay has fallen sharply for those on the bottom rungs of the earnings distribution.
- The living standards of low-paid American workers are far below those of low-paid workers in Europe and Japan.
- There is rising disparity in hours worked, with the high-paid working more hours and the low-paid working fewer hours, producing even greater disparity in annual earnings than in hourly pay.

Solution: Skill/Knowledge-Based Pay[30]

In light of this situation and managers' limited spheres of influence, an effective way to promote a living wage is through redesigning jobs so as at once to require greater skill or knowledge and to enable workers to acquire the requisites in service. Generally, the more skilled the work, the easier it is for the firm to pay a living wage.[31] Skill-based pay is attractive because it fosters the conditions under which companies can pay a living wage without suffering net competitive disadvantages.[32] Within the means available, managers can help lower-skilled, less-educated workers achieve living wages *not* by simply paying them more (that is, at the risk of economic chaos). Instead, managers can train and develop employees in tandem with redesigning their work, with the aim of increasing the work's economic value and returning that value to the employees. This clearly parallels our discussion about job design in chapter 4. If firms can "smarten" the job through training and skill development, they not only contribute to the human development of the employees, but also make employees more marketable by making them more efficient and productive. Consequently, this promotes organizational conditions favorable to paying a living wage.[33] One limited study in the U.S. found that company-based training increased wages from between 4.4% to 11%, with a corresponding 17% increase in productivity.[34]

Skill-based systems not only increase wages, they enrich work's subjective dimension. When employees participate in their own skill development, they begin to take ownership not only of the conditions affecting their rate of pay, but also of the whole of their work. Skill development, for example, promotes employee self-management. By training employees in necessary skills, organizations in effect "push" knowledge, information, and decision making to lower levels of the organization. This is a practice of the classical principle of subsidiarity, but it is often also a real efficiency. Meanwhile, employees' work becomes more human simply by becoming more intelligent and more intelligible. By increasing their knowledge, employees come to understand their own work in relation to the work of the whole organization. Thus, skill-based systems promote highly beneficial social developments. When employees come to understand and to undertake their work as a community of action, their increased satisfaction is matched by enhanced organizational effectiveness. Moreover, employee participation in skill-based systems of pay connects directly to their responsibility for achieving living wages: if employees fail to seize the opportunity for self-advancement, then they must live with the consequences. Such responsibility also promotes and is an essential part of human development.

Joining the two components of virtue, a good end and effective means, Reell Precision Manufacturing established what they call a "target wage." A target wage integrates the good of a living wage and the effectiveness of skill-based pay in a creative way. At Reell, a Salary Review Committee establishes a target wage based on a rough idea of a reasonable local standard of living. In 1996, this target or living wage was $10.91 an hour ($22,500 a year). Some employees hired at RPM fell below the target wage, due to their lack of experience or weak skills relative to those of other workers. Market factors dictated that these employees should be paid as little as $6.80 an hour. But Reell did not simply capitulate to the mechanical force of the market. Rather, it enriched the jobs of the lowest paid employees so they could earn the target wage and still be competitive.[35]

Reell redesigned its manufacturing work to include more skill and decision making from employees, thus creating organizational conditions which require less supervision, allow faster set-up times, and reduce the need for quality inspection.[36] Together, these improvements reduce overall costs, allowing Reell to pay its own target wage. The institution of the target wage owes nothing to an attitude of "enlightened self-interest," but rather was inspired by the founders' deep sense of stewardship for the growth of employees.

The Christian social tradition, especially as it is articulated in Catholic social teaching, does not hold that Reell (or any firm) is obligated to pay employees in excess of an economic wage (a wage consistent with the sound financial management of the firm), even if that wage falls below a living wage.[37] To do so would unjustly place Reell—and all the firm's employees—at risk of economic failure. It would also create in employees an unhealthy dependence on Reell for a standard of living that they could not otherwise obtain elsewhere, since in a market economy the economic wage and the market wage converge. In a market economy no firm can be obligated to set a wage without regard to the effect of labor costs on its competitive position, since that would amount to the imprudent choice of self-defeating means.

Nevertheless, Reell—like all firms—does have a just obligation to work with employees toward a living wage. At Reell, this cooperative pursuit of justice takes the form of the "target wage" system: the firm supplies employees with the training that advances them toward the target wage, while employees are held responsible for learning as much as they can and for working as diligently as they can.

With this approach, Reell's managers have been able to meet the strategic demands of efficiency, productivity, and quality, while simultaneously satisfying the basic human needs of their employees.

The firm's experience underscores the essential concept that the just wage is not a static concept, not a flat demand laid upon the firm or society. It is, rather, a dynamic one, a goal which is established through a common regard for justice, and pursued with a prudent regard for concrete possibilities in the here and now.

Here we need to evaluate a logical tension arising from our insistence on *the principle of need* at the root of the very notion of the living wage and the emphasis we have placed on *skill development* as a condition for the achievement of just wages. We asserted that a living wage depends not upon the work done, but upon the dignity of the laborer. At the same time, we argued that the value of skill-based pay consists in enhancing the employee's economic ability to justify the payment of a living wage. Some may argue that our reliance on skill-based pay surrenders the principle of need to market pressures, treating human labor as just another form of capital, what is often referred to by the unfortunate term, "human capital."

It is important to reiterate that our argument concerns the *manager's* sphere of influence, and so concentrates on the means available to the manager for providing a living wage. Given the competitive price system which governs most managers, the most direct, effective means that managers command of promoting a living wage within the organization involve developing employees' skills—that is, making employees more efficient, productive, and cost-effective; and redesigning work processes to take advantage of employees' enhanced skills. These means all increase labor rates while decreasing labor costs.[38]

To be just, managers must pay a living wage, but he who wills the end must will the means: without a prudent, concrete means of sustaining them, just wages will be short-lived. In other words, justice without prudence (organizing the appropriate means) is merely an exercise in moralism, which cannot deliver on its promise. For this reason, employers are not solely responsible for achieving living wages because they *cannot* be. In a real sense, any firm's living wage can only be a *result* of a *social* achievement founded in cooperation with other employers, employees, unions, government and other "indirect employers."[39] Without making a comprehensive social commitment to a living wage, those who decide unqualifiedly to pay living wages in highly competitive, commodity-driven, price-sensitive markets, risk economic disadvantages that cannot long be supported or subsidized. If the market wage in the industry is below a living wage, and some employers decide to raise their wages unilaterally, they will price themselves out of the market. Obviously, this constraint becomes increasingly decisive in international markets.

It is precisely this competitive price system that tempts managers to apply an exclusively strategic view of pay. Proponents of strategic pay may often acknowledge the importance of a living wage: they know, as Edward Lawler writes, that low base pay "can cause significant problems in recruiting and retaining the best and the brightest individuals. It can also lead to an internal culture of low esteem and to feelings that the organization in general is second best and lacks the resources to do a first-rate job."[40] Yet, the strategic logic here still subjects a living wage and the human person to a closed economic system.

For example, what happens when wages that are strategically advantageous for the firm are at a rate that fails to meet the basic needs of employees, such as in developing countries where labor protection is nonexistent, labor unions are suppressed, and labor markets are flooded? What happens when "human performance is not a major determinant of organizational performance?"[41] If we take the logic of strategic pay seriously, the answer is to forfeit the needs of employees. As one human resource strategist put it, if jobs require "a low level of skills and enjoy a large labor supply, then a strategy of high pay may not be appropriate; in this case, increasing labor costs may produce a minimum number of benefits."[42] But benefits for whom? The strategic approach narrowly defines "benefits" only as they affect the strategic worth of the organization, tacitly classifying the employee among the other means of producing greater profits and increased shareholder value. It is clear that Reell did not develop a target wage on strategic grounds alone. The firm's leadership first desired just and right relationships with its employees.

2. An Equitable Wage

The Principle of Contribution

If a firm's compensation for full-time adults fails to provide for their basic needs, something is fundamentally wrong with the organization, with the larger economic and political structure, or with both. Still, just compensation presupposes a complex system within a complex organization. It cannot be determined by one principle, such as need, alone.[43] The principle of need is foundational in determining a just wage, but it is insufficient, since it accounts only for the material needs of employees and does not include their productive contributions. By their effort and sacrifice, as well as by their skill, education, and experience, some employees contribute more to the organization than others, and are "due" more pay.

In the Middle Ages, Thomas Aquinas noted the failure of justice when quarrels and complaints arise because workers are paid the same wages for unequal work, or unequal wages for equal work.[44] On a purely pragmatic basis, employee morale is always jeopardized when people receive pay based on job titles, rather than on their actual contribution to organizational success.

Although equal in their dignity, and thus equal in their right to the fulfillment of their human needs, not all people are equal in their efforts, sacrifices, and productive capacities.[45] In other words, a *living* wage, while a minimum floor, does not complete the structure of a *just* wage. To honor someone's humanity in the wage relation, we must also recognize his talents and efforts.[46] An equitable wage, then, is *the measure of the contribution of an employee's productivity and effort within the context of the organization's existing profits and resources.*[47] The difficulty with equity is to find a measure which is neither narrowly mechanical nor rigidly quantitative at one extreme, or too broadly impressionistic or vague at the other.

Problems

One of the most contentious and explosive issues in organizations today, an issue that calls the principle of equity into question, is the alarming and widening disparity between employee and executive compensation.[48] The main reason for the growing income disparity between executives and other workers lies in the allocation of incentives to executives: bonuses, stock options, stock grants, restricted stock, and cash payouts.[49] Who participates in incentive programs raises the prior question of who is responsible for the success of the company. Some executives tend to pay like cowboys, but talk like monks: they sermonize on the importance of employees' contribution, but pay as though the executive is the Lone Ranger of corporate success.[50] This is not to deny that executives should be paid according to the rarity and sophistication of their talent and decision-making abilities, but as Michael Novak points out, most of the high compensatory rewards

> do not go to inventors or discoverers, but rather to managers of large corporate enterprises, of which top managers are only small, if crucial, parts. There is something supremely social in their achievements. What they did, they did not do alone. Their achievements rest upon the intelligence, enterprise and creativity of many others in their firms—and upon the social system (the U.S. political economy) that make their efforts possible. It is wrong to reward them as if they were Lone Rangers.[51]

As Dean McFarlin explains, "company performance rarely, if ever, hangs on the work of just one individual" or even of a small group.[52]

Stock options and other incentives, we are told, motivate executives to perform. But here is precisely the problem. Executives do not perform alone, but rather in concert with other people in the organization. If the new knowledge economy reveals the inability of managers to master the range of specialized knowledge required for organizational success, executives should be making less in comparison to other employees, not more, since they no longer dominate a uniquely valuable niche in the hierarchy of talent.[53] It is a sad irony that the recent growth of executive salaries parallels the recent increase in the number of knowledgeable workers and work teams who have been introduced into organizations in response to the idea that employees should take on more responsibility and decision-making authority.

It is no surprise that employees compare their pay to that of those higher on the organizational ladder. When employees conclude that differences among the incentives offered to groups are a matter of arbitrary status and do not correlate with workloads or other objective criteria, right relationships are impossible to establish. When mission statements philosophize on reward by merit for all while pay practices provide rich pickings for the few, a company will be culturally dysfunctional at its core, never realizing its full potential.[54]

Solution: Pay for Performance[55]

Pushing pay for performance incentives downward or outward within the organization can facilitate the development of a more equitable compensation system by inviting employees to share in the rewards as well as the risks of the enterprise. In fact, many firms are spreading their incentives throughout their organization, and the concept of performance incentives appeals to employees. One study found that 63% of employees stated that they would like "to see their pay more closely tied to their company's annual performance, and an even higher percentage—75%—indicated they'd like to see their pay more closely tied to the annual performance of the operating unit they work in."[56] Many people want to be paid according to their contributions. A new employment covenant may emerge in which employees do more, are better equipped, and share proportionately in the risks and rewards of the company's performance.

Gainsharing is one way of building equity into the pay structure (although it, too, has problems).[57] Gainsharing focuses on the improved productivity of the individual worker, work team, or department. Since profits and productivity do not always increase in tandem, gainsharing establishes a direct connection between worker productivity and pay.[58] It is based on a formula that connects increased productivity of the individual or team to increased bonuses, independent of the company's financial performance. In short, gainsharing rewards those who make the improvements. This system has proven effective from the standpoint of justice because it encourages organizations to offer financial incentives and rewards to even the lowest organizational levels, thereby increasing equity within the organization.[59]

Successful gainsharing plans are based on two factors: formula and culture. A gainsharing formula should measure well-defined goals clearly and precisely, so employees have no doubt about what they have to do to receive bonuses. Gainsharing, unlike profit sharing, allocates bonuses quarterly and sometimes monthly to reinforce behavior with reward.[60] Under a gainsharing plan of the furniture company Herman Miller, employees negotiate with management to determine goals in four areas: effective customer service, effective use of money, effective use of materials, and effective use of labor.[61] The focus of the plan is not only on greater output, but also on reducing production costs while increasing product quality. This is a critical point, since in the past too many individual incentive plans focused on increased output and then the company suffered in product quality. One nagging difficulty with gainsharing's structure is that often the people providing auxiliary services make critically important contributions to the success of a team or department, but may not share in rewards that are dependent upon their support.

No successful gainsharing plan can function purely as a productivity technique operating with the right formula.[62] Its success will owe much to the ingrained culture of the organization, and especially to the concept of the person that shapes the organization's purpose. Again, we return to the subjective dimension of work. Gainsharing should not be viewed simply as a strategic tool to motivate workers toward greater productivity; rather, gainsharing should be considered intrinsically connected to the larger purpose of the company, particularly as it relates to human development.

Herman Miller, for example, sees its gainsharing plan as embedded in an organizational culture that fosters the subjective dimension of work by creating conditions of *participation, transparency, ownership, and equity.*[63] Employee *participation* plays a critical role in the effectiveness and acceptability of gainsharing programs, because their own participation assures employees that the program is fair and equitable. Participation supposes a high degree of *transparency*, that is, information is regularly and openly disseminated throughout the organization. Herman Miller's management spends one day each month informing the employees of the status of productivity, profits, and employee suggestions. The conditions of participation and transparency connected to employees' performance and their financial reward has increased worker awareness of the financial situation of the company, and has partially flattened the organization's decision making and informational structure.

Herman Miller also provides an employee stock *ownership* plan calculated to foster an ownership culture in which power and authority derive from demonstrated competence, knowledge, and skill, not from opaque sources of seniority or favoritism. Herman Miller has instituted an *equity* ratio, which provides that the highest paid employee, usually the CEO, cannot be paid more than 20 times the pretax income of its manufacturing employees.[64] In the 1980s, when compensation committees were designing golden parachutes for top executives, Herman Miller's former CEO, Max De Pree, designed silver parachutes for *all* employees, protecting the whole workforce—not just a select few—from raiders.[65]

Herman Miller's gainsharing program fosters equitable pay precisely because it is embedded in an organizational culture that takes the subjective dimension of employees' work seriously. A gainsharing program can avoid the great stumbling block of appearing manipulative to employees, if it is managed in an organizational culture that has just relationships at its operating core, and is shaped by participation, transparency, ownership, and equity.

3. A Sustainable Wage

The Principle of Economic Order
Pay is not only income for the worker; it is also a cost to the employer that has a significant impact on the economic order of the organization. A just wage cannot be determined "without reference to the quantity and quality of available resources" or to the effects present wages and incentives will have on future resources.[66] An ecological principle operates in pay systems: actions cannot be taken without consequent reactions. As a prime regulator of every business, profits play a critical role in the determination of any pay plan. Paying a just wage without foresight about how a living and equitable wage will affect the economic order of the organization, becomes a high-sounding but practically empty moralism. The principle of economic order, then, *is the examination of the employer's ability to pay wages that are sustainable in view of the economic health of the organization as a whole.*

Problems
Throughout this chapter, we have criticized the strategic view of pay as a form of instrumentalism. As we have stated, the critique does not imply a wholesale rejection of strategic thinking, but rather of the thinking of those proponents who fail to recognize that the strategic

understanding of pay is intrinsically limited. In order to illustrate these limits, we will explain the important distinction between techniques and virtues, which in turn will help us to articulate an integrated, strategic, *and* just understanding of pay.[67]

Strategy is a technique for adopting courses of action (whether planned or emergent), and for allocating resources necessary to an organization's long-term, economic viability. Since pay is a significant part of the organizational cost structure, its design should furnish a competitive advantage in the strategic direction of the company.[68] As a way of thinking, strategy is *necessary but not sufficient* to a full understanding of the reality of pay. It is necessary because it maps out the economic and productive implications of the organization's system of pay, for the sake of safeguarding economic order. But strategy is insufficient because it disregards the moral and imaginative resources that put people in right relationships.

Because strategic thought is the examination of *all possible* means for achieving precisely defined economic/financial objectives, it must treat human beings and "human factors," such as the skills of managers, the loyalty of customers, the efficiency of suppliers, as well as the labor of employees as "organizational resources." Put another way, strategic thinking is *constrained* thinking: it is the discipline of thinking *as if* "good" could only mean "good for earnings" or "good for net profit," etc., so as to achieve the most exact and detailed view of how earnings or profits can be increased *by all possible means*, i.e., maximally. If we are purely strategic thinkers, therefore, we do not *allow* our wider knowledge of relationships among various goods—our practical wisdom or prudence—to interfere and complicate the exercise; this deliberate withdrawal from "thinking in the round" is the essence of technique. Its technical character should warn us that *strategic thought is itself a good only as the instrument of prudent concern for the comprehensive human good,* the good "in the round." That prudent concern examines first the justice of policies that define relationships among employees and between employees and employers, as pay policies do.

Volumes of materials written on business strategy indicate that the technique of strategic thinking has advanced tremendously in firms in recent years. Unfortunately, its ascendance has not been combined with concerns about justice.[69] A virtue such as justice is an habitual human action directed to a good end that renders the acting person good; that is, it completes or fulfills the person *as* a person. Virtue thus qualifies a person comprehensively. When we say, "This person is just," we are saying something about the whole person. Technique, on the other hand, qualifies a person partially. When we say, "This person is productive," we are saying something about what she does rather than about who she is. We describe activity, not identity.

Similarly, strategic thinking describes the pay relationship in partial, technical terms. By contrast, a just wage describes the pay relationship comprehensively. It can do so because it seriously examines and includes the *subjective* dimension of the person at work without totally discounting strategic factors. Strategic thinking restricts the pay relationship to a technical practice subordinated to economic goals, and thus subjects the person to a technical system measured only by "economic value added." Consequently, this "enslaves the human person through a lack of understanding of his moral dimension, to the detriment of human dignity."[70]

These are harsh words, but justified, as an example will help to illustrate. H. J. Heinz Company instituted a management incentive plan (MIP) based on the company's strategic goal of "consistent growth in earnings."[71] Rewards and penalties assessed under the plan corresponded strictly to the company's projected earnings. When division management met their targets, they earned bonuses of up to 40% of their salary. When they failed to reach their targets, they suffered great pressure from corporate headquarters to rectify the situation.

The flat demand from corporate headquarters to achieve "consistent growth in earnings" in an "inconsistent marketplace" pressured Heinz's divisional managers into extreme, and at times illegal, accounting practices in order to guarantee their rewards, or at least to avoid the costs of failure. Some, for example, transferred reported income and expenses from one fiscal year to the next. Even though Heinz touted a code of ethics, internal forces within the company made it extremely difficult for employees to follow the principles of the code. By focusing only on the quantitative criteria in its incentive system, Heinz created a culture of economism: the only value of anything was economic value. By building its whole incentive plan on one strategic goal—consistent growth in earnings—Heinz rewarded economic success, but only by unjustly penalizing those who failed to meet the goals, even for legitimate reasons.

More can be learned about an incentive system by what it penalizes than by what it rewards.[72] Heinz created a punitive system that failed to deal honestly with the abuses it inspired. Not only would noneconomic goods, such as honesty in exposing fraudulent accounting practices go unrewarded, they might even have been penalized. Heinz subordinated justice and at times set it aside entirely in favor of a kind of utilitarian calculation, even when officials were actively breaking the law. When a company can define only narrow strategic goals and economic self-interest as the basis for human motivation and decision making, human relationships within it become distorted and fragile.[73]

Solution: Integrating Just and Strategic Pay

The alternative to purely strategic thinking does not follow a program such as skilled-based pay or gainsharing; rather, it involves a habit of integrative thinking. We cannot get this habit by pulling a plan off the shelf. The integration of just and strategic pay systems occurs through the slow, at times tedious and painful, process by which we get all habits: practice. In this case, a practice that consistently poses the profound human question: "Is the person made for the purpose of work, or is work, including technology, meant to serve the person?"[74] Certainly, the possibility of an integrated system of pay that is both just and strategic hangs upon this question and its possible answers. Those who would honor the Christian tradition must answer the question with an affirmation of labor over capital, of person over object, of virtue over technique.

We need to go a step further here and explain the dynamics of this priority. A helpful distinction for thinking through this integration comes when we ask, as we did in chapter 2, "What is most *foundational* and what is most *excellent* about a human organization?" What is most foundational to an organization concerns its economic viability. By enhancing profitability and efficiency, strategic pay strengthens a firm's chances of surviving. Heinz's incentive plan was clearly driven by the judgment that consistent earnings would guarantee survival of the company.

Yet, what is foundational to an organization is not what is most excellent about it. Organizational survival is a means to the development of the person and community. While pay strategies focus on the viability of the organization, they tend to ignore those questions of pay that concern the most excellent, human, dimensions of the firm: Does it pay justly? How does the pay affect the subjective dimension of workers and not merely their productive capacities? Does the pay foster authentic human development? Entrepreneurs and human resource managers face the difficult challenge of integrating the subjective and objective dimensions of work without marginalizing one for the sake of the other. In this regard, the Heinz incentive episode amounts to a cautionary tale in which Heinz encouraged managers to become economic giants at the expense of becoming moral dwarfs.

The integration of strategy and justice is most critical for organizations in times of economic crisis, when wage rates conflict with falling revenues. Because compensation represents one of the highest costs of production in some companies, managing wages and bonuses is critical to the economic order and sustainability of such an organization when revenue decreases. Addressing this problem in a way that takes full advantage of strategic insight while anchoring the solution in a framework of justice can strengthen human relationships within the firm, even as it helps safeguard the firm's fiscal integrity.

For example, in 1995–96, when one of Reell's largest customers, Apple Computer, cut back its orders, Reell's revenue fell 23%. Reell reacted in a fully "strategic manner." Recognizing that its economic health was at stake, Reell addressed its shortfalls by reducing wages and salaries, and also by seeking a wider customer base in international markets, by looking for greater efficiencies, reduced costs, new products, customer retention, and so forth. But Reell's response to this economic crisis proceeded in the context of what is at the heart of the firm as a human enterprise: the growth of people. When reducing wages and salaries, Reell executives took the proportionally larger cuts, and those employees under or at the target wage were exempted from reductions. Layoffs were seen as the *last alternative* to solving Reell's revenue shortfall because of the relationships the firm had established as a workplace community, thereby preserving the most excellent goods of their organization. Reell's management, guided by their understanding of the subjective meaning of work, considered layoffs in the spirit in which a surgeon contemplates the amputation of a patient's leg: a grave decision that is justified only when the life of the body is at immediate risk.

While all at Reell found these experiences painful, they also found them to be a catalyst of workplace solidarity. Organizational crises tend either to divide workplaces or unite them, but they never leave them the same.[75] If the leadership of the company can respond to a crisis justly and competently, by means that call for equitable sacrifice from—as opposed to sacrifice *of*—employees, sacrifices themselves can prove a tonic for a work community. These sacrifices not only create a sounder economic organization (promoting foundational goods), but also actually foster a real sense of community (promoting excellent goods). It is that reality which those at Heinz apparently could not imagine or address, since they failed to move beyond foundational goods. Most employees are willing to make sacrifices when they believe it will be *shared*, a sacrifice which addresses a *common* threat, such as a revenue shortfall.[76] A preexisting culture of ownership (as promoted by Reell's ESOP) will go a long way toward eliciting voluntary sacrifice when business conditions make sacrifice unavoidable. Reell presents an example of a company that has learned to integrate justice and strategic thinking. Reell managers understand that human development, as the company's overarching end, must be pursued through the virtues, with justice foremost among them. They employ strategic techniques—carefully keeping them in their proper place—as the means of sustaining the company's human vocation.

A Brief Summary

A Living Wage: The Principle of Need. A living wage is *the minimum amount due to every independent wage earner by the mere fact that he or she is a human being with a life to maintain and a personality to develop.*

Issues: What criteria are used to determine a just wage that serves as a minimum floor? How does one overcome the obstacles of a market wage that falls below this minimum floor? What role does the state have in determining living wages?

An Equitable Wage: The Principle of Contribution. An equitable wage *is the contribution of an employee's productivity and effort within the context of the existing amount of profits and resources of the organization.*

Issues: How does one know if they have become too narrow or quantitative or too broad or vague in determining contribution? How does one attract the necessary human talent and maintain internal equity? How does one avoid short-termism, poor morale, and manipulative politics when instituting incentives?

A Sustainable Wage: The Principle of Economic Order. *The principle of economic order examines the employer's ability to pay wages that are sustainable for the economic health of the organization as a whole.*

Issues: Sustainable = Livable + Equitable. How many people can an organization afford to pay living wages? What is the role of part-time work? When is it ethical to lay people off and move a company because the labor costs are no longer sustainable? What is the role of automation?

CONCLUSION

There are, of course, various ways to examine the question of just wages. The Chicago-based group "Business Executives for Economic Justice" who meet to reflect on the importance and challenge of faith within business, examined this issue and came up with the following guidelines for a just wage:[77]

1. You cannot assume a wage is just because someone is willing to accept it.
2. The lowest full-time paid person at a company ought to be earning enough money to allow the worker a standard of living consistent with human dignity.
3. A manager's first obligation is maintaining the company as a going concern for the benefit of all the stakeholders (investors, employees, customers, and community).
4. The right of all employees of the company to be paid a living wage prevails over the right of owners/investors to earn a reasonable rate of return on their investment in the company.

5. If the above four criteria are met:
    • Because they risk their capital, owners/investors are justified in earning a higher level of compensation than generally prevails among their employees.
    • Because of their assumed responsibility, level of talent and experience, managers are also justified in earning a higher level of compensation.

Whatever guidelines one may develop, it is critical for the manager and entrepreneur to break away from a purely instrumental or market-based approach, and to think broadly and deeply from a faith perspective.

Were a company committed to achieving a just wage tomorrow, what steps should it take today? Three seem critically important:

Articulate a pay philosophy: Every company adheres to an implicit philosophy of compensation. Relatively few companies adequately explain it to themselves.[78] The three principles of a living wage (need), an equitable wage (contribution), and a sustainable wage (economic order) make for good starting points. Of course, a philosophy of pay only makes sense for an organizational culture that finds its purpose in the common good of its members, and those in communion with wider society.

Evaluate present pay practices: The three principles also make for critical standards against which to evaluate the present pay system, with the aim of establishing a better fit between principles of justice and concrete practices.

Align pay practices with pay philosophy: Initiate policies that clearly are connected to the principles of pay. For example, institute a "Living Wage Policy" which establishes a "floor" and connects skill development to wage increases, or a "Wage Differential Policy" which confines wage-extremes within fixed ratios, so that the highest paid employee will not receive more than 10 or 20 times the wage of the lowest paid employee. Whole Foods, for example, pays no one more than 8 times the average salary of the company. Announced principles must receive concrete expression. Without concrete application, organizations usually find it better "to have no principles than to have principles that are not lived up to."[79]

These steps are not a recipe for the solution of the problem of just pay. They will not create a beatific vision of "pay nirvana." They will not relieve managers of their burdens, and may even multiply them. Managers may find some comfort in the thought that the burdens involved in the quest for just wages are borne for the sake of the common good, and that success in bearing them is itself growth in virtue. A compensation system based upon justice and the common good will set organizations on the long and arduous path toward developing organizational conditions that foster human development not only materially, but also morally and spiritually.

Entrepreneurs and human resource managers would do well to be more candid, especially to themselves, about the ethical traditions and the perception of the human person that they use when examining issues of compensation. Often an unstated, unexamined utilitarianism undergirds the purely strategic thinking that reduces human beings and human communities to so many "human resources." Once again, we must say that our criticisms of strategic pay are offered without prejudice to strategic theory's technical successes. Our point throughout this chapter has been that through prudent use, strategic thinking should itself become a "human resource."

STUDY QUESTIONS

1. What is the end or aim of pay within the Christian social tradition? In your answer focus on the tension between a strategic and Christian view of the pay relationship/exchange. Be sure to bring in the subjective and objective dimensions of work in your answer.
2. What means are suggested in this chapter to foster a just wage?
3. How did Reell Precision Manufacturing respond to market circumstances in order to pay a living wage?
4. Why is strategic thinking both critically necessary but fundamentally insufficient in understanding a just wage?

VIDEO SUGGESTION

A Just Wage from *Religion and Ethics News Weekly* (202-216-2380). Reports on the importance and difficulty of paying a just wage in a free market system.

6

Corporate Ownership

Temperance and Common Use in Finance

*The paramount problem is not how to stop the growth of property,
and the building up of wealth; but how to manage it so that every
species of property, like a healthful fruit tree, will spread its roots
deeply and widely in the soil of a popular proprietorship. The
paramount problem is not how to crush, or hawk at, or hamper the
corporation, merely because it is a corporation; but how to make this
new form of property ownership a workable agent toward
repeopleizing the proprietorship of the country's industries.*[1]

—Peter S. Grosscup
Judge of the U.S. Circuit Court of Appeals

WRITTEN IN 1905, JUDGE GROSSCUP'S COMMENTS capture both the free-market system's strength and its weakness: its ability to create wealth, and its inability to distribute it equitably. Ownership of the corporation, according to Grosscup, lies at the heart of the distribution problem in free market economies where the corporation is the main generator of wealth. Those who own corporations will enjoy far more of the distribution of that wealth. For Grosscup, a principal issue for corporations is the development of a structure of ownership that distributes the wealth of society more effectively, without sacrificing the corporation's wealth-generating ability.

The problem of wealth disparity that prompted Grosscup's comments at the beginning of the twentieth century burdens us in a particularly global way as we enter the twenty-first century. For example, The United Nations Development Program concluded in 1996 that 100 countries found themselves worse off than they had been 15 years earlier. It is estimated that the combined wealth of the 224 richest individuals in the world equals the combined annual incomes of the poorest 47% of the world population, that is, of some 2.5 billion people.[2] A variety of evidence indicates that even in the U.S., where there has been significant economic growth over the last two decades, the gap between the most affluent Americans and everyone else in the nation is the widest it has been since the end of World War II.[3] Although the *average* income for households increased 10% between 1979 and 1994, the top 20% of households claimed 97% of that growth. This has resulted in a wide economic disparity where the net worth of the top 1% is now greater than that of the bottom 90%.[4] While mutual funds and 401(k) plans have fueled much-celebrated gains in capital participation, one study showed that 71% of U.S. households hold no stock, or hold stock valued at less than $2,000.[5]

For the reader who may find these numbers too abstract, Jeff Gates cites the rise of "Tiffany/Kmart" marketing strategies. Kmart and Tiffany, which represent the low- and high-end retail markets, reported increased earnings in 1997, while midscale chains such as J.C. Penney suffered significant losses. National retailers are setting up two-tiered, high-low marketing systems, as advertising and investment houses warn of the erosion of traditional, "middle-class" mass-markets. Retailers see that a shift in income patterns is polarizing markets to the disadvantage of operations aimed at a shrinking class of middle incomes.[6]

For some, wealth disparity simply represents a natural economic force we must accept in a free market. Paine Webber Inc., for example, simply readjusts its investment flows by advising investors to "avoid companies that cater to the 'middle' of the consumer market."[7] However, others see wealth disparity more as a function of choice than market determination. William McDonough, president of the Federal Reserve Bank of New York, insists,

[i]ssues of equity and social cohesion [are] issues that affect the very temperament of the country. We are forced to face the

question of whether we will be able to go forward together as a unified society with a confident outlook or as a society of diverse economic groups suspicious of both the future and each other.[8]

For McDonough, unless we take seriously the idea of the common good as it relates to wealth distribution, we may find our cultural and political arenas too fragmented to support a healthy free market system.

Many complex causes account for widening income disparity. One key cause, particularly in the U.S., has been the interplay of *productivity gains, wages,* and *capital.* Since 1974, productivity increased by 68% in manufacturing, and by 50% in the service sector. During this same time period, however, employee wages stagnated. The rewards of productivity consequently went to capital. With the richest 25% of the population owning 82% of corporate stock in the U.S., the clear winners were capital owners. Consequently, income disparity increased.[9]

The problem, as Grosscup suggested, is not the magnitude of capital owners' gains, but the system's tendency to restrict rather than to promote participation in capital ownership. When the power of the ownership of productive capital is highly concentrated in the hands of the few, the income of the nonowning majority grows uncertain; when capital is *disconnected* from labor, its use may be determined without regard for its impact on labor or on society at large.[10]

As Peter Drucker said, "A change in property ownership always results in a change in power. We've had a change in property with the emergence of institutional investors. That is a change in power."[11] Power in this case has gone to depersonalized capital markets, which have no concern for employees or particular communities beyond their ability to increase wealth. The markets' relentless pursuit of maximum investor return compels corporations to "unleash what the *Wall Street Journal* characterizes as the 'four horsemen of the workplace': (1) downsizing; (2) moving operations to low-wage countries, (3) increased automation and (4) the use of temporary workers."[12] Most people—certainly most wage earners—might concede that firms might use one or more of these expedients legitimately to meet economic crises, but few would consider their combination as a legitimate, ordinary business practice. Nevertheless, they have become

Pockets of Prosperity, Holes of Disparity:
Some Numbers to Ponder

- The United Nations Development Program (UNDP) reported in 1999 that the world's 200 richest people have more than doubled their net worth in the four years to 1998, to more than $1 trillion. That's equal to the combined annual income of the poorest 47 percent of the world's people (2.5 billion).
- The wealth of the top three billionaires now exceeds the combined GDP of all the least developed countries and their 600 million people. The assets of the 84 richest individuals exceed the GDP of China with its 1.2 billion people.
- UNDP reported in 1999 that 80 countries have per capita incomes lower than they were a decade ago. Sixty countries have been growing steadily poorer since 1980.
- In 1960, the income gap between the fifth of the world's people living in the richest countries and the fifth in the poorest was 30 to 1. By 1990, the gap had widened to 60 to 1. By 1997, it had grown to 74 to 1.
- Over the past three decades, the poorest 20 percent of the world's people saw their share of global income decline from 2.3 percent to 1.3 percent.
- In 1996, the Census Bureau reported record levels of inequality, with the top fifth of U.S. households claiming 48.2 percent of national income while the bottom fifth gets by on 3.6 percent.
- The United States leads all OECD nations in the disparity in both wealth and income.

Source: Jeff Gates, "From Containment to Community," forthcoming in *Perspectives.*[13]

staples of those who drive "disconnected" capital's pursuit of ever-increasing returns, regardless of the social effects.

In order for people to participate effectively in the market system's distribution of wealth, they need access to two main sources of income: labor and capital. Restricting their income effectively to one source—labor—through the concentration of ownership, increases the probability that their access to goods will fall short of their needs. This effect is intensified in an economy such as our own, where capital income increases faster than labor income. For many people, the wages alone of even two earners are no longer adequate to secure a just share of wealth over the long-term. When John A. Ryan wrote in 1935 that an employee's rise to ownership "relieves him from complete dependence upon his wages,"[14] he already understood "relief" to mean relief from bearing an inequitably large share of the market-economy's risks and an inequitably small share of its rewards.

We need a view of capital property that asks the fundamental questions, *What is property for?* and *Whom does it serve?* Within our diverse society, answers to these questions will vary significantly. As we saw in chapter 2, the main reason for these variations will be the divergent views concerning the purpose of the corporation. Within the last thirty years in the U.S., two men have played critical roles in addressing these questions, and have brought about two important financial trends: mergers and acquisitions, and employee ownership. These two men place property and finance within two different philosophical paradigms, one individualistic and the other communitarian. Their views of the nature and purpose of corporate property provide a context in which to appreciate a Christian ethic of property and ownership in respect to the modern corporation.

Two Conflicting Views of Property: Individualistic and Communitarian

The first of our two figures is *Jerome Kohlberg*. The founder of Kohlberg, Kravis, and Roberts & Co. (KKR), and often considered the father of leveraged buyouts (LBOs),[15] Kohlberg's main concern was the separation of corporate ownership and control.[16] As corporations have grown larger, capital holdings have been dispersed to larger numbers of shareholders, reducing shareholders' control of the company. The largest shareholder at a company such as General Motors may own only 1% of the shares. It is likely that this "owner" will actually be a pension fund or some other institutional shareholder. This dispersed ownership structure diffuses shareholders' influence, and prevents them from taking a decisive hand in maximizing the return on their capital. Kohlberg's solution to this problem is acquisition through the leveraged buyout. By replacing diffuse public shareholders, who exercise little control over the corporation, with a small group of highly motivated investors who exercise considerable control over a small group of highly motivated executives, owners can be in a better position to maximize their wealth (this partially explains why executive bonuses are so high—there is an alignment between stock price and executive salary).[17]

As for the issue of the common good, Kohlberg understands property primarily as a private and particular good—a tendency shared by many of us in the Western world. For him, a corporation is an investment that should maximize the particular goods of *individual* shareholders on the basis of two dimensions: risk and return. It has no inherent or "natural" *common* purpose of wealth creation for distribution, nor of building community or promoting virtue. Finance serves as a technique to maximize the particular wealth of individual shareholders, who in their private lives can determine what they want to do with it. Thus, corporate property is reduced to a "financial asset owned for its return/risk characteristics and with a view to its eventual sale."[18] Underlying Kohlberg's understanding of corporate property is a philosophical individualism that implies at least two things: first, exclusivity of ownership, that is, "*this property is mine and not yours*"; and second, control, that is, "*it's mine, and I alone determine its use.*"[19]

Quite different from Kohlberg, and often considered the father of employee ownership, *Louis Kelso* viewed property in communitarian and democratic terms. Kelso maintained that Employee Stock Ownership Plans (ESOPs) would serve as an effective corporate financial technique to distribute wealth in the economy.[20] Applying his two-factor theory (that income derives from one's *labor* and/or

FIGURE 6.1

	Kohlberg	Kelso
Definition of Problem	Lack of Control by the Few	Lack of Participation by the Many
End of Property	Individual Gain	Just Distribution
Means of Finance	Leverage (LBOs)	Leverage (ESOPs)

one's *capital*), Kelso wrote in the 1960s and 70s that, owing to increasing use of technology and to international competition, capital would play a greater role in wealth distribution than wages from labor. Kelso believed that a company's employees and customers were its logical and natural shareholders.[21]

Kelso saw the ownership of the capital of corporations as the main vehicle for wealth distribution, and a necessary condition of human development (promotion of the common good). For him, financing companies is a means to a social end, namely, to build enterprises capable of long-term growth *by creating conditions for a just distribution of wealth*. In Kelso's view, corporate property has the important social purpose to make capital acquisition accessible to all, especially to those without the financial means to secure access to credit. An ESOP is one way to finance wider ownership, or in the words of Judge Grosscup, to "repeopleize" corporate property (in Europe, cooperatives have been the main means to that end).[22] As a financing device, an ESOP turns labor workers into capital workers, which in turn links the structures of ownership with social equity. (The mechanics and problems of ESOPs are examined in greater detail in the last section of this chapter.)

Because the lives of Kelso and Kohlberg were directly entangled, their differing views of property are all the more striking. In the 1960s, Kelso supposedly introduced the technique of leveraging corporations to Kohlberg. To leverage a company is to buy the company using borrowed money, with the company itself serving as collateral. Kelso envisioned leveraged financing through an ESOP as an effective means for employees to participate in the ownership of a company, thereby creating the conditions for a more just distribution of wealth. Since employees would never be able to save enough money to buy shares, they would have to borrow. Kohlberg adapted Kelso's technique of leveraged financing, but applied it to a different end, based on his different view of property. Indifferent to wealth distribution and income disparity, Kohlberg leveraged companies so that outside investors or executive management (that is, his clients) could buy the company and exercise control for the sake of maximizing shareholder wealth.

Kelso and Kohlberg used the same *technique* of leveraged financing for two radically different *ends* based on two different philosophical traditions of property (see figure 6.1). As we mentioned in chapter 3, techniques such as financial leveraging become an opportunity for virtue only when they are directed toward the common good. For Kelso, the technique of leveraged financing can be a powerful means for expanding ownership in the interest of a just distribution of wealth. For Kohlberg, however, this technique served the particular, private and exclusionary good of shareholders and nothing more.

Kohlberg's use of leveraging infuriated Kelso: "I taught them [Kohlberg and others] the art of the leveraged buyout. Now they're just using it for the wrong *purposes*, to make themselves and a few people richer."[23] Kelso saw leveraged financing for the goal of concentrating wealth as an abuse. His case is not unlike that of the researchers who developed the drug methotrexate to fight cancer and save lives, only to see other researchers adapt it to take lives as one of the main ingredients in abortifacients. Techniques can be used for good or ill. For Kelso, to make the technique of leveraged financing into a means for private gain alone is a perversion: "instead of making economic power more democratic, they [Kohlberg and others] make it more plutocratic."[24] That is, Kelso denounced Kohlberg's use of leverage as a capital finance tool for an existing elite group of owners. It did nothing to increase the ranks of capital ownership.

This conflict between Kohlberg and Kelso represents a similar conflict concerning possible responses to the questions, *What is property for?* and *Whom does it serve?* Kohlberg's ideas represent an individualistic understanding of property that denies there is an authentic social and spiritual purpose to the corporation. Kelso represents the near opposite communitarian vision of corporate property that coincides with that of the Christian social tradition. We can see in the visions of these two men the concrete and practical implications of philosophical beliefs concerning property. We must probe deeper into the roots of the communitarian understanding of property underlying Kelso's goals, as it appears in the Christian tradition. By retrieving this tradition concerning property, and on employee ownership in particular, we can provide a solid basis for reexamining the ownership and distribution of productive capital. It is precisely here that an investigation informed by the Christian social tradition can help to answer *why* a just distribution of income in terms of capital and labor concerns all people.

A Christian Property Ethic as It Relates to the Ownership of the Corporation

It is important to recognize that the idea of ownership is one of the fundamental ideas of Western civilization. Most major philosophers and theologians have written about property, and all economists and business people are dependent in one way or another on these philosophical principles. At root, the way we organize property is a means of organizing social relations, and so it has a powerful influence over the goodness—or lack of it—in people's lives. We can characterize an understanding of property on four levels.

The Christian understanding of property is, first, theological. It arises out of our belief in a God who created the world "and saw it was very good," and who, as part of that creation, gave humankind the gift of dominion over the earth. In other words, the basic, core idea that grounds the Christian understanding of property is the reality of it being a *gift*, that is, a *gift from God*.

While we are familiar with the experience of giving and receiving, we tend to see it as a private and individual exchange. This understanding of gift, however, is not universal. When Native Americans encountered Europeans in the gift encounter, they were baffled by their possessiveness over gifts given them. Native Americans expected their white visitors to give back their gifts so as to keep them moving. This idea of setting gifts in motion equally baffled Westerners, who coined the pejorative phrase, "Indian givers."[25] What Native

Americans understood, and what we should take heed of, is that when a gift is not shared, it corrupts the holder. The one who makes the gift an occasion for selfish hoarding, rather than keeping the gift in motion, becomes corrupted by the gift itself.

In the West, we tend to regard property as a private matter, as Kohlberg did: "As long as it doesn't hurt anyone, I have the right to do whatever I like with what is mine." Yet, our "private" interpretation of property should give us pause for thought. St. Augustine pointed out that the word *private* comes from "privation," signifying a certain loss of meaning or substance.[26] To understand property *only* in private terms is to refuse to recognize its inherent "giftedness."

Humans do not create anything, but rather inherit everything from God and others. Our human ownership of things is not an absolute dominion over property (absolute dominion belongs to God alone), but rather a limited and responsible dominion best characterized as stewardship. An insistence on a solely private interpretation of property, then, asserts a dominion human beings do not and cannot exercise.

If we are to truly understand property, we must face the universal experience of property, which is that, in the end, everything is given back. At a rich man's wake, someone asked, "How much did he leave?" The simple conversation stopping answer: "Everything!"[27] Property—all wealth—is a gift, of which our "ownership" is no more than a temporary stewardship. We neither arrive in this life with property nor leave with it, and as owners we will be called to a steward's accounting of our use of property.

Christian managers and entrepreneurs, if they *manage as if faith mattered*, must come to understand that their property and their work are not ultimately theirs and that they will be accountable not just to stockholders, but to Him "who knows how to ask questions."[28] They need to keep in mind that they will be judged with mercy, but also with justice: Have they been stewards or exploiters of the property and wealth committed to them?

If to possess property is ultimately to receive a gift, then ownership inherently involves entering the *second level* of the Christian property ethic, summarized in the principle of "the universal destination of goods." Possession is for the sake of use, and the gift of created goods is made to all human beings alike, not only to the brightest or the richest, not to one country rather than another, not to one generation rather than another. Inscribed within the very makeup of useful goods is a "universal destination": their goodness is for all alike, so that all people can benefit from God's creation. To use the terms of chapter 3, the fruits of creation must be made available to all human beings at the level of use. St. Ambrose, with the directness and confidence that characterized the Fathers of the Church, declared, "The earth belongs to all, not to the rich."[29]

Embedded in God's gift of creation is the right of all people to the *common use* of created goods. To subdue the earth is to command its fruits not only for oneself, but also for others through increasingly comprehensive spheres of community: for family and friends; for co-workers, and for fellow citizens and colleagues in the political enterprise; for fellow members of the body of Christ, and for one's neighbor—that is, for anyone in human need. The duty to subdue the earth, then, cannot be realized unless all people can share in the means of dominion (raw material, technology, education, credit, etc.), in order to reach a sustainable decent standard of living.[30] Consequently, any idea of an absolute right to the possession or use of property is alien to Christian social thought, since property is neither the creature of its owner, nor is it destined unqualifiedly for its owner's use.[31]

The *third level* of a Christian ethic of ownership and property considers what conditions foster greater common use of God's creation. We argued in the first several pages of this chapter that a wider distribution of *productive property or capital* is necessary for greater common use.[32] To serve labor, property and capital must be reconnected to labor through ownership. This is why within the Christian tradition, and as the subject of special attention in Catholic social teaching, employee participation in the ownership of business organizations is strongly emphasized. As John Paul II has stated, while various employee ownership plans may or may not be applicable in specific situations, "it is clear that recognition of the proper position of labor and the worker in the production process demands various adaptations in the sphere of the right to ownership of the means of production."[33]

Jeff Gates points out that the more *connected* capital can be to labor and to the communities that supply labor (that is, through ownership), the more it can serve the common good. (He, Norman Kurland, Robert Ashford, and others propose not only ESOPs but also CSOPs— Customer Stock Ownership Plans, RESOPs—Related Enterprise Share Ownership Plans, and other stock ownership plans to reconnect capital to the communities that generate it.) Gates aims for an "up-close capitalism" in which those who stand to be affected by the uses of corporate property consider those uses from the perspective of owners, and speak for or against them with the voices of owners.

Thomas Aquinas made a similar point in the thirteenth century. He explained that private possession can serve the principle of common use because it creates three important conditions: *personal initiative, productivity,* and *peace.*[34] These three criteria do not guarantee the common use of property. They do, however, create conditions that facilitate the individual's access to the goods of creation by overcoming the disparity in wealth we described at the beginning of this chapter. We will examine these three conditions with employee ownership in mind to illustrate how a Christian ethic of property ownership can function.

1. Personal Initiative and Motivation

When people own something, they are more likely to use it in a considered, enterprising way. The person is more likely to dedicate time and talent to caring for and developing his own property than to caring for another's, and is more likely to show consideration for properties that are owned by some person or agency than for those which belong to no one. For example, a person shows more initiative for the care of an owned house than for a rented apartment, and people generally treat city parks with more consideration than they do vacant lots. For the individual employee, worker ownership can serve as a means to a greater sense of self-direction at work, since when people "know they are working on what belongs to them, they work with far greater eagerness and diligence."[35] Many employees are not concerned solely with the foundational, financial goods they receive from their labor, they also want to know that they are working for themselves, and that their work is a matter of personal achievement and even of excellence. Employees who do not participate in the ownership of the company find it more difficult to make a personal connection with what is not their own. Worker ownership can serve as an aid to employees' development by fostering responsibility and accountability.[36]

2. Long-Term Productivity and Efficiency

This personal initiative encourages greater productivity and efficiency, and less waste. Jack Stack, CEO of Springfield Remanufacturing Company (SRC), emphasizes this point when promoting his company's ESOP. In his view, employee owners tend to shift their thinking entirely when they consider the whole question of what it means to benefit from the company. They think of "sacrificing instant gratification" for long-term stability and longevity. Stack explains, "[If] you have equity and understand it, you know why it's important to build for the future. You can make long-term decisions. You will pay attention to the day-to-day details, but you're doing it for the right reason: because it's the best way to achieve *lasting* success."[37]

3. Social Peace

When people possess the things they need to meet their responsibilities, keep their promises, and realize their ambitions, they are simply more at peace and more disposed to harmony with others than they are when they cannot own or control these things. This simple fact has become very evident in the downsizing of corporations. Employees may have large pensions at stake, but because they are not owners they lack any control over the disposition of their company. In such cases, employees' anxiety and hostility are likely to run in direct proportion to the size of their stake in outcomes over which they have no say. The more people who participate in the ownership of property, particularly productive property, the better the chances that wealth will flow like blood through the human body, as a force for health and social cohesion.[38]

When employees are not interested or not allowed to participate in the ownership of their own organization, a divergence of economic interests is created that makes peace more difficult to achieve. When shareholders and management seek higher profits, lower labor costs, and greater efficiency, while at the same time employees seek higher fixed wages and stringent work rules, the ownership structure breeds distrust between employees and management. This weakens a company's competitiveness in the marketplace and inhibits mutual cooperation for the good of the whole organization.[39] A house divided against itself, as the Scriptures note, cannot long stand—let alone prosper.[40] Isolating the means of production "as a separate property in order to set it up in the form of 'capital' in opposition to 'labor'" makes the possibility of peace ever more difficult.[41] Jack Stack explains, "[Y]ou have to knock down the barriers that separate people, that keep people from coming together as a team."[42] At SRC, he saw the lack of shared ownership between management and workers as a critical barrier to overcome. By connecting the perceived goods of employees and managers through stock ownership, SRC could act as a cohesive unit with increasing confidence that all were working for each other.[43]

Personal initiative, long-term productivity and peace are necessary conditions for making corporate property common in use. They do not, however, complete a Christian property/ownership ethic. The common use of property requires that we do not regard property as something to be distributed and used merely for our own particular ends. We need to go to a *fourth level* of this ethic, which calls us to use our property for the development of "a community of work," with its roots in participation toward common ends and virtues.

All property, Aquinas explains, should be seen "as common so that, in fact, a person should readily share it when he sees others in need."[44] A more equitable distribution of particular goods by individual ownership is not enough: employees and management alike must understand and treat their shares in the ownership of the company as instruments of others' good, and not merely of their own particular interests. This necessary regard for others' good is twofold. First, it involves participation in seeking the good of each and every member of the firm by promoting the firm's success. Second, it involves arranging the activities of the firm to promote the good of the wider community and its members (including, of course, the members of the firm).

The fact that a company is widely owned by employees, or that its financial success is immediately distributed among its employees, does not in itself prove that the firm is pursuing the common good. Neither is the enthusiasm of a company's employees, or their dedication to its business plan, a sure sign that they form a genuine communion. Pornography and tobacco companies can be employee-owned, and criminal enterprises often generate considerable élan. In comparison to the overall good of the (political) community, *the common good*, the ends of even the largest business organization are private, *as are the ends of individual persons.* Business organizations' fundamental contribution to the common good, like that of private individuals, is observance of the law. And like private individuals, their more mature contribution involves participating in the promotion of the goods of the whole community (we will examine the social role of products and services in chapter 7).

Real ownership of the organization by employees offers an occasion of virtue. When an employee sees her contribution to the organization as the source of benefits not only for herself and her family, but also for her coworkers, and when her contribution to the success of the firm is also of clear service to the community at large, she participates in a *fuller way*—through virtue—in her work. In the words of Aquinas, "a man's will is not right in willing a particular good [such as property], unless he refers it to the common as an end."[45] The equitable distribution of corporate property is welcome for its own sake, but even more for the sake of establishing a community of work through which the firm's success promotes both the employee's individual good and the good of the whole community. Employees are connected not only in the pursuit of economic gain, but also in the fulfillment of organizational purpose that is social at its core.

This discussion of property suggests an answer to the unsettling scriptural question: *Why is it hard for the rich man to enter the kingdom of God?* If we fail to direct our own particular goods to a common life, our lack of intent to build community is not neutral, but, rather, a decisive refusal to take up the duty incumbent upon citizens of the kingdom of God. This theme is particularly strong in Luke's Gospel, in which Jesus tells the story of the rich man's quandary over what to do with his surplus harvest.

> "What shall I do?" he asked himself. "I have no place to store my harvest. I know!" he said. "I will pull down my grain bins and build larger ones. All my grain and my goods will go there. Then I will say to myself: You have blessings in reserve for years to come. Relax! Eat heartily, drink well. Enjoy yourself." But God said to him, "You fool! This very night your life shall be required of you. To whom will all this piled-up wealth of yours go?" That is the way it works with the man who grows rich for himself instead of growing rich in the sight of God.[46]

The point of the parable is clear: the use of property must be directed to the good of others if it is to serve as a means to the rich man's development, especially to his ultimate development, which is salvation and happiness with God. When property is not directed and used for the common good, it becomes a kind of evil, and an occasion for regression from human virtue. As the rich man's failure to use his full granary for those in need corrupted him, so our property, whether individual or corporate, can corrupt us if we fail to use it for others.

This idea of property as intimately tied to common use and virtue may sound too idealistic, too communitarian, or too impractical to some. If it does, we should ask why. Is it because we live in a culture that reduces all goods to commodities for particular, private consumption? Or is it because we have disconnected our faith from daily life to such an extent that we no longer see its social and practical implications? Whatever the reason, we should take care to reexamine how we regard our property, since it affects our perception of other dimensions of our life.

The strictly private, strictly individualistic view of property is similar to the idea that sex is exclusively for personal pleasure. While pleasure naturally accompanies healthy sexuality, the pursuit of sexual pleasure alone—sexual hedonism—has always been a sign of personal futility and emptiness. That perception degrades both the hedonist and the objects of his desire (for indeed, they become nothing more than objects to be possessed). So it is with wealth. While it "naturally" accompanies healthy enterprise, the quest of wealth alone degrades the human dignity of businesspeople, and denies the integral importance of the broader community, which alone makes the ownership of property possible and meaningful.

Thus, an understanding of the "big picture," and especially an avoidance of any myopic view regarding profits or wealth maximization is necessary for understanding the ownership of the modern corporation.[47] We call this habit the virtue of *temperance*. As we mentioned in chapter 3, temperance is that virtue which curbs and restrains our desire. The amount of wealth to be gained or lost in market economies is so enormous that St. Paul's warning about the love of money as a root to all kinds of evil should not be far from our minds.[48] The individualistic view of property has no means to curb the "all-consuming desire for profit" borne in all of us.[49] If this generation of money-denominated returns represents for us the whole purpose of corporate property, it is the result of intemperance, the excessive pursuit of wealth at the expense of all other goods.

Kenneth Goodpaster calls this intemperance *teleopathy*. Combining the Greek roots *telos,* for end or purpose, and *pathos*, for disease or sickness, he defines teleopathy as an "overemphasis on limited purposes by individuals and corporations," or a sickness of purpose.[50] Wealth is a limited goal; it should not be a governing purpose. To use our earlier terms, wealth generation is a means that cannot serve to guide us as an end.

In business, as in any other profession, the practitioner is constantly tempted to value certain limited goals, such as wealth, over larger goals, such as human development. Teleopathy or intemperance is the bad habit of regarding wealth maximization "as supremely action-guiding." Wealth, or any possession of goods, such as sex, power, fame, food, drink, etc., can be corrupting because it tends toward excess, and so requires an extrinsic limit—an outside control. The limiter or controller of one's possessions is the opportunity to distribute them to relieve others' needs, and for the promotion of the common good, such as the need of one's family, friends, coworkers, neighbors, or fellow-citizens

Augustine states: "The temperate man finds confirmation of the rule forbidding him to love the things of this life, or to deem any of them desirable for its own sake."[51] Wealth generated from property should not be maximized for its own sake; rather, the generation of wealth, if it is to avoid becoming pathological, must be directed to the common good. Temperance, in regard to our property and wealth, helps us to overcome our fixations and addictions by harnessing our *intense desire* for a narrow goal, such as profit maximization, in order to redirect us toward a much broader one, such as the common good. When they recognize this broader goal of the common good, managers have a better chance of creating conditions amenable to the development of a real community within the firm. Without temperance, most companies focus exclusively on financial goals and cease to even consider using the tool that is their capital for a broader social purpose.[52]

A close analysis of the Christian concept of property reveals what is really at stake in the corporation. The following ESOP case clearly illustrates some implications of a Christian property ethic and the ownership of an organization.

CASE: PHELPS COUNTY BANK

All kinds of U.S. companies have ESOPs. Large companies, such as United Airlines and Cargill have them, as well as smaller and medium-sized companies, such as Wierton Steel and Springfield Remanufacturing Company. We examine here the Phelps County Bank (PCB), an independent community bank in Rolla, Missouri, with 60 employees, in order to explain how an ESOP works, its benefits, and its shortcomings.[53]

PCB has a leveraged ESOP.[54] The leveraged ESOP can be described through the following four stages:[55]

Stage 1: The board of directors and representatives of the current owners agree to sell part or all of the company to the employees. They appoint trustees of the ESOP who set up the ESOP trust.
Stage 2: A financial institution lends money to the ESOP trust, usually at a reduced rate because of U.S. tax advantages to banks. The ESOP is subject to the same feasibility standards and corporate guarantees as direct loans to the corporation. For example,

the credit for the loan is secured by and repaid from the existing capital and future profits of the company. The ESOP trust in turn buys the stock from existing owners and sets up a temporary stock account.

Stage 3: As the loan is paid back, shares are released from the temporary stock account and distributed to individual employee stock accounts. Norman Kurland explains that "shares of stock are allocated to the individual accounts of workers only as blocks of shares are 'earned', i.e., the company contributes cash out of future pretax profits to the trust. The cash, which is treated as a tax-deductible employee benefit, is used to repay the stock acquisition loan."

Stage 4: When employees retire, they usually sell their shares back to the ESOP, from which new employees can then purchase them.[56]

When PCB's management presented the idea of an ESOP to employees, they were greeted with skepticism. From the employees' perspective, nothing changed noticeably in the organization, except that the ESOP would replace future wage increases with shares of stock. Most of the PCB employees were raised in homes where incomes were earned through wages.[57] Apart from this cultural dependency on wages, younger parents found the deferred income idea difficult to take. Faced with real economic pressures, and influenced by the consumer culture, many employees—and particularly younger employees—"have a relatively strong preference of current over future consumption; they do not wish to save 25% of their compensation to secure future pension benefits."[58]

Yet, through its ESOP, PCB has created more wealth and has distributed that wealth more justly throughout the organization, over the long term. In the first year of the ESOP (1980), a junior officer's total contribution to the plan was $456. In 1994, that same officer's contribution to the plan was $29,300, with an accumulated account balance of more than $200,000. An ESOP is like a house mortgage. At the beginning, payments to the loan take very little off the principal, but as the house appreciates and as the interest is paid off, equity in the house increases at a faster rate.[59]

A critical underlying problem in setting up the ESOP at PCB was resistance to the culture of ownership. For the ESOP to take hold at PCB, it was imperative to educate those involved in an ownership philosophy. Ownership must exist not only on the books, but also in the culture: employees must take ownership over their own work and they must equip themselves with knowledge and skills to be *real* owners of the firm. PCB undertook an educational program soon after initiating its ESOP. All employees became more familiar with PCB's own products and with the firm's financial status, and they developed a wider understanding of the banking industry in general. The new training and education were very costly and time-consuming. They required more meetings and new job duties, which added more hours to the day for most employees.

Not everyone found ownership appealing. The transition to employee ownership at PCB required additional time and energy from all employees, which caused problems and created resentment. Between 1986 and 1988, PCB experienced a turnover of approximately 40% in nonmanagement and 25% in management staff. As PCB's new culture became more widely known, however, the firm began to attract employees who wanted to learn and grow with the ownership of the company. Original employees who had remained with PCB found the transition from a conventional to an employee-owned corporation painful, but in the end also discovered that the change made their work more rewarding and fulfilling. The transitional problems at PCB appeared not because of the ESOP itself, but because of a change in the culture of the bank. The initial, high turnover principally included employees who objected to allocating a larger share of their energies and time to their work.

Management at PCB realized that for the ESOP to be successful, employees needed to participate to the fullest extent possible in their work. Education was critical. By training their employees and sharing more information about the company and the industry, PCB increased participation in three ways:

1) *Giving more authority to employees over their own jobs (subsidiarity):*
   CEO Emma Lou Brent explains, "Employee-owners were given authority to use their own judgment to do what they felt

necessary to retain a customer's goodwill. This included the right to negotiate interest rates, refund charges, or use creative options in solving customer problems."[60]

2) *Providing more opportunities to participate in group decision making:* Because all employees are now owners, they have a greater stake in all areas of the company, including the board of directors. At PCB, employees are elected by their peers to be members of the ESOP committee that oversees the communication and implementation of the ESOP. Committee members attend the national ESOP meeting to educate themselves in the broader ideas and philosophy of ESOPs.

3) *Better communication throughout the organization:* As Brent noted, at PCB more upward communication began to occur. "Sometimes it isn't what you want to hear, but you're making progress because now you're hearing it. It's been there all along. Employees just made sure it didn't get back to management in the earlier stages."[61]

By increasing accountability and responsibility in the organization, PCB has effectively used their ESOP to create conditions that allow employees to develop in their work. In other words, by putting the ESOP technique at the service of excellent ends, PCB has given it a "soul," based on the full participation of their employees.

The Common Good Challenge

ESOPs are not without their problems, however.[62] In some organizations, the sole principle guiding ESOPs is utility; for example, they serve as a technique for increasing productivity by motivating employees to work harder and more efficiently. While utility must be one guiding factor, not only of ESOPs but also of any organizational program, we should remember that utility itself is only one aspect of the effectiveness of certain kinds of means; ultimately, utility must be measured against an organization's highest or final ends. For example, one CEO we interviewed argued that he instituted an ESOP strictly for the strategic purpose of stabilizing his workforce, that is, his end was to reduce turnover through an ESOP that would make employees reluctant to leave the company. Any other reasons, he thought, were not good business thinking, as if to assume that good business reasoning must be instrumental reasoning.

When ESOPs are used in organizations simply as a productivity technique or a tax shelter, the full moral vision of an organization is truncated by what we termed in chapter 2, *instrumentalism*, that is, employees are seen primarily as tools—as means—and not first as ends. To consider ESOPs only as a productivity trick or tax advantage misses the larger objective of establishing an ownership culture that both distributes wealth justly and develops the person. ESOPs can create conditions for human development only if the common good in its fullest sense animates the whole business.

While we have found PCB to be a successful ESOP both morally and economically, the company, like all companies, faces a constant challenge in maintaining a principled approach with its ESOP. In chapter 2, we criticized the shareholder model for instrumentalizing the purpose and mission of business solely to the maximization of shareholder wealth. Employees, as owners, are not above adopting the shareholder model. They can adopt a financial philosophy of maximizing their own shareholder wealth, causing what could be called the "financialization of ESOPs," leading to overworked owners, among other things.

One issue at PCB causes us to raise some questions relating to instrumentalism. Our analysis is more hypothetical than factual; however, our hypothesis serves to illustrate how an ESOP, if it is not grounded in a social understanding of property, can decline into one more expression of economism.

Management at PCB felt that if the bank could increase the ESOP contribution from $100,000 to $250,000 in one year, they could emphasize the benefits of ownership in the bank through larger contributions to employees. In order to do this, the company had to increase its revenue. Management's target was to increase its loan portfolio by moving funds "from the lower yielding investment portfolio to higher yielding loans."[63] When PCB encouraged customers to take out higher yielding loans, employee payouts improved dramatically. By linking employee equity to employee activity, PCB was able to meet its strategic goals.

Certainly, there is nothing wrong with making financial goals and achieving them. There are, nonetheless, other important questions to

address in order to avoid allowing financial goals to become "teleo-
pathic"—sick in purpose. Are customers any better off with the higher
yielding loans? They may be. Yet, one can easily see a possible conflict
between the credit needs of the customer—particularly in a rural area,
such as Rolla, Missouri (where PCB does business)—and the higher
yielding loans which simultaneously served management's strategic
goals and employees' personal interests. For example, promoting consumer loans through credit cards rather than loans with lower interest
rates might well serve the financial interests of employees, but not the
good of the community of Rolla, and of PCB's customers in particular. The point here is that employee-owners may be as guilty as any
other owner of the "maximizing," strategic mentality that pursues the
firm's interest at the expense of the customer, the community and the
common good. This same maximizing mentality can result in overworked employees, which was one of the reasons why some employees left at the beginning of PCB's ownership venture. ESOPs are a
powerful, and to that extent a "good," technique, but they do not guarantee that employees will direct their particular goods toward the
common good.

There is a caveat here. Unlike an investment financier, the PCB
employee sees the customer regularly and is confronted with a face,
a family, a fellow-parishioner—a real person. The PCB employee's
stake in the ESOP is what Gates calls "connected capital," and dealings with PCB's customers generally involve Gates' "up-close capitalism."[64] It is easier, for example, to say, "I'll maximize my wealth,
and let the customer take care of himself," when the customer is faceless and the community a set of demographic profiles. The situation
is different when one shares with that customer the ordinary daily life
of the community outside the business relationship. This "connected,
up-close capitalism" may not be virtue, but it is certainly an occasion
for virtue.

CONCLUSION

This chapter rests on the belief that a wider ownership of productive
property promotes employees' development and ultimately serves the
common good. We see ESOPs as a particularly effective way of con-

verting corporate workplaces into work communities open to the deliberate promotion of common goods. ESOPs can be run in such a way that employees and managers become conscious participants in redirecting productive property toward the development of the members of the firm and the strengthening of the wider community.

Employee ownership supplies an indispensable condition for employee-management solidarity: it shares in a relatively undivided good of the company. It guarantees that management and employees alike can cultivate their individual interests only by building up the organization as a whole. As Charles Avila reminds us, "[W]ithout something materially concrete to share, we could no longer speak of a *koinonia* [community], a sharing in common."[65] However, even with something concrete to share, cooperators in a business organization will fall short of community unless they also share some ends that cannot be reduced to a dividend, converted to a price, or otherwise realized singly. That is to say, ownership in the sense of commanding a share must be tied to ownership in the sense of taking responsibility both for cultivating the good that the firm is, and for pursuing the good that the firm can do.[66]

The concept of worker ownership is consistent with the Christian social tradition in general, and advocated in the Catholic social tradition in particular, because it tends to serve the *end* of property. It does this not only by distributing wealth in service to human needs, but also by fostering a real community of work. The very difficulties people face in making the transition to an organizational culture of ownership are training themselves in the habits of solidarity, that is, of considering one's own good, and of deliberating and acting with the common good in mind.

While ESOPs as a *means* will not magically transform organizations into the very incarnation of the common good, they can certainly move them in the direction of greater community. Employee ownership provides one condition for employee/management solidarity by creating a community of work. Such a community must rest on a sound economic basis, which makes competencies in finance, marketing, operations, and so forth, essential preconditions. ESOPs provide wider ownership of productive property in a workable fashion, correcting a market economy's inherent tendency to concentrate ownership. Furthermore, ESOPs are doubly attractive in their effect of moving us closer to the common good because they tend to make responsible participation in the ends of enterprise the "flip side" of distributive ownership.[67]

The *circumstances* under which ESOPs can be implemented are contingent on many things, and the implementation of an ESOP bristles with details, each a potential source of friction: the current culture of the company, access to credit, future cash earnings, board representation, diversification of risk for employee retirement, assessment at sale, and the like. These details and their specific circumstances call for practical wisdom in managers and employees—people who can evaluate the situation as it is, and avoid plunging ahead with a generic "cookie-cutter" approach. This is no easy task, but the Christian vocation was never said to be easy.

STUDY QUESTIONS

1. Describe the fundamental differences between Kelso and Kohlberg's conceptions of property. How do their understandings of property shape their use of leveraged techniques?
2. Summarize your own ideas concerning property. Now, summarize the Christian view of property. Does the Christian concept match your own? Where are the points of convergence? Where are the points of tension?
3. How does PCB illustrate a Christian understanding of ownership? Where does it fall short?

VIDEO SUGGESTIONS

The ESOP Advantage, see http://www.esopassociation.org/prodcat/audiovis.html

The Anatomy of a Corporate Takeover (PBS) part 5 of the Ethics in America Series (1989) 1-800-LEARNER

The Mondragon Experiment (BBC Documentary "The Third Way")

7

Marketing Communication &
Product Development

Solidarity and Courage in Marketing

"Happiness is the condition of being well deceived."
—Jonathan Swift

"Better to be Aristotle dissatisfied than a fool fully satisfied."
—J. S. Mill[1]

"MARKETING IS EVERYTHING," WRITES REGIS
McKenna in *Relationship Marketing*.[2] While many
of us have heard it and might find that claim exaggerated, marketing does affect all aspects of the firm's activity. Consequently, all members of the organization should be aware of marketing's impact on their work. McKenna states,

> Marketing is not a new ad campaign or this month's promotion.
> Marketing has to be an all-pervasive part of everyone's job description, from the receptionists to the board of directors. Its job
> is neither to fool the customer nor to falsify the company's image.
> It is to integrate the customer into the design of the product and
> to design a systematic process for interaction that will create substance in the relationship.[3]

In other words, marketing is "a way of doing business."[4] We could
say that marketing is the channel through which the organization

relates to the world: "The marketer must be the integrator, both internally—synthesizing technological capability with market needs—and externally, bringing the customer into the company as a participant in the development and adaptation of goods and services."[5] For many management theorists, marketing is the central, integrating function of the whole business.

In this chapter, we will examine how marketing functions through organizing and monitoring communications between the business and its customers, and through initiating and regulating the development of new products or services. Obviously, marketers are involved in many business activities beyond these two areas, but they are key activities for managers who wish to ensure that their firms contribute to the common good.

First, we will survey the various underlying philosophies that marketing departments may have, and how these influence all their activities. Next, we will consider the communication process, and suggest that the idea of integrated marketing communication is most in accordance with the Christian tradition. Finally, we examine the new product development process (NPD), and suggest that Quality Function Deployment (QFD) represents a means of integrating faith and work while it makes the NPD process more effective.

How Does Marketing See Itself?

In chapter 2, we argued that a wealth-maximizing philosophy for the firm, especially when it influences the finance department, would adversely affect the way the firm was run and organized, and would distort the contribution of the firm to the common good. Similarly, how marketing people understand their function has a significant influence on how they communicate and how they approach the process of new product development. For the manager committed to the common good, a principal aspect of marketing communication will be honesty and relationship building, and for NPD, it will be the question of whether a proposed new product is truly good or only apparently good. Marketing approaches to these issues can be effectively divided into "relationship-based" and "postmodern" models.[6] In the first case, building commitment with the customer is a crucial element;[7] in the second, marketing sees itself as a contributing participant in a fragmented, ironic society, in which paradox and loss of commitment are simply features of life.[8] If the marketing department sees itself as promoting postmodern culture, then it will run itself and its communication programs very differently than one that is concerned with building long-term relationships with customers.

1. Postmodern Marketing

Some thinkers suggest that, far from being about building relationships, marketing is actually about the development of a postmodern world. One group of writers asserts that "marketing was born postmodern." "Postmodernity" names a set of ideas and attitudes that are still quite fluid, but we can outline some elements common to those who identity themselves as postmodern:[9]

*   *Hyperreality characterizes marketing and life.* Fashion goods represent the ultimate in hyperreality. Branded jeans, for instance, when they are promoted as giving a message to others about the wearer—a certain style, sexual attractiveness, mystique—actually take on this reality for those caught up in the sway of these images. At the same time, however, we would not want to say that all these uses of hyperreality are necessarily bad. Apple, for instance, realized the potential of hyperreality in its computer products and used it well: "Apple Macintosh's computer was not a consumer-driven innovation, but a compellingly seductive vision of a computer that could be a *friend* to one ('friendly') worked out by Steve Jobs and his design team. The computer— the product—was then developed to fill this vision. Marketing practice, therefore, is not driven so much by the ideal of a sovereign consumer as by the quest for a powerful hyperreality that consumers and marketers can believe in."
*   *Fragmentation.* The world is full of different people with different life experiences and backgrounds. At one level, the recognition of difference is very important, and opens the way for respect and openness to the other. But postmodernism goes

further, and implies that the differences between us mean that we cannot really communicate with each other. At the end of the day, we are each caught in radical isolation from everyone else; no one else is able to share our experiences, nor can they fully understand us. Similarly, we "wear different masks": we are different people in different situations. What might be right in one situation is wrong in another. There is no continuous identity for us. We live in the transitory present and wear a shifting face that fits our shifting situation.

- *Production and Consumption.* According to postmodern marketing, all of life is production and consumption. Indeed, even production is liable to be subsumed under consumption, as the consumer has more and more control over the producer. (Perhaps we could say that the consumer "consumes" the producer?) In the past, the producer may have been able to dictate to the consumer, as in the famous statement of Henry Ford ("You can have any color, as long as it's black"), but this has long been replaced by a much more complex relationship between consumption and production. Consumption in a postmodern world is the "means through which individuals define their self-images for themselves as well as to others." Yet producers, especially in fashion markets, effectively mold and influence what consumers think and do. Consumers seem to be powerful, yet at the mercy of these strong marketing messages at the same time.

- *No inherent meaning.* The "message" (whether text, pictures, film or whatever) is invested with meaning by the reader, listener, or viewer. The signifier can have no inherent meaning intended by the author, or if it does, the author's intention is something entirely separate and distinct from what the customer makes of it. This disjunction between "author" and "reader" is connected to the radically fragmented society that is a feature of postmodern thinking.

- *Juxtaposition of opposites.* Playfulness and paradox are hallmarks of the postmodern approach. The juxtaposition of ideas or artifacts that we do not normally expect to go together, or that even contradict each other, shocks or gives pleasure or both. It is these momentary forms of reaction and stimulation that we can count on, since we cannot count on shared meaning.

- *Loss of commitment.* Given the changing flow of life and the different characters that the same person plays in different contexts (such as work and home), commitment in the long term has no meaning. Without an assurance of some kind of consistent behavior and identity, how can one make a commitment? What would one be committing to?

Postmodernism is in some ways just a new version of the old skepticism, the idea that one begins with the fundamental doubt that we can truly know anything about the world; postmodernism spirals outward from that seed of doubt. All we have to go on are our impressions, which may or may not coincide with others' impressions. Whether they have anything to do with what is "out there" or "beyond me" is a meaningless, unanswerable question. From the viewpoint of postmodernism, then, long-term relationships are a deeply ambiguous, if not an absurd, undertaking. Moreover, postmodernism offers no way of distinguishing between true and apparent goods. Words such as "good," "bad," or "indifferent" have no meaning and are entirely relative to the perceptions of those involved.

Despite the criticisms we will direct toward the postmodern view of marketing in this book, we nevertheless recognize that the position has some validity. Images and messages, especially those delivered through advertising, are so numerous and varied, and pass so quickly across our field of view that they at once dominate, and yet hardly touch our lives. Completely absurd messages can be transmitted through advertisements, even though the absurdity and confusion may be due, ironically, to the power of advertising itself. The Eveready battery advertisement featuring the tireless marching bunny offers a striking example. The campaign was so successful that it was "named one of the top commercials in 1990—*for Duracell.* In fact, a full 40% of those who selected the ad as an outstanding commercial attributed it to Duracell."[10] Duracell's market share went up slightly; Eveready's dropped back! As McKenna says, when it comes to advertising, "it's a jumble out there."

Furthermore, postmodernists do have a point when they insist that everyone's voice is important. In a way, they express here a concern for justice that others may overlook for the sake of unity and respect for tradition. Since every person is made in the likeness of God, everyone *does* have something important to say, to which others should be willing to listen. On the other hand, postmodernists would not recognize the right to challenge another's viewpoint, because they perceive no real possibility of doing so. According to postmodernists, all we can do is allow people a voice; we cannot by discussion or deliberation come to a common view because none of us can really understand the other. We cannot share common conceptions of justice and the good, so there is no point to discussion or common evaluation of our desires. To speak of "true" versus "apparent" goods is to name a meaningless opposition; all that is true is "true for me."

Needless to say, postmodernism is an impotent principle in the face of unjust structures or systems of domination, despite its concern for giving everyone a say. Since they can appeal to no overarching conception of justice, postmodernists cannot provide any consistent critique of totalitarianism or anarchy. Is a system barbaric, cruel, inhumane? It all depends on one's point of view.

2. Relationship Marketing

In the chapter on job design, we discussed the development of "human-centered" (HC) technology, and suggested that this was an important development for the engagement between faith and work. "Humanistic marketing" is not a current term; perhaps because the dangers of dehumanizing people through marketing are not as obvious as the dangers posed by technology in the workplace, nevertheless we know that some kinds of marketing can undermine the human community and the human good.

What has developed at about the same time as HC-technology is the idea of "relationship marketing." In many ways this approach is the marketing analogue to HC technology. Indeed, it has been most thoroughly developed in the Scandinavian countries, where HC technology has a strong following.

The idea of Relationship Marketing (RM) arose in the late 1970s, largely within the industrial and services markets.[11] It was consciously developed to counteract the view that marketing consists solely of the manipulation of "the 4 Ps" (product, price, place, promotion). The central idea is that long-term and enduring relationships are the bases of marketing. C. Grönroos gives a clear definition of RM:

> Marketing is to establish, maintain and enhance (usually, but not necessarily long term) relationships with customers and other partners, at a profit, so that the objectives of the parties involved are met. This is achieved by a mutual exchange and fulfillment of promises.[12]

The goal of marketing from the RM perspective is to "create involvement and product loyalty by building a permanent bond with the customer . . . to increase sales in the long term."[13] The relationship is built up around an exchange of goods and services in return for some other needed good, usually money. The idea here resembles the thinking behind business networks. Suppliers try to build predictability into their market and, in the case of industrial customers in particular, to be involved in new product development. Customers try to obtain a group of preferred suppliers in whom they can trust and with whom they can work for the future. Not all relationships can be pursued to the same lengths or preserved at the same costs, but all are seen as valuable. Both customers and suppliers try to surround themselves with their "own" suppliers or customers, with whom information sharing and shared product development are possible. In the kind of highly competitive markets that these companies face, some kind of stability is needed in order to manage competitive pressures, and these long-term, highly cultivated relationships provide some of that stability.

The business network literature has developed the most extensive understanding of these types of relationship, seeing them as a true form of business organization, not just a halfway house between the open market and the big, vertically integrated firm. The fabric processing networks of central Italy, for instance, have become famous for their flexibility and responsiveness to product changes required by the volatile fashion market. These company networks are highly successful primarily because they have developed long-term, stable relationships that have allowed them to work together while maintaining their individual identities.[14]

When marketing is considered part of developing business networks, that is, as fundamentally about cultivating relationships, it is a short step to regarding marketing communication as being primarily about managing relationships. How do such relationships relate to virtue and the common good in the Christian social tradition? Within this tradition, these relationships would be treated according to the principle of *solidarity*.

Products and services "bring us into relationship with other people, including future generations" and can be the "major means of integrating us into a community, of giving us a place, status, belonging, and value."[15] They are a means of binding us together in mutual concern, and mutual service, and a crucial part of promoting and preserving the common good. In trying to live the principle of solidarity, we come to know that we are "all really responsible for all."[16] In his writings before becoming pope, John Paul II described the principle of solidarity as the constant readiness to accept and to realize one's share in the community because of one's membership in it.[17] Concerning friendship, the ancient Greek proverb holds that *koinê ta tôn philôn*—all things that concern friends are common to them. Analogous to friendship, solidarity involves developing a "third viewpoint" that is focused neither on oneself nor on the group, but on the good of both.

We can see within the idea of solidarity an obverse principle that one would follow when faced with an unjust situation: the *principle of opposition*. Solidarity, in fostering the common good involves opposition to whatever does not foster it. Such opposition is aimed at restoring conditions that promote the good of all. Opposition is a constructive attitude, an invitation to dialogue, and an avoidance of self-righteousness. It shares with solidarity an unswerving, primary dedication to the common good.

John Paul II calls the lack, or the opposites, of solidarity and opposition "conformism" and "noninvolvement." The first implies uniformity rather than unity, and thus a participation more akin to servility than to genuine cooperation among persons of equal, human dignity. Noninvolvement implies surrender to existing conditions, perhaps through despair or cynicism, marked above all by passive inactivity. We see here the emergence of a deeper view of the common good, incorporating its subjective aspect: the common good is much more than a set of conditions. It relies on the "subjective community of action" that develops out of participation.

Clearly, postmodern marketing relies on people's noninvolvement and on their servile conformity to the fashions and consumer fads of the day. It is contrary to the principle of solidarity in that it breeds vice, and systematically suppresses the human development of relationships. Since marketing communication depends so much on good relationships, a postmodern marketing department also has a negative impact on the communication process, though the damage may take a while to emerge.

Conversely, relationship marketing requires our active responsibility in our relationships with others, and in this sense is an approach to marketing that promotes human goods and human growth overall. Relationship marketing requires further development, however, at the fundamental level of analysis, which determines whether a product is a true or an apparent good. Relationship marketing scores well with regard to the virtues related to relationships, but it curiously avoids facing one of the basic questions which determines whether those relationships are truly developed by a product or not, that is, the questions whether the product is truly a good for those to whom it is offered.

Relationship marketing, like all the possible ways of implementing a more human, integrated workplace that we have identified, can be abused. In a *Harvard Business Review* article entitled "Preventing the Premature Death of Relationship Marketing," the authors paint a graphic picture of how the whole RM idea can be grossly distorted. In the quest to address customer needs more closely, customers are hounded for information, and must deal with a plethora of new, nearly indistinguishable products. When RM comes to mean this sort of approach to marketing, the authors suggest, "Perhaps we are skimming over the fundamentals of relationship building in our rush to cash in on the potential rewards of creating close connections with our customers."[18] They clearly show that firms often make use of the *idea* of building relationships with customers for ends that have nothing to do with establishing and maintaining vibrant relationships. We welcome the possibility that marketing may take a genuine approach to relationships with customers as the basis for policy, but, as always, we are aware of the possible misuse of a good idea.

MARKETING COMMUNICATION

"In truth, all marketing is communication and almost all communication can be marketing." This adage is from the authors of a book on "integrated communication."[19] If they are right, then communicating, especially with the customer, is the *raison d'être* of the marketing function. What does this mean, and what problems does it pose?

In an article on marketing communication, Ray Mackenzie relates an interesting story from an ethics class. The students were discussing the advertisements for a brand of jeans targeted at women. These advertisements contained no direct product information, but rather suggested that the wearer of the jeans would become more sexually attractive, and, therefore, more fulfilled. Mackenzie continues the story:

> I was making the point that seemed to me to be rather obvious—
> that the ad was in fact making a claim, that it was implying that
> the jeans would effect some sort of profound transformation in
> the person who wore them. And I went on to say what also
> seemed to me to be indisputable, that this claim was clearly
> ridiculous and amounted to a species of lying. But at that point,
> I began to feel that many in the class were no longer with me. The
> room grew quieter than it had been, and then one student, who
> seemed particularly troubled by the discussion, raised her hand
> and asked with some poignancy, "But what's wrong with selling
> dreams?"[20]

Mackenzie's story raises an important question. What are we marketers trying to communicate through advertisements and other devices? The student in Mackenzie's class seemed confused when it was suggested that the claims made by advertisements should be true. To her, it was sufficient if they gave people a dream, true or not, to believe in. In other words, the truth or falsity of what was said in the

FIGURE 7.1 Relationship Marketing[21]

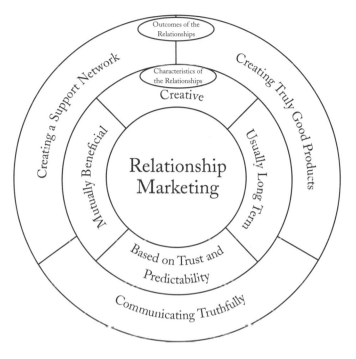

advertisement was virtually irrelevant. However, the *way* we say things, and the moods we evoke, have acquired great importance. Mackenzie writes, "Dreams are evidently what we have, not facts and realities." We want to feel good, and we are not especially concerned with whether those things that gratify us are genuine or even whether our gratification is justified. Jonathan Swift's ironic statement at the opening of this chapter could apply to many of us: "Happiness is the condition of being well deceived." Christian social teaching encourages us to root our lives and our goals in reality, and not to waste our lives trying to live a fantasy. John Stuart Mill's comment, when paired with Swift's, challenges us to put truth and the living of a real, genuine life before the aim of simply "feeling good."

Mackenzie suggests that the perceptions in marketing communication today have developed because we are required to play fragmented roles in our lives: we find ourselves communicating and promoting mutually inconsistent ideas at different times. Since marketing communication raises the question of integrity so urgently, it returns us to the heart of this book's aim: reconnecting our business lives with the kind of ethical, human life that we desire, for the sake of those we love and our own sake. How, then, can we communicate truthfully in business as we communicate truthfully with our friends? How would marketing communication look if we put this way of thinking into practice? One possible answer is that it would look like integrated marketing communication.

1. Integrated Marketing Communications (IMC)

Like relationship marketing, integrated marketing communications (IMC) is an idea that emerged in the 1990s as a way of making the communication between a firm and its customers more effective. It aims to solidify the relationship between a firm and its customers by enriching and clarifying exchanges of information.

Marketing approaches have changed much since the Second World War, with the general trend always toward a sensitivity to the needs of the customer.[22] At the same time, advertising is required to produce more direct results. In response, agencies are moving toward focusing on the particular customer, rather than focusing on the promotion of particular products or classes of products. In other words, agencies are moving toward developing an expertise at selling all sorts of products to members of socioeconomic group "A," rather than being expert at selling product "A."

While advocates of RM abandoned the idea of "the 4 Ps" in favor of cultivating relationships with customers, the proponents of integrated marketing communication list "4 Cs" as a means of focusing on marketing's communication with the customer. "Product, Price, Place, and Promotion" become "Consumer need, Consumer Cost, Convenience, and Communication." The idea behind each of the "4 Cs" is a close focus on communication with the customer. IMC is based on respect for, and dialogue with, the customer.

In order to develop the ability to respond to customer needs, a marketing department must have a database of customer information that is maintained and actively used to communicate with customers. Ongoing development and updating of the database should solicit and reflect customers' preferences. The HBR article already cited offers startling, cautionary examples of the consequences of the failure to do this.[23]

The customer database must be as complete as possible, maintaining information not only about present customers, but also about prospective ones. Getting this type and volume of information can be very difficult. Automobile manufacturers and direct-marketing organizations, like credit card companies, have developed methods to create extensive databases on customers and potential customers, as well as procedures to maintain them. This sort of effort is essential, for if a company is to have any hope of meeting the customers' needs, the firm's information about them must be as extensive and as specific as possible.

One text on integrated marketing communication suggests that a minimal customer database should contain statistical data on demographics, psychographics and purchase history, as well as how customers associate products in a "category network."[24] It should be clear already that the focus here is on the characteristics of the customer, not on the characteristics of products. In this approach, the customer and prospective customer database is more important to the success of the company than the persuasive or manipulative skills of marketers. This underlines the importance of categorizing the customer base as finely as possible in such terms as "loyal" customers or "competitive" or "swing" users, for instance. Each category of customer requires its own strategic matrix, involving interrelated strategies for managing contact with these customers, for communications, and for expanding use of the product more widely among the members of the group. Managing customer contact involves finding a time, a place, or a situation, or common reaction, and the communications strategy supports this by devising a message that is tailored to the context in which it is presented.

Interestingly, many of the cases cited in texts on integrated marketing communication concern public health or education campaigns. The American Cancer Society (ACS), in response to research that showed a significant correlation between skin cancer and exposure to the sun during adolescence, initiated an IMC program through a Chicago-based communications company. The aim was to encourage teenage sunbathers to use sunscreens rated SPF 15 or higher, in order to reduce the incidence of future skin cancer and premature mortality.

At first, the ACS thought that all it had to do was to promote the line "Save your life!" backing this up with information about the sunscreen available. Instead, when they talked to teenagers, they found that twelve- to eighteen-year-olds were decidedly unimpressed by the idea of saving their own lives. Death seemed so far away from them that they seemed to feel themselves to be immortal. It was far more important to them to sit in the sun, get a great tan, and be more attractive to the opposite sex. Their social life in the present was most important to them. As a result, the ACS realized that they had to convince teenagers that sun protection would allow them to stay out in the sun longer, and so become even more attractive. In order to reach these young people, the ACS had to understand how they thought, and how to speak to them in a way that was relevant to what they considered important.

The next important stage in the IMC procedure was to categorize the "customers" for ACS's message. Five different groups were identified: manufacturers and distributors of sun protection, health professionals, coaches and recreational professionals, parents, and finally the potential users themselves, the recalcitrant teenagers. Each group was approached and through listening and careful discussion, ACS came to understand their various perceptions of the problems. ACS identified buying incentives for each group, and then strategies were developed for communicating with them. Special effort went into understanding and communicating with the potential users themselves. The contact plan included posters for home and school, radio and TV slots, newspaper and magazine advertisements, T-shirts, bathing caps, sunglasses, and so on. The breakthrough selling idea came when the ad agency hit on the idea of using the models from the swimsuit issue of *Sports Illustrated* to promote the ACS message; this amounted to an end run around the sources of teens' reluctance.[25]

Thanks to its clear and focused message, the campaign was a great success. It gained coverage in all the newspapers, several minutes on prime-time TV and radio news programs, and many interviews in different media. Furthermore, the campaign did not stop after a short burst, but lasted several years. As a result, it will contribute much to saving lives.

2. Problems with Integrated Marketing Communication

As the description above illustrates, even a relationship marketing regime in which integrated communication is pursued can be problematic from the point of view of the Christian social tradition. First of all, in this context "integrated" means something closer to "systematic, interlocking and exhaustive" rather than "whole." The "integration" pursued by IMC is a kind of technical perfection, by which a uniform message—any message, regardless of its content—is delivered with maximum clarity and coverage to a well-defined audience. While this is clearly an important part of any "integrated" approach to communication, it leaves out the most important aspect of integration, which is that our messages express what we understand to be true. Technically, integrated programs of marketing communication may simply make us "more happy" by deceiving us more effectively. If so, they are the antithesis of the kind of integrated communication we want.[26]

There is much more at stake in the movement toward integrated communication than the integrity of the company and its members. There is also the wider and potentially more devastating problem of the misuse and consequent degradation of language. Constant bombardment by messages that we know to be untrue gradually and inevitably produces certain effects. Language becomes as an instrument of raw manipulation, a means of using and misleading people, and not a means of real communication, which is to say, of communion and community.

Mackenzie points out that within the Christian tradition, St. Augustine provides us with a theory of language that explicitly connects what we truly think with what we communicate to others. Augustine sees words as signs that convey truth when we use them to communicate. More important, he understands the word as a sign of the "internal truth" which resides in the mind of the receiver of the word:

> We consult, in the case of all the things which we understand, not the external speaker but that internal Truth which presides over our minds; the words of a speaker are, perhaps, but an admonishment to this consultation.[27]

In other words, as Mackenzie says, truth is communicated to us by God, by means of his grace, and by this means we can recognize the truth of the communication from another. This process is not limited to believers; Augustine thinks we all work in some way like this by virtue of being human. Similarly, he suggests that the word we speak is a sign of inward truth, a "sign of the word that gives light inwardly; which latter has the greater claim to be called a word."[28] The spoken word simply clothes in a physical form the word that already resides within us, just as the Incarnation clothed the Word of God, Jesus Christ, in the physical form of a human person. Furthermore, just as the Christ entered into human existence to share the life of God with us, so our spoken external language is the means given to us by which to share our inner understandings with each other.

This profound theory of language requires reflection and development so that it can help marketers to begin developing truly *integrated* communication. What is the true good that a product offers; that is, how may the product be expected to perfect or complete the persons to whom it is offered? What are the human needs of the community that this company will address (at a profit)? What are the true objectives of a marketing plan, and how can genuine relationships with customers promote the development of the company? We need to examine our hearts, our motivations, and the true goals behind our actions. We need to begin to create integrated communication programs that are in every sense worthy of the term "integrated," and are thus unambiguously in the service of the most profoundly sharable, least dispensable of our common goods: truth.

PRODUCT DEVELOPMENT

Product development is a firm's first and most central activity. Producing goods or providing services are the reasons we form businesses in the first place. Thus, to ask, "What do we make products or provide services for?" is like asking, "What is the company for?" Many people would give the same answer to both questions: "To make money."

Nevertheless, just as "To make money" does not adequately characterize the purpose of the firm. It does not begin to account for the variety of goods and services that crowd the market, nor for the ingenuity behind so many of them, or the persistence with which their makers and providers typically resist all opposition to keep their products before the public. Product development, like the firm itself, is about much more than making money, and should be approached with that fact firmly in mind.

When entrepreneurs start businesses, they may have all sorts of reasons for producing their products or performing their services: a way of making a living, to use their capital, to exercise their special technical skills or experience, to get rich quickly, for independence, creativity, service to the wider community, and so on. Once the company is up and running, employees within it also have their various reasons for getting involved with the company, and come to identify with it in some way.

In times past, even people's surnames (Baker, Farmer, Smith, Tanner, to name a few) signified their occupations. Today, when we are asked, "What do you do?" we answer, "*I am* a teacher (or manager, or designer . . .)," rather than "I teach (or manage a production line or design domestic appliances)." In other words, our idiom suggests that we believe that we are what we do. This connection between self-identity and work arises from the fact that in a real way our labor is "in" the good or service we produce. Part of our work (and part of us) leaves its mark on the product, and so our identity is tied to the product.

This identification with our work draws us to two major conclusions. As a result of being produced by the means of human labor, and thereby contributing to human development, goods and services are part of the practice of virtue.[29] Producers and consumers develop themselves through making and using products and services such as shelter, food, energy, medicine, and entertainment. A lack of some of these kinds of products can limit human development. In mismanaged economies, or in countries ravaged by war or subjected to rule by cronyism, even basic necessities such as food or shelter can be scarce. An excess of products and the attitude of consumerism, which turns owning and using products into ends in themselves, also fundamentally distorts and damages our true human development. Genuine human development, for both producer and consumer, resides in a healthy attitude toward products and services that are widely available and beneficial to all.

Second, there must be a respect for both the customer and the supplier in the development and use of products and services. We often hear the remark, "The customer is king." The phrase implies that the customer enjoys a right of command to which the supplier owes unquestioning obedience. In many respects increased attention to the customer increases the good, although the rise of "customer service" owes at least as much to the struggle for competitive advantage as to an awakening ideal of service in community. However, something is wrong, when we hear, for example, that in Japan the relationship between customer and supplier "approaches a master/slave relationship."[30]

As we wonder how "master-slave" relations can possibly serve "free markets," we encounter a problem endemic in modern market systems: the human being as worker or producer is pitted against the human being as consumer. Since we are all both customers and suppliers in one way or another, a simplistic slogan like "The customer is king" divides us against ourselves. As customers, we should have absolute power to define what we want; as producers, our products (and therefore an important part of our productive lives and self-identities) are to be totally defined for us by others. Furthermore, taken as a principle, "the customer is always right" can lead to some strange outcomes, at least, from the perspective of the common good. If the customer is always right, can the supplier ever be wrong to market "high octane" beer in the inner city? Or to design "youth friendly" tobacco mascots? Or to impute therapeutic value to untested "nutritional supplements"? One honest commentator puts the matter this way:

> Since the consumer ultimately decides, the enterprise cannot be blamed if the goods produced are trivial in value, noxious, dangerous to health and fail to meet basic needs. The business community thus escapes responsibility for socially objectionable production. If an irrational public demands stupid and dangerous goods, the business world can only in duty comply.[31]

First, from the perspective of Christian social thought, the "principle" of consumer sovereignty is nothing more than a high-sounding evasion if it allows the producer to abdicate his moral responsibility for what he produces. In regard to the common good, the concept suggests that the producer is unrelated to the ends of community except as the consumer's instrument, and that like an instrument the producer is morally neutral. In this view, only the consumer—who supplies the ends to the producers' mere means—can be virtuous or vicious. The Christian social tradition stands to remind producers that *as* producers, as users of the goods of the earth, they also have a duty to direct their production to the common good. The producer cannot transfer all moral responsibility for what he produces onto the consumer (at the very least because products shape consumers' preferences in the very act of their responding to them).

Second, the Christian social tradition also reminds customers that they have no right to require of producers whatever products meet their whims. Consumers have no right to demand products whose use degrades morals, or wreaks havoc on the social or physical environment. Consumers may not demand products whose very production would place workers at unreasonable risk of injury. The Christian social tradition stands to remind consumers and producers alike that their preferences are subject to the higher requirements of human development and the common good. Indeed, they ought not to be guided by preference at all, but by a careful selection of the true over the merely apparent goods (see chapter 2).

1. New Product Development and Quality Function Deployment (QFD)

How do we know whether a product we propose to produce is truly good or not? How do we know whether we are marketing it truthfully? We have already addressed these questions to some extent through our discussion of the common good, and we will extend that discussion here. There are at least three questions we must ask ourselves to determine whether our product is consistent with the common good:

1. Does the product harm or injure?

That is, *would society be better off without this product?* For whole classes of products, we could answer this question in the negative: wholesome foods, many forms of transportation, many clothing items, many forms of information technology, and the like would be included on that list of socially beneficial products. Similarly, we could easily compile a list of products that injure and harm: pornography, quack cures, pyramid-marketing schemes, cigarettes, and so on. We can compile the first list if we concentrate on products that directly sustain or speed our participation in the political community, which is the locus of common goods. The second list will practically compile itself if we include those products that are injurious no matter who uses them, or when, or for whatever reason, under any circumstances.

The case is altogether different for most products. Most will not fall unambiguously into either list. In part, the ambiguity stems from contemporary standards of judgment. It is not that we lack any notion of the good life by which to measure products' usefulness or harm; it is rather that our ideas tend to be purely formal, that is, abstract. Concepts of the "good life" which roughly translate into "my right to pursue my preferences in any way that does not interfere with your right to pursue yours" do not address the questions: "Is this product something we should do without? Is it something we need not, or ought not, do without?"

The ambiguity is also a reflection of the sober fact that mitigation of an evil is often the closest we can come to the good, and that mitigating one evil frequently requires tolerating other, lesser evils. In no area are the problems clearer, or their right resolutions more obscure, than in the tangled world of health products. Consider the sorts of questions that arise concerning products for treating chronic disease. The unambiguous good—a cure—is unavailable, and the available treatments present a complex mix of advantages and disadvantages—economic costs, side effects, sustainability over time, and on and on—against which the new products' features must be compared. Circumstances will affect the weight of each aspect in our deliberations: high cost will seem more or less weighty as the disease is more or less debilitating, more or less common, and so on.

Frequently, the whole question of whether a product is a real gain for the community depends less on applying a set of existing standards than on deciding which considerations count and which do not. Needless to say, communities of people with strong virtues and a developed sense of the common good will find the difficulties more manageable than communities where an understanding of the common good is weak or abstract.

2. Is the service or product futile or useless?
The temptation is to dismiss this concern: isn't a futile or useless product harmless or inert by definition? What real harm do weight-loss nostrums or pet rocks inflict? Perhaps little in affluent, developed nations, but the question hangs more heavily over cases like the marketing of Nestlé infant formulas in developing countries. Not only was the product not as good for the children as their mothers' milk (to say nothing of its effects when the local water supplies were impure), but it also absorbed limited, precious family income.

The exculpatory argument usually made in such cases is that no one forces families to buy such products. Since we are working in a "free" market, the argument goes, we must allow the customer to decide for good or ill; we ought not anticipate customers' free choices by excluding products *a priori* from the market. We might counter that customers are exactly as free as they are informed and prudent, and that they are as prudent as they are able to be independent of manipulative marketing campaigns, such as those Nestlé ran among largely illiterate populations. However, we should not evade the unstated, major premise behind this argument concerning consumer sovereignty and free will.

That premise is that apart from a consensus expressed in individual consumer's choices, there is no common good, or at least there is no access to knowledge of it. "Common good" means either an accumulation of individual preferences, or it merely expresses the preferences of those who invoke it (and their willingness to impose their preferences on others). The first three chapters of this book are a sustained argument against this premise, and we repeat: the premise is false. But it is worse than false. It is used to disarm the moral structure of the community, and to induce a voluntary abdication of duties that are justly owed to the whole commonweal. It was no medieval theologian and no enemy of the market society who warned against this premise as the refuge of what he called "the wealthy criminal class". It was Theodore Roosevelt, the Republican 26th president of the United States, who pioneered anti-trust legislation and presided over the rise of the U.S. to industrial world eminence.[32]

3. Does the product prey on inexperience or human weakness?

All human beings suffer some weakness of character, such as tendencies to violence or addiction, low self-esteem, and so on. All such weaknesses impair practical wisdom and make one less able to discern and pursue one's true good. Practical wisdom is also lacking in the young, since its development usually depends on a length and variety of experience that the young simply have not acquired. Products are sometimes developed or marketed to take advantage of the more common weaknesses of human character, or to exploit a lack of judgment thought to be typical of persons of certain ages, sex, socioeconomic, or ethnic backgrounds.

This sort of marketing can take relatively mild forms: the old standby "keeping up with the Joneses"—the appeal to envious competition—still has an influence in marketing everything from automobiles to landscaping services. It can also take forms that more immediately undermine and degrade the society that tolerates their use. The furor over the "Joe Camel" tobacco logo (cool and friendly, and designed to undercut responsible adults' attempts to tell children that cigarettes will hurt them) might have also been directed against billboard advertising for alcohol that targets the inner city and suggests the product will transport users in spirit to this or that exotic locale, or will confer the aura of success, glamour, sophistication. Less dramatically, perfume, hair treatments, or particular types of clothing are often marketed to women through suggestions that they can help them seem more confident or alluring to others. This approach depends upon the documented psychological phenomenon that women often suffer from a lack of self-esteem. Even if these products may be in themselves genuine goods, marketing them through manipulation of anticipated weaknesses in the judgment of some people is an affront to the very basis on which a community is built. Only those operating from a postmodern marketing perspective (for whom meaning and commitment are considered irrelevant) could develop, produce, and market products with such a thorough disregard for the common good.

Of course the number of truly good products vastly exceeds the number of products whose apparent goodness conceals futility, harm or exploitation. Moreover, products that are inconsistent with the good of the whole community or of its individual members seldom last (there are, of course, outstanding exceptions), and so do not enrich their makers. This makes it all the more disappointing that some business concerns persist in developing products that serve some apparent good end, but which actually damage and undermine the human community they purport to serve.

The virtue that is particularly important in the development of new products is courage. It takes courage for managers or entrepreneurs to strike out on a new path and develop a new product, since the outcome of the process cannot be wholly foreseen and some risk must be accepted. This is especially the case with new generations of products developed with new concepts or technologies. Courage is also required of one who opposes development of a product on the ground that it will serve no real good, or because it is solely the vehicle of others' ambitions.

Courage is always personal: companies run worthwhile risks or decline meretricious undertakings only because individual managers or entrepreneurs accept personal responsibility for their decisions. In the final analysis, there are no courageous companies, rather, there are companies that enjoy courageous leadership at every level of their operations. Such organizations are equipped for prudent, calculated risk-taking, and for the perseverance that is so often necessary to bring business decisions to fruition. Moreover, because courageous businesspeople inspire others to step beyond the boundaries of the safe and comfortable and to take worthwhile risks, in time, such companies reap the benefits of a risk-tolerant, resolute workforce.

Without the kind of everyday courage of the people making business decisions, economies would come to a standstill. Without the particularly striking form of courage that is required to develop a whole new product line or area, economies would gradually stagnate. Aquinas called this intrepid form of courage, "magnificence," by which he meant the courage needed to take on large risks and expenditures in pursuit of a good that benefits the community as a whole. The crucial difference between a manager who takes risks for purely financial ends and the courageous manager is that the latter incurs substantial risk for the sake of the good of the community (which includes his own financial good) rather than solely for private gain. Oswald von Nell-Breuning, an influential thinker within the Christian social tradition, describes the courageous manager as one who

> in his enterprise and in his means of production employs his working men for the creation of goods of true worth; who does not wrong them by demanding that they take part in the creation of futilities, or even harmful or evil things; who offers the consumer nothing but useful goods and services rather than taking advantage of the latter's inexperience and weakness, betraying him into spending his money for things he does not need, or that are useless or even injurious to him.[33]

Courage, in the harness of prudence, is the key virtue in driving a healthy business and a healthy economy.

There are new procedural tools recently developed that aid in new product development and which can also help to foster the common good through their application. One such tool is Quality Function Deployment (QFD), developed by the Japanese. One writer characterizes Quality Function Deployment as "a system for designing a product or service based on customer demands and involving all members of the producer or supplier organization."[34]

The basic goal of QFD is to systematize customer information and then to prioritize company responses to customer demand. Like other approaches of its kind, it requires systematic coverage of the stages of the product design process, which can be split into four phases: the organization of the project, its descriptive phase, the breakthrough phase, and project implementation. Quality Function Deployment itself is particularly important in the second and third phases, but is useless without careful project organization and effective implementation.

QFD reorganizes the new product development process by minimizing the normally lengthy redesign time. Redesigns may be necessary because of a lack of communication between people working in different departments, particularly in the crucial product definition phase, or because of a lack of documentation throughout a project. The latter case is particularly difficult to handle, since often people leave projects for personal or business reasons without leaving a written account of their work on that project. Without adequate documentation, new people who join the project may need a long time to fully absorb what the rest of the group already knows, which lengthens the design process.

Quality Function Deployment emphasizes the importance of product definition and process documentation. "The QFD approach *expands* the time it takes to define the product. It shortens the time it takes to design the product by focusing priorities, better documentation and communication during the process. It virtually eliminates the need for redesign, especially on critical items."[35]

The Quality Function Deployment process organizes the descriptive and breakthrough phases of the project through a series of charts that members of the design team must produce. The charts form the heart of the process, particularly because they are a means of integrating information from different departments, thus allowing them to communicate information in a structured and exhaustive way.[36]

One key to achieving a breakthrough in product design is the charting of one product or quality characteristic against another in a systematic way, which generates new insights over the full range of relevant product characteristics. In this way, QFD significantly increases the chances of discovering some kind of innovative product design, which enhances the product development process. Since that is crucial to the firm's success, Quality Function Deployment is a technique that can promote the firm's good and indirectly enhance the firm's contribution to the good of the whole community.

2. Limitations of the QFD approach

The main strength of the Quality Function Deployment process is its systematic nature. QFD's emphasis on this system also aids communication and documentation, and thus, promotes the participation of different groups in the design process. This not only makes it more effective, but also makes it more responsive to the common good. However, like the human-centered approach (with a weakness in its individualistic conception of the person), QFD has the fundamental weakness of ignoring the issue of whether its product is a true or apparent good. It serves more as a technique to support the design of *any* product for which a sufficient customer base can be found.

In general, techniques such as Quality Function Deployment do not supply the whole solution to new product development problems, since they do not touch the fundamental question of whether a particular product represents a genuine good. Dealing with this question in the product development process requires, as we have emphasized in this chapter, the role of the virtue of courage. As we have argued throughout, good techniques and organizational structures are necessary, but insufficient. Only when they function in a context that pursues the common good and the development of each human person in virtue can these techniques find their true end.

CONCLUSIONS

Marketing plays a crucial role in the operation of the firm, and the way it is defined has profound effects on the organization as a whole and on its relationship to the community at large. Postmodern marketing departments poison the body of society through a combination of cynicism about the possibility of communicating anything that is true, and a consequent retreat into a manipulation of consumers' needs and aspirations. If we do not want to live in a world of make-believe felicity, the alternative to postmodern despair is to use marketing as a means of building relationships for the common good by communicating products' real benefits.

Solidarity is a principle that can guide our behavior in our globally interconnected world, and it sets the context within which this kind of communication is possible. If we actively try to build solidarity into our relationships within the firm, with the firm's customers, and with all those its business affects, we can hope to start moving toward genuinely relationship-based marketing and authentically integrated communication.

In today's competitive world, new product development is of such importance that every aspect of the process affects the way the whole organization functions. A new product development process that focuses on serving the common good will depend on the quality of the firm's relationship with its customers. This relationship must reflect the principle of solidarity: the firm and its customers are co-operators in the pursuit of common goods, so that serving customers in a way that supports the community is essential to the firm's new product development process.

We have argued that new product development requires the courage to overcome organizational obstacles and to persevere in the face of quality or design problems. Techniques like Quality Function Deployment can greatly increase the effectiveness of product development. QFD, while morally neutral with regard to the products that are developed (and therefore unable to address the problems of true vs. apparent goods), does promote the common good by fostering better relationships among the groups involved in the design process. We can, therefore, welcome its use, while remaining aware of its limitations.

STUDY QUESTIONS

1. What is the "end" or "goal" of marketing? How does this general "end" relate to those of marketing communication and product development? What is the relationship of all these ends to the common good?
2. How do the "means" discussed in this chapter—integrated marketing communication and quality function deployment—promote the common good and human development? What are the limitations of these approaches? Can you suggest other marketing techniques and programs that could do the same thing?
3. Using the example of the American Cancer Society program to combat skin cancer (or any other example of a marketing communication or product development program you know about or have been part of personally), discuss how the specific circumstances of the project influenced the way the means were used toward the particular ends of the project. How did the group response to these

circumstances promote or hinder personal virtue and the common good?

VIDEO SUGGESTION

ABC Nightline June 26, 1991, on marketing malt liquor in the inner city.

Affluenza (1998): analyzes the problems of consumerism in the U.S. (1-800-543-3764—www.bullfrogfilms.com)

Sustaining
the
Engagement

8

Faith, Hope, & Charity

Authentic Habits of a
Christian Spirituality of Work

*Our work appears to us in the main as a way of earning our daily
bread. But its essential virtue is of a higher order: through it we
complete in ourselves the subject of the divine union. . . .
Whatever our human function may be, whether artist or
working-man or scholar, we can, if we are Christians, rush
towards the object of our work as though along the path of the
supreme fulfillment of our beings. Indeed, without exaggeration or
excessive fervour in thought or expression—and simply by
confronting the fundamental truths of our faith with the truths
of experience—we are led to the following conclusion: God is
inexhaustibly attainable in the totality of our action.*
—Pierre Teilhard de Chardin, S. J.[1]

THERE IS A HOPE DEEP WITHIN US THAT OUR LIVES HAVE
some great purpose. We may catch glimpses or experience in-
timations of this deep meaning, which seems far beyond our
comprehension. We can sense, as Teilhard de Chardin asserts above,
the *inexhaustibility* of God's presence in our lives. This sense that our
activities correspond to a mission has been revived through a silent
revolution among people at work. Springing up in many parts of
the world are faith-and-work-breakfasts, new books on the spirituality of work, courses on faith and work at universities and colleges,
and conferences and workshops dedicated to spirituality and work.

People from all variations of faith traditions are asking, "What is the meaning of my work?" and "How is my faith expressed through my work?"

There is also a loneliness deep within us bred from the anxious suspicion that our lives might simply be an aimless drifting from one experience to another, without a unifying, transcendent thread. Modern life may have supplied us with technological conveniences, scientific progress and financial security, but many of us feel it has done so at the cost of personal integrity and the loss of community. We come to the shattering recognition that the material world cannot save us from our own human fragility. We realize that we are far from whole, and that our own resources and capacities are only enough to initiate our search for meaning and happiness, not enough to find it. If our broken condition offers us any consolation, it is that our desire for meaning survives our very brokenness.

Our search for meaning and our fear of emptiness combine to motivate us to ask *spiritual* questions, and drive us toward *spiritual* answers. Like love, spiritual experience is so expansive that it cannot be easily reduced to categorical statements or fully captured through an argument or in any number of words.[2] But also like love, "the merest hint of its absence causes immediate distress."[3] Though we struggle to describe our intuition, most of us do recognize through our own experiences that we are something *in spirit*, something more than the ensemble of our bodily parts.

Spirituality is not a consumable good we possess or command, though our consumer culture would persuade us to see it so. Unfortunately, we can treat spirituality as if it were a car or a computer: if we could just get the right one, and use it correctly, life would be easier, more productive, and successful—and, of course, more meaningful and less depressing.

Spirituality, let us repeat, is not a *possession*. It is, rather, a *participation* in the "inexhaustible" reality of truth. We often encounter the spiritual when we sense how our temporal—time-bound—experience *participates* in the infinite, when we experience and understand how our own present moment communicates with the whole of reality, past and future. We awaken to our spiritual life, then, when we grasp in the *present moment* both our *origin* and *destiny*, both our beginning and our end. Some Eastern spiritual traditions express this awakening by the term *mindfulness*. We are fully present to the moment, spiritually present, when we grasp that both our origin and destiny are operative in it. When we forget our origin and destiny, when we ignore our beginning and our end in the decisions we make here and now, we break our connection with our spiritual nature and we fail to understand what we are actually doing.

Since our work is an important element of the integration we seek, a *spirituality of work* contributes to integrity of life. A Christian spirituality of work is the divinely inspired, human capacity to pattern the work we do upon the truths to which we hold. In other words, our origin—*made in the image of God*—and our destiny—*the kingdom of God*—shape our work, fostering an integrated life through our participation in the inexhaustible but recognizable presence of God.[4]

We will examine this spirituality of work on three interconnected levels. Most people would accept that they are more than their body parts, and would probably say that they have some kind of spirit, but they still need to recognize what their *spiritual nature* is—the first level. Since God's self-revelation to people is the basis of our understanding of our spiritual nature and because we rely on others to communicate that understanding to us, spirituality is to be understood from a *religious and ecclesial perspective*—the second level. Once we recognize and understand this spirituality, we need to direct it toward the end of all spirituality—friendship with God—through the practice of *prayer*—the third level.[5] At each level of this Christian spirituality of work we ask three key questions that address the fundamentals of our identity as human beings: Where do we come from? Where are we going? Who am I?[6] In other words, we ask how each level of our spirituality of work helps us better understand our origin, our destiny, and our present existence.

THE SPIRITUAL NATURE OF THE PERSON:
THE STRUCTURE OF DESIRE

One of the most interesting aspects of the recent upsurge of interest in spirituality at work is that it did not originate in churches or synagogues, from theologians or philosophers, nor even from business schools at religiously based universities (although many of the latter are now responding to the interest). Much of it came from practitioners themselves, from employees and managers who, in their search for meaningful work, uncovered their capacity to participate in ultimate meaning. By virtue of being "spiritually hardwired," people cannot long evade a confrontation with the spiritual dimension of their practical, working lives.[7] Human beings seem to have an inherent, "built-in" desire for self-transcendence, for participation in an inexhaustible reality.

Desire for transcendence operates in our search for knowledge, and for intellectual participation in realities beyond ourselves. Knowledge is thus a spiritual good. We also see the desire for transcendence in our capacity to lose ourselves in love of others. Unlike animals, we have the capacity and the freedom to live beyond our needs and our physical limitations: we live for abundance. Actually, we know that our fulfillment as humans is linked to this capacity for self-transcendence. We know by communion with our own nature that mere material accumulation will not satisfy our desires. Our fulfillment lies in the realm of the nonmaterial because we are not simply bodies but embodied spirits, and also because only nonmaterial goods can offer us participation in inexhaustible abundance.

The spiritual element of our human nature is always a part of us, and sooner or later it will influence our view of our work. Work is an act of, and from, the *whole* person, both body and spirit; both body and spirit partake in the action of work.[8] Because it originates from our whole person, our work cannot be measured as a financial transaction, nor can we finally be content to accept only a mere financial measure of an activity that takes a third to a half of our waking hours.

To make sense of work, we seek to integrate our working with the deepest dimensions of our self-understanding; that is, we seek to integrate our working with our conviction that we are "on the way," and that we are "not yet." We associate our work with our development, precisely because we know we can *develop* through our work. Moreover, we realize that to develop ourselves, we need ever closer integration between what we believe and what we do; otherwise, we push a wedge ever deeper between work and life; we betray our search for integrity.

This openness, this desire to bring our whole selves to work, is the source of what we call a spirituality of work. In its initial expression, a spirituality of work is an attitude of the mind and a condition of the soul that constantly asks three simple, profoundly human questions:[9]

Where do I come from?
Where am I going?
Who am I?

These are not trivial questions. Their concerns describe the structure of spirituality itself. If I would understand the present, I must understand my origin and destiny; if I would understand who I am, I must explore where I came from and where I am going. If we avoid these questions, we avoid ourselves.

1. Where do I come from?

This is a fundamental question that emerges in childhood. When the child asks, "Where do I come from, mommy?" she is embarking on the natural search, proper to all of us, to discover "Who am I?" Couples engaged to be married are encouraged to discuss their "family of origin" with their future spouse on the premise that where they come from will significantly affect their marriage and future family. When their families of origin are different, couples will face conflicts over issues such as raising children, male/female roles, finances, religion, conflict resolution, and so forth. To neglect this exploration of origins is to sow the seeds of conflict for the future.

The question for us here is whether we have a common human origin, and if so, whether it reflects a common image that influences the way we work and behave. David Whyte observes that "[w]e can create only in our own image. That is, everything takes form according to the consciousness that shaped it. If our self-image is small and restricted, or cold and inert, then what we produce will most probably be stillborn, like its maker."[10] If we see our origin as a fluke, our work will be a fluke. If we are totally self-made, then our work will be only for ourselves. If, on the other hand, we are no fluke, if we are made for a purpose, for a reason with transcendent meaning, then our work will be purposeful, and we will stand ever ready to go beyond our present understanding of it.

2. Where am I going?

We are by nature teleological beings, agents who (as we saw in chapter 2) act for an end or purpose. It is impossible to talk coherently about human beings without articulating where we want to end up. All of us know we have some destiny. We refer to our lives in terms of paths, journeys, of "going somewhere." We exist in order to arrive, changed by the particulars of our journey.

When a group of older adults was asked "What three things would you do differently if you could live your life over again?" the top items mentioned were

> *I wish I could be more reflective.*
> *I wish I could have been more courageous.*
> *I wish I could have contributed more.*[11]

When these older adults had arrived, they were not uniformly happy with who they had become. Many of the regrets of these retirees centered on their work. They had worked too much and had failed to develop the more contemplative side of their nature. They had come to retirement without the reflective habits that would allow them to flourish. In their more honest moments, they could only echo the regret behind Lee Iacocca's confession on *Fortune* magazine's cover: "How I flunked retirement."[12]

Perhaps they all had worked too bureaucratically, never taking risks—especially moral risks. Perhaps they had "discovered a capacity for cowardice in the face of their own destiny, a refusal to live the life that has beckoned them."[13] And worst, perhaps they had too often worked only for themselves, strategically advancing their careers upward like an ascent of the tower of Babel: when they reached the top they realized what they had worked for was nonsense—babble that did not speak to their human and social nature. For social beings, the question "Where I am going?" always implies "Where are we going together?" It has been noted that death-bed regrets rarely take the form of wishing one had traveled more, earned more money, or achieved greater career success; rather, they take various forms of wishing one had developed meaningful and spiritual relationships with the people one lived and worked with.

3. Who am I?

Socrates' famous dictum, "The unexamined life is not worth living," compels us to ask, "Who am I?" This is a question for us now, not later. People, particularly those in managerial and professional work, are often tempted to identify themselves with their position, and with the activities and accomplishments of the organization they work in. When they do this, they ignore the soul and cut themselves off from other institutions: church, synagogue, civic organizations, community groups, and family. By discounting the world beyond the organization, "we forge a small identity held within the narrow corridors of the building in which we work."[14]

However, many of those people who are in this habit of identifying themselves with their work find it unacceptable: they know there is more to work than money, self-interest, and image; they are tired of seeing their own narrow interests as the final arbiter of reality. They know that somehow work can be a source of spiritual nourishment. Like them, we know that our own identity must reflect not how much we have, but what we are and can become. Ultimately, what counts is not how much we make, but who we become in the making. And that person we become depends on what we give of ourselves to others around us.[15]

It seems quite natural that we awaken to our spiritual nature when we begin to see in the *present moment* our *origin* and our *destiny*, when we *participate* in a meaning that exceeds what we could make alone. We grow spiritually when we see the eternal directing us to our ultimate meaning. We learn from these timeless, spiritual moments how utterly inadequate and inappropriate it is to treat our present moment in merely economic or careerist terms. We begin to see why worldly goods cannot be the basis of ultimate value in our lives. While money, work, power, status, fame, and pleasure are all good, they cannot fulfill our yearning for human meaning: no finite good can explain our origin, our destiny, or ourselves.

The Theological Virtues:
The Structure of Grace

Our human experience reveals that we are spiritual, and a merely physical or even psychological account of ourselves and of our work overlooks its mystery. We are, nonetheless, left with the question: What next? Am I the source of these profound questions? Is spirituality merely an exercise in navel-gazing? Do I have the resources to account adequately for my initial experiences? Is my spiritual nature shareable, or am I the sole arbiter of its meaning? If our searching and questioning points us to something larger, something spiritual, our own personal interpretations may simply be too small, too personal. Thus, to remain closeted alone with our own spirituality is to deny it and to warp it.

Thomas Aquinas observes that knowledge of things spiritual, and of God in particular, "when investigated by reason [and experience] comes at great length to but a few and then mixed with many errors."[16] What spirituality is, and to whom it is directed is far from clear, even in the most profound personal experience. Because our capacity for spiritual life and experience outstrips our reason and our sensibility, we are not always certain about how to respond. We need to engage in more than simply human endeavors if our spiritual life is to flourish.

Our spiritual vision is fragmented by the limits of our understanding, but because spiritual experience calls us into the presence of others, our spiritual life can call on a community of people who recognize their brokenness and seek to be made whole by more than their own efforts.[17] This is precisely why religion is so important to spirituality. The church provides a community of life and worship through which to recognize, to accept, and to cooperate with the mysterious action of God in our lives.

The word "religion" itself comes from the Latin *religio*, which means to reconnect, *to bind us back together* to God through a community of people that extends through history.[18] This reconnection occurs through "the acknowledgment by oneself of radical defect [which serves as] a necessary condition for one's reception of the virtues of faith, hope and charity."[19] Within the religious community of the church, we can be sustained and developed through participation in, and cooperation with, the God-given virtues of *faith, hope,* and *charity*. These three virtues are the bedrock of a Christian spirituality of work.[20]

As we mentioned in chapter 3, virtue involves growth toward the fullness of personhood. The key to understanding the place of faith, hope, and charity, or the theological virtues, as they are called, lies in the phrase "radical defect." This phrase does *not* refer primarily to our evil acts; even without evil we would be in need of the virtues in order to realize the full potential of our human nature. For this reason, spirituality cannot be left at its personal "natural level"[21] and endure. We need help, and the theological virtues are God's aid—His grace and gift—in our need. If we turn away from the theological virtues and fail to take God as our partner in our growth, it causes us to live only on the surface.

1. Faith and Creation: Where do I come from?

The question of human origins is addressed in the first book of the Bible with what Christian theology calls the doctrine of creation:

> So God created man in his own image, in the image of God he created him; male and female he created them. And God blessed them, and God said to them, "Be fruitful and multiply, and fill the earth and subdue it; and have dominion over the fish of the sea and over the birds of the air and over every living thing that moves upon the earth." . . . And God saw everything that he had made, and behold, it was very good.[22]

One of the foundational aspects of faith in God the Creator is that we are made in the *image of God*. No matter what we do or neglect to do, God's image can never be erased from our being. Further, the image of God we carry in our intellect, heart, and will can be developed through our activity. God calls us to sharpen His image in us by freely cooperating with His creative activity, and especially with God's continuous creation and re-creation of us.[23]

Thus, we bear a clearer image of God the more closely we *imitate* God. At the end of each day of God's creation or work, God said, "It is good." Imitating God's creative activity, the source of all good things, we, too, should look back on our work and ask, "Was my work good?" In the Talmud, Rabbi Hama comments on this imitation theme:

> Just as God clothed Adam and Eve when they were naked, *we* must supply clothes for the naked poor. Just as God visited Abraham when he was healing from his circumcision, *we* should visit the sick. Just as God buried Moses, *we* must bury the dead. Just as God comforted Isaac after the death of his mother Sarah, *we* should comfort mourners.[24]

If our work is to imitate or cooperate in God's work, it must be work for the good of others. Yet, it would be a mistake to see clothing the naked, visiting the sick, and consoling the mourners solely as acts of liberality. Rabbi Jeffery Salkin points out that the active imitation of God in these three aspects is tied to the millions of people involved in the clothing business, in medicine and managed health care, and in funeral services.

Our work, too, if it is to be good work, must imitate God's work in the sense that it must be *good work*—work that provides wages that meet the needs of employees, jobs that are designed for the whole person, ownership patterns that distribute wealth more equitably, and products that serve society. We are integrated beings that bear the image of God in every part of our existence. In creating us, God did not make a being with a life divided into separate categories— economic, social, religious, family, political. God made us one person, with one life to dedicate to His ongoing creation.[25]

Our faith gives us a deeper understanding of where we come from. Faith does not distort reality, but penetrates to its *real* meaning.

It moves us from a superficial, materialistic interpretation of human experience to a more holistic vision of what it means to be human. Faith corrects our vision of life's meaning as a new pair of glasses sharpens our vision of the world. This correction does not come from within, just as the correction of sight does not come from within. Our new corrected eyes of faith enable us to see the dignity of work rise out of creation itself. God's creative act did not stop after six days, thus, we have been called to carry on our work in collaboration with God's. If we fail to see our work in light of God's work, we misunderstand work itself.

2. Hope and the Kingdom: Where am I going?

To fully understand where we come from, we must understand where we are going. "The beginning is only truly and completely known in the light of the end."[26] To us, as pilgrims en route to a promise, faith reveals God's intention that we should share in His divine life. Our ultimate destination, for which we are made, is God's kingdom and eternal life.

While we may find it awkward to speak of salvation, and heaven, and of entering the kingdom of God, a Christian spirituality of work would be deficient, even fundamentally incomprehensible, without reference to our ultimate end. Indeed, a spirituality of work directs us to consider our end, our *telos*, so we may more clearly understand our present: if there is no eternal value to work, work can have no lasting present value, no matter how complicated the formula we use to calculate it.

Because this end of ours is one we still wait for, an important aspect of a spirituality of work is hope. Hope "fixes our attention on the best thing that can happen to us—the full assimilation of ourselves in God—and sees this as the only genuine and acceptable fulfillment of ourselves."[27]

This hope emphasizes for us two critical insights concerning our work. First, our journey can never be fully realized or completed this side of death. We must never *over invest* ourselves in work, as if it could bring us to our full completion.[28] Successful managers and professionals face a danger that is known in the Christian tradition as the

Pelagian heresy: the belief that we can achieve through our own good performance and actions our own perfection and our own salvation. Success persuades us to believe in the salvational power of our accomplishments, and as we forget our own finitude, we succumb to "a self-deceptive reliance on a security that has no existence in reality."[29]

The aggressive manager, politician, academic, doctor, lawyer may seek escape from the existential plight of uncertainty by retreating into the apparent certainty of his own skills, tools, and achievements. This is fueled by the pull of success and the repulsion of discomfort and failure we find in the stories of many professionals. The story of David Durenberger, former U.S. senator from Minnesota, provides a clear example.

At the height of his legal difficulties, and near the end of his term as senator, Durenberger gave a talk at a faith-and-work-breakfast meeting in downtown Minneapolis. He began by listing for the group all the great things people had said about him, a list of successes that had characterized his political career. At the end of this litany, he paused and confessed that he had made one mistake—he had actually believed what these people said about him! He explained that as senator, he was inundated with power, flattery, prestige, and esteem. These proved enough to persuade him that he was powerful, competent, and altogether superior.

As his political career progressed, however, Durenberger's family and spiritual life began to suffer. He retreated from his familial and spiritual problems into his political successes. He constantly said "Yes" to career and "No" to family and the spiritual life. This led to a divorce, alienation from his children, and a decreasing amount of time in reflection, worship, and prayer. His overconfidence in his own abilities, with the pandering of people who supported him, gave him a *false hope* that all would be well. But all was not well, because he depended only upon himself and his political skills. It was only through a spiritual pilgrimage that Durenberger began to see that his hope was misplaced. This gave him the insight and courage to reflect honestly on his mistakes.

The second insight hope brings to our work is that the end of this journey is inextricably linked to what we do today. We must never *underinvest* ourselves in work, as though it were insignificant. Although the object of our hope lies beyond death in the kingdom of God, that expectation which colors us, should also color all our actions, including our work.

Hope does not justify inaction as we wait for the kingdom. It does not excuse injustices and inhumanity simply because in the kingdom all will be well. Rather, hope in God's kingdom inspires and orders us toward great things.[30] While hope prevents overconfidence by tempering any mistaken belief that our achievements are our own, it does give us the courage to attempt great things that hint at the greatness for which we have been made. Hope will help us discern our vocation by asking, "Is this the work that will help me flourish as a whole person by contributing to the common good?" "Is this the work I have been called to do?" "Have I used the right principles to choose this work?" "Is this the profession where I should stay?"

What kills our desire for greatness, what kills the soul more surely than any other vice, is despair.[31] Despair has many expressions. The most obvious is cynicism, the refusal to acknowledge or partake in the present good.[32] Cynicism presents one of the greatest obstacles to the attainment of a healthy organizational culture, for it is particularly attractive to those who experience failure at work, and especially to those who see their own failures as undeserved. All employees experience failure, and few credit failure to themselves, thus, workplace cynicism is like a smoldering fire, never short of fuel and always threatening to spread.

Most people who enter organizations arrive with great expectations for good and a desire to make useful contributions. If they do become cynics, deep disappointment or a series of disappointments are usually the cause: lack of promotion, poorly designed jobs, the frictions of a dysfunctional culture (which includes the society of accomplished cynics). As a defense against future disappointment, they develop the attitude that the organization lays traps for the unwary. They then suffer a more serious loss than any disappointment: loss of the capacity to judge and direct their actions in the service of present good.[33]

We overcome cynicism and its root of despair through the daily habit of hope. To hope is to rest in God's assurance that all will be well. That is to say, hope is *not* a naïve, sentimental denial that life can be brutal. It is, rather, the eschatological confidence, a confidence that the full fruit of actions and intentions inspired by God's grace will bring us to the kingdom of God. Hope provides us the art of not yielding to despair and the resources not to capitulate in our crises of finality. By creating a joy in us that cannot be corrupted by disappointment and failure, a joy that—though incomplete—sustains us through the toil of our work, hope brings us an inkling in the present moment of the end we have been created for.

Hope prevents us from both overrating and undervaluing work. It is the sustaining virtue in a world that wears us down and obstructs our approach to our true good. However, because hope lives as our confidence that God is for us, as we are for Him, hope cannot exist apart from charity, which is friendship with God.

3. Charity and the Incarnation: Who am I?

"So faith, hope and charity abide, these three; but the greatest of these is charity."[34] The virtue of charity, or love, is the greatest virtue because through the gift of this virtue we become what we ultimately can become: friends with God.[35] This is the radical claim of Christian spirituality: our vocation in life, in all that we do, is to deepen our participation in the friendship God offers without distinction or favor to the human race. In so doing, we truly enter onto the road toward genuine and full personhood. God's revelation in Jesus, the Incarnation, whereby "the Eternal enters time,"[36] establishes through Jesus' life, death, and resurrection what it means to be friends. Jesus tells his disciples, "No longer do I call you servants, for the servant does not know what his master is doing; but I have called you friends."[37] In charity, that is, in God's friendship and God's self-communication to us, we come to know ourselves and come to know our work. Thus, Augustine prays, "God, let me know you and know myself."[38]

Benevolence,[39] seeking another's good, is critical to authentic friendships. True friends have each other's good at heart; they take what John Finnis calls a "third viewpoint," which is neither theirs nor their friend's, but a good that is shared in common. Benevolence is to *work* for the well-being of another, not just to wish for it. Certainly, it is not the glad-handing bonhomie that so often camouflages self-interest. True friends delight in each other's happiness and actively will each other's good. Because God knows the good of all infinitely better than we know our own good, friendship with God is the foundation to being authentic friends with others.

To know another's good is to know what makes that person suffer. A story of two drunken peasants illustrates a deeper notion of friendship:

> A rabbi was visiting the owner of a tavern in the Polish countryside. As he walked in, he saw two peasants at a table. Both were gloriously in the cups. Arms around each other, they were protesting how much each loved the other. Suddenly Ivan said to Peter: 'Peter, tell me, what hurts me?' Bleary-eyed, Peter looked at Ivan: 'How do I know what hurts you?' Ivan's answer was swift: 'If you don't know what hurts me, how can you say you love me?'[40]

If we do not know the sufferings of others, we fail to share the depth of true friendship, because we fail to understand what is good for them.

Our love and friendship for others cannot be understood without the cross, that is, without understanding the other's suffering. We can ascend to the height of friendship only by descending to where we are "in touch with the depths of human misery."[41] Hence, the cross and death of Christ became, for the earliest Christians onwards, cornerstones of Christian spirituality: they sound the uttermost depth of true friendship.[42]

Christ's love for us, expressed through the cross, deepens our sensitivity to those who suffer around us. When we share the sufferings of others, we imitate Christ's emptying of himself for the sake of friendship.[43] A mark of spirituality, then, would be a person's increased *vulnerability* (which means "capable of being wounded"), enabling one to comprehend and serve the good of another.[44] Thus, Christian spirituality is not a course in how to find emotional comfort in a cold world: it is the discipline of love at any price. Bernard Lonergan observed, "[W]hen everyone is dodging suffering, when no one accepts it, the burden is passed on forever."[45] Christian spirituality is the refusal to pass the burden on under any circumstances, including those burdens of work.

We cannot, then, have an authentic spirituality of work unless we understand the sufferings of those in the workplace: those who suffer from subliving wages, dehumanizing job processes, and products that harm the body and the soul. As Christ seeks our good by suffering on the cross, we must seek the good of others by taking on their sufferings. A Christian spirituality of work shaped by charity aims to alleviate as much suffering as possible in the workplace by developing a "disciplined sensitivity to the sufferings of others."[46] The failure to develop this sensitivity turns spirituality into a form of angelism, a disembodied spirituality, which is the failure of the "spiritualizers" we met in chapter 1.

We can respond more fully to our spiritual vocation when the Spirit of God guides our lives. This guidance is revealed through our participation in the graced life of virtue. Charity, our participation in the love of God, moves us to collaborate, in faith and hope, with Him, to create organizational conditions *suitable for friends*. By prudently designing human work processes, justly establishing livable wages, tempering the disparity of wealth, communicating honestly, and courageously developing socially useful products, we create these conditions. A spirituality of work brings us to a clear recognition that people are the subject of work, not the objects, not the instruments of our strategic maneuverings. Faith, hope, and love provide us the habits, in the words of Charles Handy, "to live so that others can live better after I have gone."[47]

THREE RHYTHMS OF PRAYER:
THE STRUCTURE OF PRACTICE

The third level and the heart of a spirituality of work is prayer.[48] If we are to build upon our natural spiritual desire and nurture the graced habits of faith, hope, and love, we must order and structure our day "to practice the presence of God."[49] We need first to realize Teilhard de Chardin's insight: "Nothing here below is profane."[50]

Each of our days is an occasion to practice the presence of God. The heart of living our spirituality is the way we order our day: we want our day-to-day activities to aid our participation and flourishing in the Spirit of God.

There are many ways to structure a daily spirituality of work. We offer one possibility, which we call the three rhythms of prayer: rhythms of the body, the church, and the day.[51] The focus here is how we start our day. What is the first thing we do when we wake up? With what habits do we start our day and to what rhythms are we attentive?

1. Rhythm of the Body: Daily Silence[52]

In July 1995, we were presenting talks in Calcutta, India. Our Hindu host arranged a meeting for us with Mother Teresa. As we were leaving, Mother Teresa said, with a chuckle in her voice, "Let me give you my business card." It held no address, e-mail, fax or telephone numbers, but was inscribed with an insight into how we should order our day:

> The fruit of SILENCE is prayer.
> The fruit of PRAYER is faith.
> The fruit of FAITH is love.
> The fruit of LOVE is service.
> The fruit of SERVICE is peace.
> Mother Teresa

What we have in Mother Teresa's business card is a profound insight into a spirituality of work. Silence is first, since "only the silent hear."[53]

A precondition of any spirituality of work is silence. We live in a very hectic, noisy world, where spiritual wisdom is drowned out by the constant hum of information. We need time in our day to hear things that are difficult, if not impossible, to hear at work. Thus, time for self-reflection in silence is not a luxury. It is the wise person who "seeks the silence that deafens every fool,"[54] for the wise person knows that we cannot develop our soul's capacity to perceive the reality of the world without silence. In silence we confront our "inner emptiness" in the hope of *kenosis,* that is, of offering our emptiness to God to receive God's fullness. Through silence, as Johan Verstraeten explains, "[i]nstead of controlling or managing the universe, one develops an attitude of pure receptivity."[55]

Practice

How can we bring our overstimulated mind to a rest, to a stillness that leads us *to* re-collection, *out* of our mental dispersion of our many concerns and obligations, and *into* a source of unity for our lives? The monks of the early church practiced what they called *hesychia.*[56] *Hesychia* means silence, a silence that is not only noiselessness, but more essentially, the inner silence of the soul's power to receive the reality of the world. "*Hesychia* means silence, not negatively in the sense of an absence of speech, a pause between words, but positively in the sense of an attitude of listening. It signifies plenitude, not emptiness; presence, not a void."[57] *Hesychia* is a silence essential to a spirituality of work; however, it is a silence busy people find most difficult to practice.

Begin your day in silence. When we come to prayer, that practice of the presence of God, many of us come with so many distractions that our mind is like a "drunken monkey," stumbling over a multitude of thoughts.[58] One method for settling our mind into silence is breathing. If we practice silence on a daily basis and quiet ourselves, we can begin to feel the rhythm of our breath as we inhale and exhale. We do not breathe as though we control life, "but breathing out is first of all letting things go, and breathing in, receiving."[59] Our breathing itself can become our prayer, by incarnating the awareness that, like our breath, our life is the gift of Another.

Attentive breathing is used by many religions. It settles the body, which then settles the mind. Just being mindful of our breath has a way of grounding us in our awareness of a reality that escapes us in our frenetic activities. When our breath attaches itself to a word or phrase about God, we begin to recognize God's presence in the present moment. For example, take a short text and divide it into two parts for breathing. In exhaling, say aloud, "Come, Lord Jesus." In inhaling, say aloud, "so I may serve you."[60] By spending several minutes with this prayer, repeating it with each breath, we focus on our being with God, conscious of God's presence.[61]

2. Rhythm of the Church: Daily Scripture

As we come to the end of our repetition, we have prepared ourselves to receive God's word as mediated through the Scriptures. The church provides us a liturgical year, the recurrent rhythm of Advent, Christmas, Lent, Easter, and Ordinary Time, each supplied with its appropriate daily scriptures. Through its scriptures, the order of the liturgical year helps us participate in God's mysteries on a daily basis. During Advent, for example, the church's rhythm follows a time of quiet reflection, of silence, of waiting and expectation for God's Son to be born in humility and poverty in a stable where shepherds bring themselves to pay homage. Scriptures in Advent bring to mind the Incarnation of God's indwelling in human affairs.

Even as the liturgy of Advent encourages us to slow down, to pray more, to relive the expectation and anticipation of Christ's coming into our lives, our work and culture foster a different rhythm and message. Particularly for those in education, retail, and transportation, December is an intensely busy time of the year. Not only is the pace of work accelerated, but also many of us are caught up in end-of-the-year parties and gift purchasing. One could hardly invent a starker contrast between images and values than the contrast between Advent and the frenzy that marks the commercial "holiday season."

Nevertheless, for many of us, that very contrast characterizes the world we live in. And because it is the world we live in, we will lose Advent's message if we fail to be in daily contact with it. Our working life will also lose another opportunity to be transformed by God's grace. Unless we cling to the counterculture of the church, we may find ourselves going places that have nothing to do with the kingdom of God.

Practice

Within the Anglican, Catholic, Orthodox, and some Protestant traditions, there is a liturgy of the hours, or the readings of the day, which matches the rhythms of the liturgical year. These churches provide books that contain the readings of the day for each day of the year. Find one, and after centering yourself in the hesychastic prayer, let these scriptural readings be the first thing you read for the day. Pray with the church by participating in its liturgical life and calendar. By following these readings, we participate more fully in the rhythm of the year, which provides a healthy counter to the often-chaotic turbulence of our culture and our work.[62]

3. Rhythm of the Day: Daily Reflection

As we practice silence at the start of our day and participate in the rhythm of the church, we prepare ourselves to "pray our calendar," and see our present situation with new eyes. What we find as we pray our calendar is that we do not bring God into work, rather, we begin to see God already acting in our work. With a play on words, John Haughey explains, "God is at work at work."[63]

Our problem is that too often we do not have the eyes and hearts to see our work as God sees it—that it is His work. We do not often see God in our work. We do not see the joy in our work, and we do not see opportunities to help others to grow in their work, not least by repairing injuries we may have caused. When Mother Teresa went to the slums of Calcutta, she did not see herself as taking God to Calcutta. Rather, she encountered Christ in the sufferings of Calcutta's teeming poor. She saw God in the poor. Her spirituality of work allowed her to see God where most don't.[64] This holiness, this ability to see God at work, is not restricted to a privileged few: all who are called to work in any way are called to it.

Practice: Pray Your Calendar
After breathing your prayer and reading the scriptures, prepare for your day by asking, "What do I desire out of my day?" Think about those you will encounter in meetings and presentations, in the hall, at lunch. "Using your appointment calendar if that helps, face your immediate future. What feelings surface as you look at the tasks, meetings, and appointments that face you?"[65] While it can be difficult to know what to make of our feelings, they often indicate where our prayerful attention should be directed.

To pray over our calendar is to offer our work, our family, and our experiences to Christ for His insight, seeking help to know our feelings and to move us toward fulfilling our vocation the only way we can, day by day. It is here we see that God's ways are not always "my" ways or the organization's ways. Seeing our day through God's eyes enables us to pray for our "enemies" at work: those we do not care for, those we are jealous of, those who get under our skin. In praying for our enemies, God changes first, not them, but our attitudes and actions toward them. For God's instrument in changing their attitudes and actions is our own conversion of heart.

The purpose of praying our calendar daily is not simply to have God with us ten to fifteen minutes a day, but to begin to develop a discernment that sees God in everything we do, because everything we have is a gift from Him. Our prayer, if it is from a grateful heart and to God, will begin to transform our actions and attitudes at work. It will no longer be only we who work, but God who works with us.[66]

CONCLUSION

The message of a Christian spirituality of work can be summed up in the words of a Baptist preacher: "A religion that ain't good on Monday ain't no good on Sunday."[67] A Christian spirituality of work should lead us to greater interiority, without leading to individualism. It should lead us to greater social awareness, without allowing us to fall into that idolatry which is ideology. A Christian spirituality of work is not another set of ethical rules, but a way of life that recognizes God's rule through our participation in the life of the Spirit. In the final analysis, *a Christian spirituality of work is based on friendship with God, for the sake of the human race, in the work we do.*

By nature we are spiritual beings. We may suppress this dimension of ourselves through consumerism and egoism, but we can never remove it. It remains with us as long as we remain human. We develop this spiritual dimension through the theological virtues of faith, hope, and, above all, charity, that is, through gifts of grace that serve to integrate our lives in ways we are unable to attain ourselves. Charity, for example, is not our love, but God's love dwelling in us through our free acceptance of the relationship God offers us. Christian spirituality—our dialogue with God—provides us with the capacity truly to transform our intentions, to challenge our apparent self-interests, and to avoid our tendency toward instrumentalism in our working relationships with others. Its end is integrity of the deepest kind: spiritual integrity.

This spiritual integrity has the capacity to transform us according to the beatitudes: "Blessed are the pure of heart, for they will see God."[68] It shatters any illusions that our work is our own, that we are ultimately in control of our destiny, or that our good works are our own doing. To create a pure heart, especially in our work, is ultimately beyond our abilities. It is finally God's work.

STUDY QUESTIONS

1. Why is a spirituality of work critically necessary to a better understanding of work?
2. Why are the theological virtues necessary for our work?
3. How do you structure your day? In particular, what are your habits in the morning?

VIDEO SUGGESTION

On the Waterfront: Confronts the abuses of an overly private spirituality of work in the face of serious work injustices.[69]

9

Liturgy

The Source and Summit of Our Work

The Liturgy is the indispensable basis of Christian social regeneration.

—Virgil Michel[1]

W HY A CHAPTER ON LITURGY IN A BOOK ABOUT THE engagement between faith and work? Engaging work with personal spirituality seems to fit, but engaging work with communal acts of worship? Isn't this pushing the engagement too far?

Indeed, it might at first seem strange to connect liturgy with work. Yet, the connection exists and was already made many centuries ago. Our word "liturgy" is the transliteration of the ancient Greek, *leitourgia,* a compound word translated literally as "the work of the people" or "the work on behalf of the people." In the world of Greek antiquity, *leitourgia* could describe any activity—including religious activity—undertaken on the authority of the commonwealth and for the good of all.[2]

We can see the wisdom of the ancient Christian thinkers who used the term "liturgy" to describe the central acts of communal prayer in the life of the church. A true liturgical celebration draws up all of our lives, and all of every life, into the common praise of God, in thanksgiving to Him for all He has done for us. If it is true that in work we become more fully human, then our work must be included in our liturgical celebration, if we want to include the full range of our humanity in our celebration.

Unfortunately, the experience that many people have of the liturgy does not support what we have just said. Young people in particular seem to complain that liturgical celebrations are boring, irrelevant, or lifeless. Their complaints point to a disjunction between the liturgical celebration and their ordinary life experience. They object because they think that the liturgy should connect to their lives, and their criticism thus shows that they believe the liturgy should be relevant to them. Their very criticism underscores the wisdom of the ancient thinkers: our human experience should be central to our liturgy, and our liturgy should challenge and strengthen our Christian lives beyond the church door.

The disappointment many people feel about the liturgy is no argument against the topic of this chapter. If our working lives and our liturgical celebration have moved apart, that must be addressed. The perception that something has gone wrong does not mean that the deep relationship between liturgy and work we have been talking about does not really exist. On the contrary, the very fact that we are uneasy testifies to our sense that liturgy and life are, and should be, intimately connected.

Karl Rahner, one of the greatest theologians of the second half of the twentieth century, has traced the deep links between the liturgy and our workaday lives. Rahner claims that our basic, fundamental openness to God, and our ability to communicate with Him is the essence of what it means to be human. Openness to God is thus part of every aspect of our lives. However, in the liturgy our openness to God is made most clearly manifest *to us:*

> knowing and responding to the absolute mystery of God are implicit in all our daily activities . . . when we worship, the relationship with that unfathomable mystery which is a secret ingredient of every moment of our daily lives is expressed and manifested.[3]

The significance of our human existence becomes difficult, if not impossible, for us to grasp without the liturgy: how can we imagine alone that all our lives, all our "ordinary" experience, *must* be significant, *must* be meaningful, even if that meaning is hidden from us? Our experience at work, in the family, at play—our whole existence—

is lived in communion with God. The liturgy is the means by which our experience in communion *with* God is translated into experience *of* communion with God. If we consider it, our everyday experience is an experience of grace, and all things conspire to teach us that we are creatures of One Creator:

> The dynamic process of God's self-communication and our acceptance of it, as this process is experienced in daily life, is the original experience of liturgy. Every type of explicit worship is a symbolic manifestation of this original form of worship, the liturgy of the world.[4]

In other words, the world is liturgical—it is a vast work of praise. In the church's liturgy—its work of praise—the end and meaning of that vast world and its work is made present. "The Church, then, is the permanent presence in the world of the fulfillment of the liturgy of the world."[5]

Rahner's insights touch upon the profound bond between liturgy and everyday work. If he is correct, it is not only helpful to speak about the engagement between liturgy and work, but also it is essential to the discussion:

> The experience of the everyday as seen through the eye of faith on the one hand, and the celebration of the Eucharist on the other, must be correlated and made complementary. Each must be interpreted in the light of the other. Only when we do this do we achieve a real and effective encounter with Jesus Christ, our Lord, our life, our judgment, our eternity.[6]

If we may rely on Rahner, this book could not be complete without a discussion of the connection between liturgy and work. Without liturgy, the interconnection we seek between faith and work would be baseless, and would ultimately collapse.

LITURGY AND SPIRITUALITY

In the chapter on spirituality we discussed the role of the life of faith in the business organization and the need for each of us to link, or to integrate, our working and spiritual lives. Liturgy takes us one step closer to integration. We can suggest liturgy's integrating power through an analogy: As liturgy is to personal spirituality, the common good is to personal virtue.

Personal virtue—that is, pursuing good ends by effective and efficient means—directs us toward the good through ever-expanding circles of community, each circle offering its opportunities for the pursuit and attainment of good in common with others. At the level of the business community, as at every level, the personal virtues of those people in positions that allow them to act—especially their prudence and their justice—are the sources of structures and policies that promote the common good. Thus, we may realistically say that the common good depends on personal virtue.

Justice, magnanimity, benevolence, and the like, are outward looking and other-regarding: their exercise and perfection are motivated and inspired by community life. The realms of fully human action are the realms of community, of common ends and goods, where temperance and courage serve primarily to discipline us for justice. That is why it has been said, as long as justice is virtue entire, there is no personal virtue apart from the common good.

Personal spirituality and liturgy are mutually supportive in a way that recalls the reciprocity between personal virtue and common goods. Spirituality feeds liturgy, which is, after all, a work "in spirit and truth." Just as the pursuit of the goods common to the circles of community to which we belong summons, extends, and refines our virtue, so the common prayer, worship, and teaching of the church summons, extends, and refines our spirituality.

It is a sober truth that spirituality degrades easily into a narcissistic attention to our own individual needs that cuts us off from others. It is easy to imagine how the justice of a recluse could decline into mere self-righteousness. With little social contact, dedicated to purely private ends, he will come to view the "good of the other" (the formal object of justice) only in the context of his own needs and inclinations, for he will have shut out the light of all others. A purely personal, private spirituality runs the immanent risk of mistaking self for spirit.

Authentic spirituality craves and seeks grounding in the community of faith. Authentic spirituality is eager to measure itself against a comprehensive tradition: it is bold (with the boldness of hope) to believe that it can contribute to such a tradition, and it is humble (with the humility of hope) to believe that the tradition offers counsel, discipline and encouragement. Clearly, spirituality can forge the link with that wider tradition through a deep engagement with the liturgy:

> The Liturgy of the Church stretches us to be for others—not for ourselves—from the liturgy of initiation where even our renewal of baptismal promises is not done for ourselves but in the context of the baptism of others, right through the liturgy of Christian burial where the proclamation of resurrection is boldly made that we may, in Paul's words, "comfort one another." The Liturgy of the Church . . . takes us beyond letters and beyond numbers, beyond self-fascination and beyond self-fulfillment into the mystery of God where the God-become-flesh is the center and where human life, yours and mine, is transformed into the divine.[7]

In the liturgy, the whole church is praying with Christ, the head and leader of the church. Through the liturgy, our own personal prayer and our own spiritual lives are taken up into the great, common prayer of the whole church. Thus, through liturgy we become full participants in the church, members—as Saint Paul does not tire of saying—of one body and sharers in one great hope. Thus, we come to God, our final common good, not merely individually, but through and with one another. Just as virtue can only be truly itself if it is open to the promotion of the common good, so spirituality can only be genuine if it is open to participation in the liturgy, the common work of worship.

Modern Western Christians often have great difficulty in recognizing the need to ground their spirituality in liturgy. This difficulty is akin to difficulties they have accepting a life of virtue dedicated to promotion of the common good. In most Western nations, the ideal of common values and of a common worldview is in eclipse, although in practice, common values are what hold together even "advanced" societies. In order to celebrate common values, however, we must recognize that sharing them by participation is itself a common end and good. It is not a restriction of personal choice and freedom, but a condition of our flourishing together.

Thus the problem we have with the liturgy today is that we come to it with individual rather than communal expectations.[8] Or to put it bluntly, we come making demands and wanting to be heard; we come wanting to "get something" for our time. It hardly occurs to us that our contribution to the liturgical work might involve heeding some very old, authoritative advice recorded in the Psalms: "Be still, and know that I am God."

Liturgy is our work, a human work, and so it runs a risk common to all human works. It may decline into routine, becoming a purely formal, external ritual. Those who collaborate in liturgy, like those who participate in the pursuit of common human goods, must be cultivated and trained to the work if they are to do their parts well. When the ends and goods in view belong to the political or business communities, the collaborators' personal virtue is the condition for their promotion. Thus, besides personal virtue, the instruments forged for promotion of the good—laws or policies, customs or procedures— are, at best, reduced to rote and empty rules. Unless its participants cultivate their personal spirituality and a life of prayer, liturgy can disintegrate into a quasi-mechanical exercise from which the hearts and minds of those present are disengaged. The liturgical work demands their active participation in the celebration, the engagement of their personal spirituality with the prayer of the community as a whole. Conversely, the liturgy may also be degraded through the assumption of a kind of false "otherworldliness." Liturgy that leaves the participants with the impression that what they do outside the sanctuary is disconnected from what they do within it promotes their disconnection from the world.

Liturgy disciplines and refines personal spirituality: if we enter into the liturgy, we will find our spirituality opening to fellowship; we will find our views undergoing correction in light of a comprehensive vision; and we will find ourselves far less confident of our own spiritual maturity. Liturgy challenges spirituality to openness, objectivity, and honesty. Vital personal spirituality turns liturgical celebration toward the spiritual lives of those celebrating,[9] thus, in the liturgy all that we do in the world, together with our own personal spirituality, are drawn together and directed toward the most excellent activity in which we can participate on earth: the worship of God.

It is vital to remember that in every liturgical celebration, we have both the descent of the grace of God (through the Holy Spirit) and the response of the community in worship, thanks, and intercession. In other words, liturgy can never be considered merely our act toward God; it is, rather, our *response* to the action of God. God's initiative is primary. This reflects the basic "giftedness" of creation to us, something we have already noted with regard to the ownership of property.

God's gift of salvation to us is prior to our celebration of this gift in the liturgy. Just as the natural, objective world is given to us through God's creation, so our prayer and praise, and our supernatural life *in toto*, is redelivered to us through the re-creation of the redemption worked for us in Christ. Our liturgy, like our work, depends first on the gift that God has given. Furthermore, each liturgical celebration also depends primarily on the action of God's grace among us, before we even begin, and beyond all that we could ever achieve. Thus, although the word "liturgy" might come from the Greek words meaning "the work of the people," we need to remember that that work, just as our work in the world, depends first on an initial gift from God.

What Makes up the Liturgy?

All Christians regard prayer in common as a central element of their faith. Following the example of the first Christians, recorded in the Acts of the Apostles, they try to be faithful to "the apostles' teaching and fellowship, to the breaking of the bread and the prayers."[10] Critical in this phrase is the mention of the breaking of the bread, the proto-eucharistic liturgy. Today, many of the Christian traditions still regard the Eucharist as the central liturgical celebration of the Christian community. Those who participate in the Orthodox, Anglican, Catholic, and some Protestant communions recognize in the Eucharist the "source and summit" of our lives.[11] It is the source because, through the liturgy of the Eucharist, we are united to Christ and his redemptive mission in the world. We are given grace to heal the wounds of sin in our lives, and to return to the path of virtue.

What does this teaching on the Eucharist mean in terms of business? It means that in promoting the common good, we are involved in an activity no less important than the redemptive work of Christ in the world. Without sin and the structures of sin that flow from it and encourage it, we would be able to pursue the common good of this world naturally, with desires that would accord with the natural order of the world. However, we are not sinless, and therefore we need grace to achieve our natural personal and communal good in this world. The Eucharistic liturgy—through which we can be sure to receive the grace of God and union with Christ—is thus in a real sense the source not only of our Christian faith and the theological virtues, but also of our natural virtues and of our every capacity to promote the common good.

Vatican II also called the Eucharist the "summit" of our Christian lives. In other words, all that we do approaches and culminates in our union with Christ and the Church through the celebration and reception of the Eucharist. Thus, the Eucharistic liturgy represents the pledge of our ultimate goal: happiness with God. All our virtues and every common good in this life, however excellent, are means to that end.

Nevertheless, the Eucharist does not exhaust the liturgical life of the church, nor incorporate all the ways that the liturgy can relate to our working life. Between "source" and "summit," there is much room. We can point to other sacraments of the church which accompany us with the grace of God at significant points in our lives. We are reborn through the ministry of the church into new life (baptism); we are deepened in the gifts of the spirit (confirmation); we repent and are forgiven our sins, through the power to forgive that Jesus bequeathed to the church (reconciliation); we are sustained through serious sickness and in the face of death (sacrament of the sick); we give ourselves to lifelong service of others in society and the church (marriage and holy orders).

Each of the sacraments can relate to the world of business in particular ways: through baptism and confirmation we are welcomed into the church community and thus enabled to benefit from the unifying power of the Eucharist; through reconciliation, we can repent of our sins against the common good and our lack of virtue, and so can be reconciled not only with God, but also with the wider community; through marriage and holy orders, we commit ourselves to lifelong structures of love and service in the community that help to stabilize us and provide the basis for our working lives; finally, through the sacrament of the sick, we can be restored to health or can be strengthened in our last struggle and provide hope to others even through our death.[12]

There are many other aspects of the liturgy that comprise the rich fare offered by the church to her members: the liturgy of the hours, exposition of the blessed sacrament, lay fraternity prayers in common, eucharistic services in the absence of a priest, services of reconciliation, prayer services for special events, and so on. Important for the connection between liturgy and the business organization is the liturgical year, especially the feasts with a special connection to work, such as that of St. Joseph the Worker (May 1), or in the United States, the celebration of the Labor Day holiday. All these elements make up the rich and complex fabric of the church's public, communal prayer and touch many points of our personal spirituality and our virtuous behavior at work.

UNDERSTANDING LITURGY

Perhaps the best way of understanding liturgy in the context of our whole lives is to think of the *"before," "during,"* and *"after"* of liturgy. *"Before"* the liturgy signifies all that leads us to the celebration, our entry into the life of faith by means of *catechesis,* and the content of that faith to which we assent. In the words of an old Latin adage, we enter into the liturgy through our assent to the *lex credendi* (rule of belief).

The *"during"* of the liturgy is the celebration of the rite itself, the *lex orandi* (literally, rule of prayer). The crucial theological idea behind understanding the way the liturgy itself works is that of *anamnesis,* or "recollection." Put simply, it means that in our liturgical celebration, through the remembering and re-presenting of the saving action of the life of Christ, Christ himself comes to be truly present among us. The saving action of God that occurred centuries ago is recollected and made present in our day through the ritual, liturgical remembering of the worshipping community. In our celebration of the sacraments, we call to mind all that God has done for us in Christ, and this recalling makes present in our own time that saving work of God. We thus participate in that saving work and receive its benefits.[13] In the context of this chapter, we can remember that, if our happiness with God is our ultimate common good, then in making present the saving grace and presence of Christ in our midst, we are truly participating in, and receiving a foretaste of, our true common good in Christ.[14]

The most relevant to our purposes is the *"after"* of the liturgy, what has been called the *lex vivendi,* or the rule guiding our life. Out of our life of faith (*lex credendi*) and our celebration of that faith (*lex orandi*), our lived life flows, our life considered both within business and in the wider world. That life flows back into the liturgy and is taken up into it. There is a deep organic connection between the life of the liturgy and the life of society. In the liturgical celebration, we form a microcosm of society; we offer up to God all that we have and hope for.[15] The idea of the Eucharistic liturgy as the "source and summit" of our lives emphasizes this organic and integral connection between our communal celebration of the Eucharist and the rest of our lives. The source of a river becomes the river—it is not something different from it—while the summit of the mountain is lifted high because it rests on the body of the mountain. If the Eucharist is to be the source and summit of our lives, it must be as integrally connected to our lives as a spring is to the river that flows from it, or the body of the mountain is to the peak that crowns it.

MAKING CLEARER THE LINK BETWEEN LITURGY AND WORK

We have focused on the necessary and real link between the liturgy and the world of work. We have argued that conscious and deliberate attempts to "engage" our liturgical with our working lives are not a futile forcing together of disparate spheres of human existence. Liturgy and work are, of themselves and prior to our efforts, deeply engaged with one another. Nevertheless, in practice people do find it hard to see how liturgical celebration and work are connected, so we conclude this chapter with some pointers for making this connection clearer. What are some practical ways in which the link between our work and our liturgy can be strengthened? How can we more closely examine the consequences of that linkage and take them to heart?

Some simple ways are offered to us by the normal liturgical life of our parishes and communities. This is the crucial area in which a real, living connection between faith and work can be developed. Baldovin is certainly correct when he observes of the connection between liturgy and justice:

> . . . the way the liturgy is celebrated every Sunday is going to have more of an impact on the assembly's orientation toward justice than special peak moments. In a sense, the liturgical year will be successful as an agent of justice when the aspect of Christian communal existence is taken for granted—not ignored—as one of the attitudes that describe the assembly's existence.[16]

For many, the liturgical life means simply Sunday Eucharist, and thus special, prayerful attention to the themes of faith and work may seem inappropriate when so much else needs to be said and celebrated in such a short time. It is important not to overstress one aspect of our lives—even such an important one as our work—in a celebration that must touch the whole of our humanity. The revival of the liturgy of the hours in more and more parishes promises to extend the liturgical life of their members, and this would allow for the development of more themes and for deeper, sustained reflection. Nevertheless, Sunday Eucharist does offer working people important ways to reflect on the link between faith and work without overburdening the celebration.

Intercessory prayers may be offered for a deeper understanding of the link between life and liturgy, for the needs of the local unemployed, for businesses in difficulty, or for the good formation of business leaders in the principles of Christian social thought. More properly called the "Prayers of the Faithful," they are the liturgical moment set aside for lay members' direct expression of their own petitions to God. Accordingly, introduction of the themes of faith and work at this point in the liturgy gives them a special solemnity.

Homilies and post-communion reflections offer another opportunity for introducing these themes into the liturgy. Celebrants' homilies should always reflect on the readings of the liturgy of the word, and particularly on the day's Gospel. However, many Gospel passages would allow, and some would demand, reflection on faith and work. Recall, for instance, the astonishment of those who hear Christ in the synagogue (Mark 6:2–3), incredulous that a carpenter could speak in the way that Jesus does. What does their prejudgment, that no wisdom could come from a carpenter, suggest concerning our own attitudes toward the shaping of workers, our fellow Christians, by their work? Work and workers of every kind are represented in the Gospels. Jesus' parables often concern work and workers (the housewife and the coin, the vineyard and its workers, the sower) in ways that should remind us that the practice of religion extends to all authentic human action, and that no such action is unworthy of dedication to God.[17]

The rite of preparation or offertory is another important point in the liturgy at which the connection between our work and our communal praise of God can be made manifest. In the early church, the gifts presented at the offertory were closely connected with labor—each person who could, brought bread and wine, and those who were too poor to do so received whatever bread was left over after the celebration. Today, instead of bread or wine, we bring a portion of our wages. The problem here is that the check we place in the envelope does not clearly remind us of what we are doing when we make this offering, namely, giving to God from the fruits of our work.[18]

With a bit of effort and imagination it is possible to reconnect what we give at the offertory to our work. We can remember that the check or currency placed in the basket is the product of our labor. We can imagine placing in the basket our carpentry, electrical, managerial, computer, accounting, or teaching services. The gifts we give at this point in the liturgical rite really are an extension of the work we have done. Furthermore, because we give from our salaries, this rite should challenge us to ask whether the work we offer through these tokens is pure, like the unblemished lamb offered at the temple.

Most of us, if we are honest, will be given pause by such a question. Do we treat our subordinates, fellow workers and supervisors with dignity and respect? Do we make the extra effort to create conditions in our workplace that foster the virtues of justice, prudent decision making, courage, and self-control, rather than the vices of pride, gossip, laziness, and greed? Do we go the extra mile, and make the extra effort? Do we avoid allowing status, power, and prestige to overwhelm family needs and relationships?

We should pray over our gifts of money before we give them. Giving is difficult to do week after week. Often we experience a struggle when we think how we could otherwise use the money we give—a vacation, new furniture, house repairs, books. However, this giving of our money has an important effect on us. It reminds us that in the end, we own nothing. Everything, especially our work, is a gift from God and is carried out in collaboration with God. We are caretakers, and though we have been given dominion, it is a dominion within God's created order; it is not our own.

The themes discussed above can be made the occasion of postcommunion reflections by any competent member of the church community, and can be focused specifically on the goal of deepening our understanding of the profound connection between the liturgical life of the parish or community and the daily work of its members. We have already mentioned that particular feasts like that of St. Joseph the Worker could play an important role in raising awareness of the essential link between liturgy and work. On such occasions, hymns, readings, reflections, and bidding prayers can all provide different ways in which the liturgy informs working life.

Groups such as Christian professional organizations, business people's breakfast or lunch groups, or groups like the YCW or Catholic Worker can also develop their own liturgical resources and emphasize liturgical celebration as part of the pastoral dimension of their work. Conferences on the spirituality of business could be offered for the development of the link between liturgy, spirituality, and work. Local saints could also be incorporated into the liturgical calendar, unofficially if necessary. This practice could also be adopted by organizations trying to support the engagement of faith and work.[19] They could create their own parallel liturgical calendars (as many religious orders do), and add to them celebrations of lives that can inspire them in their work:

> People relate best in the final analysis not to ideas but to flesh-and-blood human beings who exemplify for them in the contemporary cultural circumstances what it means to be *in Christ*, to be grasped by the power of God. Saints here are far more than models for moral imitation; they are tangible reminders that God's power has been at work in human beings.[20]

Success in these initiatives requires the real conviction that both the liturgy and the world of work have been made poorer by their disconnection from each other. Once we are convinced of this, the sheer number of opportunities for making connections exceed our ability to pursue them. Like the practice of virtue, the initiative and the nurturing of these links depend on the situations in which people find themselves; we can offer only general outlines here. The biggest problem is not making the engagement once we realize its importance; the real difficulty lies in coming to that realization in the first place.

STUDY QUESTIONS

1. What has been your experience of liturgy? Did this experience help you understand other aspects of your day-to-day living? Why or why not?
2. What is the connection between liturgy and personal spirituality? Why do they both need and support each other?
3. How can the connection between work and liturgy be made more clear? In particular, how can we make our work express more clearly its deep connection with liturgy?

Epilogue

*[I]t is of primary importance that the economic world be
constructed and function in such a way that men do not run the risk
of sacrificing what they are to what they do; they must be inspired
to live their work as a means of achieving spiritual enrichment and
perfection.*

—Pietro Pavan[1]

O N ONE LEVEL, *MANAGING AS IF FAITH MATTERED* IS about one thing: "keeping the end in mind."[2] It is about reconnecting the *means* of management—its techniques, skills, and strategies—to its *ends*, as conceived of by the Christian social tradition. The aim of this book is intended to overcome the "divided" life, so that we do not pursue efficiency and wealth at work during the day, and happiness and goodness with our families at home at night, but instead, that we pursue consistently and everywhere the *good*. Because this chasm between means and ends is maintained and promoted by the universities, it is appropriate that this book challenge and refute this split. Only when our universities (including the religiously affiliated ones) can overcome this dichotomy of their own making, and face the question of "ends," can we expect society as a whole to object to this kind of division.

The healing of this split can be addressed in a myriad of ways, appropriate to many people and many situations. In chapter 1, we outlined three basic models for reengaging means and ends (or work and faith). It was our intention to present the diversity of the possibilities in a clear and simple way; we do not mean to suggest that there are not many more diverse ways in which such engagement can be made. Within the realm of genuine engagement, all things are possible. We do rule out the deficient models that are outside the realm of a genuine engagement, that is, the models of the secularizer and the spiritualizer. But a Reell Precision Manufacturing is not a Herman Miller, which is not again Borg-Warner. They have found their own ways of bridging the separation of faith and work. Some are more explicit than others about the source of their motivation and organizational principles, while others focus on reaching a good outcome that promotes the kind of personal development and organizational environment that is consistent with their success. Other institutions, like the churches and the universities, can contribute to the success of this engagement, through their critiques of a situation or system. Every approach has strengths and weaknesses, but each represents a form of genuine engagement. One of the main aims of this book is to make as clear as possible what constitutes genuine engagement, and to distinguish it from the artificial and incomplete versions of the secularizer and spiritualizer.

In some ways, this first part of the process is the most difficult—it is certainly the most fundamental. However, when we try to put this engagement into practice in various management disciplines, other sorts of difficulty arise. In many cases, it is simply difficult to imagine what job design or pay structures or new product development would look like if the ends of human activity were reconnected with the means of creating effective job design or pay systems. This is often harder than the first stage because it requires real practical intelligence (virtue of prudence), a commitment to right relationships cashed out in practice (the *virtue* of justice, not just its principle), an ability to control one's desires for acquisitiveness and self-aggrandizement (virtue of temperance) and the willingness to take risks and make sacrifices (virtue of courage), plus, it requires a solid grasp of the technical questions that arise in each function. It requires that every technical approach be judged by the demands of the common good and the development of the human person. Such requirements show what a high calling and vocation the manager has, and that surely special grace or help from God is needed if this engagement is to be made truly and well.

To live this grace-filled life in organizations today requires a form of everyday heroism—a heroism that is worthy of the name, in which intelligence and rational deliberation are bound to courage and perseverance. To live out such a daily witness in practice—requires the support of the deep spiritual resources of the Christian tradition, which are available to us through personal prayer, meditation on Scripture, communal worship, sacramental life, spiritual direction, and so forth. Without the constant support we receive from these channels of direct contact with God, in prayer and through the body of the Christian community, we could not go on. At the very least, we need to learn from others who are trying to do the same thing—trying to integrate their faith and their work in a way that is economically effective while it promotes the higher goods. If you would like to contact either of us about questions, comments or concerns please e-mail us (Helen Alford—Alford@pust.urbe.it, and Michael Naughton—mjnaughton@stthomas.edu), or visit the John A. Ryan Institute for Catholic Social Thought Web page at www.stthomas.edu/cathstudies/cst, for more information on the relationship between Christian social thought and management.

The old phrase, "we should work as if all depended on us, and pray as if all depended on God," helps us to emphasize the need for action on our part. Equally true is the phrase "we should pray as if all depended on us, and work as if all depended on God," which helps us to emphasize the need for grace. As a broken and sinful people, we are reminded that we cannot work on our own. We need divine guidance in our work. We need help to overcome our weakness in the face of such a difficult task and to inspire our weak minds and wills with practical ways forward. As we begin this new millennium, may we all *work as if our faith mattered.*

Notes

1. Making Us Whole

1. Douglas Coupland, *Life After God* (New York: Pocket Books, 1995), 39. In conversation, Dr. Tom Bausch, Professor of Management, Marquette University, has reminded us that "compromise" is an equivocal term: "A person can compromise on principles—to do so is deeply troubling. A person can compromise on means to achieve a principled end without sacrificing principle. This can be the virtue of prudence. Acting in prudence can also compromise on the ideal timetable for the accomplishment of desired principles."

2. Niccolò Machiavelli, *The Prince and the Discourses* (New York: Modern Library, 1940), 56.

3. These formulations come to us from Oliver Williams *via* John Murray.

4. We use the terms "Christian social tradition" and "Christian social teaching" rather than "Catholic social tradition" because the different Christian denominations today exhibit an ecumenical convergence on this topic of work (see Lee Hardy, *The Fabric of this World* [Grand Rapids, Mich.: Wm. B. Eerdmans Publishing Co., 1990], 67ff.). It seems that where the Gospel's call to justice and to charity is so urgent and so immediate, Christians' unity in baptism overshadows their doctrinal divisions. We are confident that our debt to our own Catholic tradition of social teaching will in any case be no less clear than our debts to the thought and witness of Protestant managers whom we describe in this book.

5. The development of the idea of different conceptual models both of business organizations and of the Church is one of the most interesting and fruitful developments of our century in organization theory and in ecclesiology. Among other advantages, conceptual models encourage us to recognize the underlying *mystery* both of the Church in its divine and human aspects, and of any group of human beings cooperating with each other in some enterprise. We cannot completely explain the Church, or a

business organization; they are beyond our comprehension, albeit in different ways. Yet, they are not completely inexplicable in rational terms, and our necessarily partial accounts retain explanatory value as long as we are aware of their limitations. Diverging models resist our tendency to reduce the reality of things to our own convenient size; concurrence of different models, sometimes despite mutually conflicting aspects, reminds us that though reality exceeds us, it does not wholly escape us. Both are salutary lessons in intellectual humility.

6. Tom Peters, "Spiritual Talk Has No Place in Secular Corporation," *Minneapolis Star Tribune*, 6 April 1993, 2D. See also Michael and Kenneth Himes, *Fullness of Faith: The Public Significance of Theology* (New York: Paulist Press, 1993), 2ff., concerning the distinctions among secularization, secularism, and privatization.

7. Ibid. For a critique of the liberalism underlying Peters' comments, see Stephen Carter, *Civility: Manners, Morals, and the Etiquette of Democracy* (New York: HarperCollins, 1999), 174.

8. See also David Tracy, "Defending the Public Character of Theology," *Christian Century* 98 (1981): 350. Tracy argues for the proposition that "no major religion, properly understood, can accept a privatistic self-understanding."

9. John Paul II, *Ex Corde Ecclesiae*, 44, www.cin.org/jp2/excorde.html (1/28/01).

10. The bishops at Vatican II strongly condemned the divorcing of faith from work. In a paragraph that might be titled "Don't Ghettoize the Faith!" they proclaim that Christians are "wide of the mark who think that religion consists in acts of worship alone and in the discharge of certain moral obligations, and who imagine they can plunge themselves into earthly affairs in such a way as to imply that these are altogether divorced from the religious life. The split between the faith which many profess and their daily lives deserves to be counted among the more serious errors of our age. . . . Let there be no false opposition between professional and social activities on the one hand, and religious life on the other. The Christian who neglects his temporal duties, neglects his duties toward his neighbor and even God, and jeopardizes his eternal salvation. Christians should rather rejoice that they can follow the example of Christ, who worked as an artisan. In the exercise of all their earthly activities, they can thereby gather their humane, domestic, professional, social, and technical enterprises into one vital synthesis with religious values, under whose supreme direction all things are harmonized unto God's glory" (*Gaudium et Spes*, 43). See also Michael Budde, *The (Magic) Kingdom of God: Christianity and Global Cul-*

ture Industries (Boulder, Colo.: Westview Press, 1997), 4ff., where he writes of a "dual ethic" that has permeated the Christian tradition, especially since the fourth century.

11. Bill George, "An Open Letter to Tom Peters on Spirituality and Motivation," *Minneapolis Star Tribune*, 19 April 1993.

12. David Whyte, *The Heart Aroused* (New York: Currency Doubleday, 1994), 69.

13. Peters' problematic view of religion accompanies his problematic view of the corporation. For him, the overriding purpose of the corporation is to create conditions that enhance *competitiveness*. But to reduce working to competing, and workers to competitors (both within and among firms), is to guarantee that organizations will regard persons merely as instruments of competitive strategies. As John Paul II observes, "When a person is deprived of a transcendent reference, he becomes little more than a drop in the ocean, and his dignity, no matter how sincerely acknowledged and proclaimed, loses its most solid guarantee" (*Origins*, 23 September 1993, 257). Chapter 2 considers these concerns in detail through an examination of the shareholder and stakeholder views of the corporation.

14. The tendency to think that unjust and dehumanizing conditions in the workplace can be compensated by giving people "education" or "culture" in their off-work time is deeply entrenched in the capitalist mentality, in part because the "father of capitalism," Adam Smith, suggested it himself in the fifth volume of his classic text, *The Wealth of Nations*. See Michael Novak, *Business as a Calling* (New York: The Free Press, 1996), 58ff., for a more positive interpretation of Carnegie's role in business.

15. Thomas L. Schaffer and Robert E. Rodes, "A Christian Theology for Roman Catholic Law Schools," *University of Dayton Law Review* 14 (1988): 5–18. See also Laura Nash, *Believers in Business* (Nashville, Tenn.: Thomas Nelson Publishers, 1994), 29–30.

16. Stephen Carter finds a kind of conservatism in the attitude of those we call spiritualizers (*Civility*, 175). For an illuminating, pastoral examination both of the moral obtuseness which usually accompanies an insular faith and of the monstrous "choices" contemporary business often throws at engaged faith, see J. Irwin Miller, "How Religious Commitments Shape Decisions," in *On Moral Business: Classical and Contemporary Resources for Ethics in Economic Life*, ed. Max L. Stackhouse, Dennis P. McCann, and Shirley J. Roels, with Preston N. Williams (Grand Rapids, Mich.: Wm. B. Eerdmans Publishing Co., 1995), 707ff. Unlike the secularizer, the spiritualizer rightly presupposes that the spiritual health of persons is the foundation of the healthy organization. Spiritual health is found through prayer,

friendship, worship, family living, and simplicity. But spiritualizers tend to confine their spirituality only to (admittedly important) issues of personal conduct: whether to take a bribe, to help an employee in need, to lie to gain a sale. However, spiritualizers fail to apply the tenets of the Christian faith—including its version of social justice—to the various policy issues of organizational life.

17. See John Paul II, *Sollicitudo Rei Socialis*, 36–40, in *Catholic Social Thought: The Documentary Heritage*, ed. David J. O'Brien and Thomas A. Shannon (Maryknoll, N.Y. : Orbis Books, 1992). (NB: unless otherwise noted, all references to papal and conciliar documents are by paragraph number from this collection.) In particular, John Paul observes, "'[S]tructures of sin' . . . are rooted in personal sin, and thus always linked to the *concrete acts*, of individuals who introduce these structures, consolidate them and make them difficult to remove. And thus they grow stronger, spread, and become the sources of other sins, and so influence people's behavior" (ibid., 36). The opposite of this structural sin is commitment to the common good, which we discuss in the next chapter.

18. See Alasdair MacIntyre, *After Virtue* (Notre Dame: University of Notre Dame Press, 1981; 2nd ed., 1984); *Whose Justice? Which Rationality?* (Notre Dame: University of Notre Dame Press, 1988); *Three Rival Versions of Moral Enquiry: Encyclopaedia, Genealogy, and Tradition*, Gifford Lectures, 1988 (Notre Dame: University of Notre Dame Press, 1990).

19. See MacIntyre, *After Virtue*, chapters 5–6, pp. 51–78.

20. See Basil Willey, *The Seventeenth Century Background* (London: Chatto & Windus, 1950), 4. Willey explains that the scientific methods developed in the seventeenth century became more satisfying in explaining reality because "instead of the kind of 'truth' which is consistent with authoritative teaching, men began to desire the kind which would enable them to measure, to weigh and to control the things around them; they desired, in Bacon's words, 'to extend more widely the limits of the power and greatness of man'. Interest was now directed to the *how*, the manner of causation, not its *why*, its final cause. For a scientific type of explanation to be satisfying, for it to convince us with a sense of its necessary truth, we must be in the condition of needing and desiring that type of explanation and no other." Michael Buckley provides an integrated view of these two searches for truth: "The fundamental proposition of the Catholic [and Christian] university is that the religious and the academic are intrinsically related. Any movement toward meaning and truth is inchoately religious. This obviously does not suggest that quantum mechanics or geography is religion or theology; it does mean that the dynamism inherent in all inquiry and knowledge—if not inhibited—is toward ultimacy, toward a completion in which

an issue or its resolution finds place in a universe that makes final sense, i.e., in the self-disclosure of God—the truth of the finite. At the same time, the tendencies of faith are inescapably toward the academic. This obviously does not suggest that all serious religion is scholarship; it does mean that the dynamism inherent in faith—if not inhibited—is toward its own understanding, toward its own self-possession in knowledge" ("The Catholic University and the Promise Inherent in Its Identity," in *Catholic Universities in Church and Society,* ed. John P. Langan, S.J., [Washington, D.C.: Georgetown University Press, 1993], 82–83). See also Terrence Nichols, "Aquinas's Concept of Substantial Form and Modern Science," *International Philosophical Quarterly* 36 (September 1996): 303–318.

21. Alasdair MacIntyre argues that managerial effectiveness that is conceived as morally neutral and indifferent to the ends it serves is a pernicious illusion; see MacIntyre, *After Virtue,* 74ff. MacIntyre's description of managerial practice may not seem altogether accurate, but his analysis of the normative in social practice is compelling.

22. In a 1994 report, the Hastings Center of Values on Campus in the Undergraduate Curriculum ". . . suggests that the erosion of structured opportunities for moral development occurred as the academic value of research rose and the development of disciplines resulted. This discipline, narrowing and professionalization in most fields, removed from contact the dilemmas of human experience and resulted in silence about critical questions of personal and social choice. An unforeseen consequence was a crisis of purpose and mission as students had fewer formal opportunities to pursue questions of ethics and values" (John A. Ruhe et al., "Values Traits Reinforcement and Perceived Importance: Does Context Matter?" *International Journal of Value-Based Management* 11 [1998]: 105). Even where theology or philosophy courses are regularly required, students tend to regard them as involving one more sort of distinct, specialized knowledge alongside other sorts. Philosophy and theology rarely function as integrating studies. Comparing religious and public universities, Ruhe et al. report that business students in the former ". . . seem to compartmentalize their ethical instruction, and do not generalize it to business" (ibid., 117).

23. Robert Bellah et al., *The Good Society* (New York: Alfred Knopf, 1991), 289. In their report on management education in the U.S., Porter and McKibbin argue that schools of management adequately prepare students to perform entry-level tasks, but fail to equip students with the larger historical and philosophical framework required of critical practitioners and effective future leaders; see Lyman W. Porter and Lawrence E. McKibbin, *Management Education and Development: Drift or Thrust into the 21st Century?* (New York: McGraw-Hill Book Co., 1988), 104ff., 310ff. The failure is

critical, since free and responsible agents are always characterized by their conception of the whole and how they relate their own particular interests to it.

24. Neil Hamilton, "The Legal Profession and the Common Good," talk at St. Olaf Catholic Church, Minneapolis, Minn. (17 September 1998).

25. Quoted in Willey, *The Seventeenth Century Background*, 9.

26. Porter and McKibbin, *Management Education and Development*, 187; see also ibid., 192. Nor do the liberal arts faculties see much of a need to interact on an academic level with the school of management. This lack of interaction translates into a segmented curriculum that has lost "vision about ways to achieve 'an amalgamation of the two'" (Michael C. Jordan, "The Tension between Liberal Education and Career Education," in *Papers 1987: Faculty Seminar on the History of the College of St. Thomas*, St. Paul, Minn.). Meanwhile, students are left with the uneasy sense that they participate in two types of education: one that makes them more human, another that makes them more money, but they are unclear about how—or whether—the two fit together. Required business ethics courses (increasingly common) may help students take a broader and more social view of business. However, too often they are not integrated with the balance of the curriculum, and they separate ethics from religion, and thus from the sources of many students' sense of obligation. They encourage the idea that ethics can be reduced to a kind of strategic casuistry, the skillful invention of a rationale for doing "what pays."

27. Ruhe et al. ("Values Traits," 117) point out that the moral imagination of students from both religiously affiliated and public universities was minimal. One reason cited for this lack of difference may be the prevalence of the sort of insular faith that we have ascribed to spiritualizers: "students in the religious, co-ed schools might have perceived reinforcement of these traits [generosity, loyalty, etc.] in their religious classes, but did not perceive that these traits would help them achieve success in a business career—especially if these heart values were also not integrated or reinforced in their business studies" (ibid.).

28. G. K. Chesterson, *Orthodoxy* (New York: Image Day, 1990), 14. See Bernard Lonergan, "*Existenz* and *Aggiornamento*," in *Collection: Papers by Bernard Lonergan*, ed. Frederick E. Crowe (New York: Herder and Herder, 1967), 240–251, wherein Lonergan discusses authentic and inauthentic traditions, 246–247.

29. Vatican II, the Second Council of the Vatican, was a general council in which all the Catholic bishops of the world met in several sessions

from the years 1962 to 1965. See the Council's *Pastoral Constitution on the Church in the Modern World (Gaudium et Spes)*, 33–39, 76.

30. See John Paul II, *Fides et Ratio*, 104, www.cin.org/jp2/fides.html (1/23/01). Michael and Kenneth Himes (*Fullness of Faith: The Public Significance of Theology*) propose an hermeneutical, as opposed to apologetic, public theology, as the means of rendering Christian symbols (in the senses both of "sign" and "creed") understandable to ordinary people of other persuasions and faiths, and to the end of opening for them the resources of Christian theology.

31. Jacques Maritain, *Man and the State* (Chicago: University of Chicago Press, 1951), 77. One should note well that Maritain's focus on practical agreement does not lead him into indifferentism; quite the reverse: "I am fully convinced that my way of justifying the belief in the rights of man and the ideal of freedom, equality, and fraternity is the only one which is solidly based on truth. That does not prevent me from agreeing on these practical tenets with those who are convinced that their way of justifying them, entirely different from mine or even opposed to mine in its theoretical dynamism, is likewise the only one that is based on truth. Assuming they both believe in the democratic charter, a Christian and a rationalist will, nevertheless, give justifications that are incompatible with each other, to which their souls, their minds, and their blood are committed, and about these justifications they will fight. And God keep me from saying that it is not important to know which of the two is right! That is essentially important. They remain, however, in agreement on the practical affirmation of that charter, and they can formulate together common principles of action" (ibid., 77–78).

32. Ibid., 77. Maritain goes on to write that the extent of such agreement "is doubtless very little, it is the last refuge of intellectual agreement among men. It is, however, enough to undertake a great work; and it would mean a great deal to become aware of this body of common practical convictions" (ibid., 77–78).

33. Nash, *Believers in Business*, 246–247.

34. Nash (*Believers in Business*, 247) records the opposite dynamic in the case of James Burke, former CEO of Johnson & Johnson , who presided over the deletion of "with God's grace" from the company's Credo in 1979. See also the discussion of the religious influence exercised by business leaders Adrian Cadbury (Cadbury Schweppes), J. Irwin Miller (Cummins Engine), and Max DePree (Herman Miller), in Patrick Murphy and Georges Enderle, "Managerial Ethical Leadership," *Business Ethics Quarterly* (January 1995): 117–128.

35. For Beré and other religious managers in secular organizations, two disciplines are paramount: public intelligibility and public accessibility. These disciplines are described by Michael Perry, *Love and Power* (New York: Oxford University Press, 1991), 106. According to Perry, public intelligibility is "the habit of trying to elaborate one's position in a manner intelligible or comprehensible to those who speak a different religious or moral language." Public accessibility is "the habit of trying to defend one's position in a manner neither sectarian nor authoritarian. . . . A defense of a disputed position is sectarian if (and to the extent) it relies on experiences or premises that have little if any authority beyond the confines of one's own moral or religious community. A defense is authoritarian if it relies on persons or institutions that have little if any authority beyond the confines of one's own community."

36. Max De Pree, former CEO of Herman Miller, goes to the heart of the danger that "common ground" will slip away into "prevailing ground": "Unless somebody articulates something different, you are going to adopt a secular standard without even thinking about it" (Nash, *Believers in Business*, 262).

37. See Nash, *Believers in Business*, 102ff. See also the web site www.scruples.org (1/28/01) for information on Christians in the marketplace.

38. See Walter Kasper, "The Theological Anthropology of *Gaudium et Spes*," *Communio* (Spring 1996): 133. To articulate the mission and identity of the company only in natural law terms surrenders *a priori* "the chance to secure an ecumenical consensus."

39. See Kenneth E. Goodpaster and Laura L. Nash, *Policies and Persons*, 3rd ed. (New York: McGraw-Hill, 1998), 135–150.

40. The phrase and the thought are owed to Ernest Pierucci, Esq., whose insights on these matters have been invaluable to the authors.

41. Michael Buckley, S.J., "Father Buckley to Prof. O'Brien," *America*, 11 September 1993, 22.

42. As Alasdair MacIntyre observes in a related—and equally vexed—connection: "If we do not recover and identify with the particularities of our own community, then we shall lose what it is that we have to contribute to the common culture. We shall have nothing to bring, nothing to give. But if each of us dwells too much, or even exclusively, upon his or her own ethnic particularity, then we are in danger of fragmenting and even destroying the common life." Alasdair MacIntyre, presentation on the nature of the Catholic university, University of St. John's, Collegeville, Minnesota (September 29, 1990).

43. See Nash, *Believers in Business*, 260–261.

44. See Gene G. James, "Whistleblowing: Its Moral Justification," quoted in W. Michael Hoffman and Jennifer Mills Moore, *Business Ethics: Readings and Cases in Corporate Morality,* 2nd ed. (New York: McGraw Hill, 1980): 332–345. The engineers in question were almost certainly required by their professional codes of conduct to question this situation.

45. Isaiah 58:3.

46. Prophetic voices need not thunder in denunciation, as one of the twentieth century's most notable voices shows. Peter Maurin, co-founder with Dorothy Day of the Catholic Worker movement, "never had more than the clothes on his back, but he took the Gospel counsel literally—'if anyone asks for thy coat give him thy cloak too.' He went in all simplicity to men like Thomas Woodlock of the *Wall Street Journal,* and John Moody of the Moody Investment Service, and not only asked them for things, but also discussed finance capitalism, unemployment and usury with them" (Dorothy Day, *The Long Loneliness* [New York: Harper and Row, 1950; reprint, San Francisco: HarperCollins, 1981], 179). The financier, manager, or entrepreneur who fails to listen, even to the "still, small voice" of the marginalized, risks failing to hear his God.

47. See Bernard Brady, *The Moral Bond of Communication* (Washington, D.C.: Georgetown University Press, 1998).

48. Joseph Cardinal Ratzinger, "Market Economy and Ethics," in *Ordo Socialis: Making Christianity Work in Business and Economy,* ed. Association for the Advancement of Christian Social Sciences (Philippines: Divine Word Publications, 1992): 62–67.

49. The elements of what has come to be called "solidarity" in the Catholic branch of the tradition.

2. The Purpose of Business

1. This chapter has been substantially rewritten with the help of Steven Cortright. For an interdisciplinary analysis of the purpose of the firm, see *Rethinking the Purpose of Business: Interdisciplinary Essays from the Catholic Social Tradition,* ed. S. A. Cortright and Michael J. Naughton, to be published by the University of Notre Dame Press. The epigram for this chapter is quoted from Robert Bellah et al., *Habits of the Heart* (Berkeley, Calif.: University of California Press, 1985), 66.

2. Thus, Studs Terkel's interview with worker Nora Watson: "Jobs are not big enough for people. It's not just the assembly line worker whose job is too small for his spirit, you know? A job like mine if you really put your spirit into it, you would sabotage immediately. You don't dare. So you absent

your spirit from it. My mind has been so divorced from my job, except as a source of income, it's really absurd" Studs Terkel, *Working* (New York: Avon Books, 1965), 675.

3. Stephen R. Covey, *The Seven Habits of Highly Effective People* (New York: A Fireside Book, 1989), chap. 2.

4. Alasdair MacIntyre, *After Virtue,* 2nd ed. (Notre Dame: University of Notre Dame Press, 1984), 148.

5. The existence of forced labor clearly proves that the ends of action can be "common" in the sense that many people work toward them without being "common," in the sense that their attainment includes their distribution to those involved. The ends of action, that is, can be common as ends without being common as goods. For example, tyranny—the antithesis of political community—is a regime that reserves for the benefit of one or a few what is achieved in common. It is a mark of community, then, that whatever goods are achieved in common are also distributed, and so are common both as ends as goods.

6. Aristotle used a famous simile to explain how the final end orders other subordinate or intermediate ends. The archer's determination to hit his target involves many intrinsically different activities, such as stringing a bow, pacing off distances, nocking arrows, forging steel, into one, intelligible undertaking called "archery." Likewise, our natural determination to seek out and do whatever promotes human happiness governs the many aspects of human action.

7. For example, Ryuzaburo Kaku, chairman of Canon Inc., has popularized the Japanese term *kyosei,* which he roughly translates as "living and working for the common good," to describe the purpose of Canon. In an approach similar to ours, Kaku uses *kyosei* to criticize the shareholder and stakeholder models (see Ryuzaburo Kaku, "*Kyosei*—A Concept that Will Lead the 21st Century" [Public Relations Department of Canon Inc., 1095P5, Japan]). In an interview, Kaku states, "Based on the concept of kyosei, I define companies in four categories. The first category is purely a capitalistic company that tries to maximize profits even if it exploits its workers. The second is where management and labor share a common destiny, and the third is where a company goes beyond working for its own well-being and considers that of the community." The fourth stage is Kyosei, the common good. He goes on to state that while personal liberty is essential to human growth, freedom alone will be insufficient to resolve the problems of our world (Joe Skelly, "Interview: Ryuzaburo Kaku," *Business Ethics* [March/April 1995]: 32). Similarly, in the pastoral letter *The Common Good* issued by the British Catholic Bishops, Dr. Zaki Badawi, head of the Muslim College in London, stated that

the common good concept has an exact Muslim equivalent (Clifford Long-ley, "The Moral of the Coke Tin," *Tablet*, 25 January 1997, 99). Timothy Fort argues that "an international business ethic will not be the result of western logic, but will come through an 'overlapping consensus' among comprehen-sive normative frameworks" (Timothy L. Fort, "The Spirituality of Soli-darity and Total Quality Management," *Professional Business Ethics Journal* 14[1995]:3–21).

8. The distinction we make between "foundational" and "excellent" goods is made by other authors with pairs of terms such as "instrumental" and "inherent," or "extrinsic" and "intrinsic." We choose the terms "founda-tional" and "excellent" because they convey the impression that both types of goods are important in their own right.

9. Some writers would call such goods "mixed"; that is, they are, in our terms, both excellent (desirable in themselves) and foundational to the at-tainment of other goods.

10. Abraham H. Maslow, *Motivation and Personality*, 3rd ed. (Reading, Mass.: Addison-Wesley, 1987), 15ff. For the "inclinations" of Aquinas, see *Summa Theologiae*, I-II, q. 94, a. 2. Maslow's hierarchy of needs is so well known to students of management that one can hardly do without it as a vi-sual aid for explaining what one could mean by a "hierarchy of goods." As the sequel shows, we are by no means in agreement with the individualism (see, e.g., *Motivation and Personality*, 31) implicit in Maslow's account of human development.

11. Note that we say here that these undertakings are the means of maturation for the *majority* of human beings. We recognize the validity of other ways of life: of single people, of those living a life of consecrated chastity, and so on.

12. Quoted in Kenneth E. Goodpaster and Laura L. Nash, *Policies and Persons*, 3rd ed. (New York: McGraw-Hill, 1998), 135–150.

13. With Thomas Aquinas, we would argue that these excellent goods include the fulfillment of our need for society. We want to distance ourselves from an individualistic notion of human development.

14. John XXIII's famous definition of the common good—". . . the sum total of those conditions of social living whereby men are enabled more fully and more readily to achieve their own perfection" (*Mater et Magistra*, n. 65)—if applied to the organization, would become *the creation of those or-ganizational conditions that foster integral human development*. In the docu-ment, *World Hunger, A Challenge for All: Development in Solidarity*, the Ponti-fical Council *Cor Unum* (Charity and Development Aid) uses the term "structures of the common good" (*Origins* 26 [7 November 1996]: para. 25).

See also Pope John Paul II, *The Dignity of Work*, ed. Robert Kennedy, Gary Atkinson, and Michael Naughton (Lanham, Md.: University Press of America, 1995).

15. In practice, at least in the U.S., financial practitioners tend to control business organizations. At one time, the majority of CEOs were engineers and production people; today, the majority of CEOs come from the finance department. The second most important person behind the CEO in U.S. organizations is typically the vice president of finance; in Japanese organizations, the second most important person is the vice president of human resources. Consequently, we should not be surprised by the fact that U.S. firms pay out higher dividends and invest in employee development at lower rates than Japanese firms (see V. J. Tarascio, "Towards a Unified Theory of the Firm: An Historical Approach," *Atlantic Economic Journal* [September 1993]: 13, and also Lester Thurow, *Head to Head* [New York: William Morrow and Company, 1992], 54).

16. E. F. Brigham and L. C. Gapenski, *Financial Management: Theory and Practice* (Orlando: Dryden Press, 1991), 10–11. Defenders of this financial approach in defining the purpose of the firm justify shareholders' primacy on various grounds: property rights, economic efficiency, agency, and contract; but upon examination, each of these considerations is tied ultimately to an argument built on social grounds: maximizing shareholder wealth is best for society at large. Financial theorists finally rely on their own account of the common good. See J. R. Danley, *The Role of the Modern Corporation in a Free Society* (Notre Dame: University of Notre Dame Press, 1994), 189–190. The argument from the position of property rights proposes that the shareholders, as owners, are due the whole benefit of the firm. The firm's managers are thus the shareholder's agents, bound by an obligation to direct the company in accordance with the purpose the shareholders express in acquiring ownership: the increase of their wealth. Yet, the modern concept of the corporation (as a legal person in itself, not as an embodiment of the shareholders' interests) makes this ownership-to-agency theory problematic. At base, the firm's management is a fiduciary—an agent in trust—for the firm, not for any one shareholder or any group of shareholders. See John Boatright, "Fiduciary Duties and the Shareholder-Management Relation: Or, What's So Special about Shareholders?" *Business Ethics Quarterly* 4, no. 4 (1994); G. A. Steiner and J. F. Steiner, *Business, Government and Society* (New York: McGraw-Hill, 1994); Douglas Birsch, "The Failure of [Milton] Friedman's Agency Argument," in *Contemporary Issues in Business Ethics*, ed. Joseph R. Desjardins and John J. McCall (Belmont, Calif.: Wadsworth Publishing Company, 1990). The "classical" discussion of these issues can be found in the following: Adolf A. Berle, Jr. and Gardiner C. Means, *The Modern Corporation and Pri-*

vate Property (New York: Macmillan, 1932; rev. ed., New York: Harcourt, Brace and World, 1968); E. Merrick Dodd, Jr., "For Whom Are Corporate Managers Trustees?" *Harvard Law Review* 45 (1932); Adolph A. Berle, Jr., "For Whom Corporate Managers Are Trustees: A Note," *Harvard Law Review* 45 (1932). Alternatively, financial theorists argue that a corporation cannot exist unless it attracts capital, while the ability to attract capital depends upon an ability to build confidence in the corporation's potential for future earnings; the confidence of the markets' influences in the firm's rate of capital investment, enhancing or impending its ability to generate returns to shareholders. The financial relationships among the firm and its employees (wages), suppliers (payments), customers (affordable products), and government (taxes), which make the firm a generator of economic benefits at large, thus begins with the motivation of maximizing shareholders' wealth. See, e.g., A. Rappaport, *Creating Shareholder Value* (New York: The Free Press, 1986), 12.

17. Clearly, there are external pressures compelling companies to interpret their purpose as the maximization of shareholder wealth. Robert Reich has pointed out that international competition and financial markets have placed tremendous pressures on American corporations, requiring them to focus "more and more intensely on increasing shareholders' returns and less and less on improving the standard of living of their workers." To reduce these pressures, Reich has suggested that the federal government provide incentives to change corporate behavior ("How To Avoid These Layoffs," *The New York Times*, 4 January 1996, A13).

18. The financial theory thus proves to be a consequentialist argument. It proposes that the single-minded pursuit of shareholders' good is justified because it causes the promotion of others' good. At the same time, the theory rests on a utilitarian idea of the common good, namely, that the ends of society are realized whenever any good is maximized for the greatest number, regardless of means. If one accepts the ideas underlying the shareholder theory of the firm, it follows ineluctably as natural law that *actions that maximize the firm's share price maximize the firm's benefit to society.* Brigham and Gapenski assemble the usual sort of package with admirable clarity: "First, stock price maximization [read: shareholder wealth-maximization] requires efficient, low-cost operations that produce the desired quality and quantity of output at the lowest possible cost. Second, stock price maximization requires the development of products that consumers want and need, so the profit motive leads to new technology, to new products and to new jobs. Finally, stock price maximization necessitates business establishments—these factors are all necessary to make sales, and sales are necessary for profits. *Therefore, the types of actions that help a firm increase the price of its stock are also*

directly beneficial to society at large" (Brigham and Gapenski, *Financial Management: Theory and Practice,* 17 [emphasis added]).

19. T. S. Eliot, *Murder in the Cathedral,* in *The Complete Poems and Plays,* 1909–1950 (New York: Harcourt, Brace and World, 1971), 196.

20. See John Paul II, *Centesimus Annus,* 35.

21. See John XXIII, *Mater et Magistra,* 83; John Paul II, *Centesimus Annus,* 41. Maximizing shareholder wealth is a clear, precise, and measurable end. Conversely, contributing to full human development as the purpose of business will always generate more questions than answers for managers. Yet, if managers see themselves as professionals and not as mere technicians, such ambiguity is inescapable. Human decision making, even in corporations, cannot be reduced to one simple formula (see, e.g., W. F. May, "The Beleaguered Rulers: The Public Obligation of the Professional," *Kennedy Institute of Ethics Journal* 2 [1992]: 28).

22. Because the basis for community formation varies, and because the ways of sharing the goods achieved through community also vary, the term "common good" must be understood *analogously.* If one considers these statements: *Julius Caesar is a man; Julia Child is a man; Jesus Christ is a man,* it becomes clear that the term "man" is used univocally, so that an aspect of its meaning can be understood in all three cases. Conversely, in the group of statements, *Post no bills; Birds have bills; Pay your bills,* the term "bill" is used equivocally, so that the context of one sheds no light at all on the other two. To use an illustration introduced by Aristotle and favored by Thomas Aquinas, analogy organizes the uses of "healthy." For example, in "Training for a sport is healthy," "Tiger Woods is healthy," and "Julia Roberts' complexion is healthy," the second use of "healthy" is primary or focal, and we understand the other two uses in relation to it. Focally, "common good" is used to name a perfection of the political community in which all the citizens together, and each one personally, share by participation. (The establishment of these goods as institutions of a way of life may be called *the* common good.) One such good is civil peace. It is an excellent example of the common good, for it provides and supports the uniquely human ability to flourish through the society of others. It can be realized only in common, that is, by all together; and it belongs especially to a complete community, that is, a political community, one which offers participants a full range of opportunity to pursue any good that naturally promotes happiness. Civil peace *is* a "communion." It benefits all alike by virtue of their participation in the community, yet belongs to the community's members singly, for each of them receives the whole benefit of civil peace and, by their keeping of the peace, bestows it on the others. Common goods *par excellence,* such as

civil peace or justice, illustrate the formal marks that identify goods that are in some degree common. Such goods are *ends* in common, i.e., their pursuit shapes some sort of human community; they are also goods in common, that is, their realization perfects the whole community as a whole. At the same time, such goods are "common" by way of being distributed. They flow back to and benefit the members of the community singly. For the uses of analogy, and for the relations between Aristotle's and St. Thomas' ethics, see Ralph McInerny, *Ethica Thomistica: The Moral Philosophy of Thomas Aquinas*, rev. ed. (Washington, D.C.: Catholic University of America Press, 1997). We argue then that the business corporation is a kind of community, shaped by ends and goods which are genuinely common. They are best and most easily attained by cooperative efforts made possible by business organizations. They benefit the firm as a whole, but they can be preserved and extended only by their "distribution" among the members of the firm. Nevertheless, the business corporation is a private community shaped by limited ends. Like the ends and goods of private persons, the firm's ends must be compared—and perhaps adjusted—to external, ultimately political and legal, standards of justice and general equity.

23. See, e.g., Yves Simon, *The Tradition of Natural Law*, trans. Vukan Kuic (New York: Fordham University Press), 99.

24. See Jacques Maritain, *The Person and the Common Good*, trans. John J. Fitzgerald (Notre Dame: University of Notre Dame Press, 1966), 50–53.

25. Antoine de Salins, "Does Finance Have a Soul?" www.stthomas. edu/cathstudies/cstm/antwerp/p2.htm) (1/28/01).

26. We concede a point of agreement here with the opposing view. Unlike the family and the commonwealth, which are communities shaped by ends uniquely theirs (so that there is no substitute either for family or for some sort of political community in human life), the firm is a human expedient. Business organizations have not always existed. They now serve as intermediary institutions to connect persons to the means of satisfying their needs: they promote many purposes, but in a sense, they have none of their own. To put the paradox more positively, the end of the firm is to serve the ends of others. However, because the business organization creates the context in which human beings may develop through their work, it has inherently excellent as well as foundational ends, and the participated goods it produces cannot become allocated goods available for distribution among the various stakeholders.

27. A government need not be democratic to be legitimate, but to rest on that point is to beg the real question: Among the legitimate forms of

government, which is best? If there is an argument in principle for the superiority of democratic forms, it is that they are more fully participative than others. They provide ". . . the necessary condition and sure guarantee of the development of 'the whole individual and of all people,'" unlike many other forms. But we can go further and argue that so far as any form of government is legitimate and genuinely promotes the common good, it is already pointed toward democratic forms. If it rests on participated goods, we can speak of the growth of community and the democratization of the regime in a single breath.

28. See, for example, Kenneth Goodpaster, "Business Ethics and Stakeholder Analysis," *Business Ethics Quarterly* 1 (January 1991): 57.

29. For example, see one of the most influential of these recent studies, Lawrence C. Becker, *Property Rights: Philosophic Foundations* (Boston, London, and Henley: Routledge and Kegan Paul, 1980), 18–19; cf. Thomas Donaldson and Lee Preston, "The Stakeholder Theory of the Corporation," *Academy of Management Review* 20, no. 1 (1995): 84–88.

30. Emphasis added. Recent developments in the law suggest that multifiduciary, stakeholder conceptions are gaining ground (see, e.g., G. A. Steiner and J. A. Steiner, *Business, Government and Society,* 636). Relevant developments in the U.S. include: (1) state constituent statutes over mergers and acquisitions which broaden a board's legal authority to consider the interests of stakeholders other than shareholders in its decision making; (2) state statutes directing boards to consider named "stakeholder" groups, as well as the community and economy overall (see, e.g., Sec. 18, Minnesota Statutes 1986, section 302A.251 Subd. 5); (3) liability and regulatory restrictions, such as product liability laws and employee protection statutes, which give stakeholder groups shareholder-like status in the considerations owed by the corporation (see, e.g., W. M. Evan and R. E. Freeman, "A Stakeholder Theory of the Modern Corporation: Kantian Capitalism," in *Ethical Theory and Business,* 3rd ed., ed. T. L. Beauchamp and N. E. Bowie [Englewood Cliffs, N.J.: Prentice Hall, 1988]). For a comparison of constituency statutes among various states, see C. Hansen, "Other Constituency Statutes: A Search for Perspective," *The Business Lawyer* 46 (1991): 1355–1375.

31. "How does a manager resolve the conflict of rights when there is no other good besides one's own particular right?" When management answers, ". . . [we] will exercise responsibility in our dealings with all our stakeholders and in the case of conflict balance the interests of employees and shareholders on an equal basis over time," the obvious question remains: "What is the fulcrum that provides the balance?" (A. Campbell and L. L.

Nash, *A Sense of Mission* [Great Britain: Hutchinson Business Books Limited, 1990], 21). As J. R. Danley points out, "From the fact that different interests [stakeholders] are involved one would expect reference to another premise, some kind of moral premise, which would license an inference to the conclusion that social responsibility requires taking into consideration the well-being and interests of each constituency (stakeholder group) and 'doing the right thing'" (*The Role of the Modern Corporation in a Free Society*, 189).

32. We are indebted to Ernest Pierucci for reminding us that, in this connection, personalism *is* realism.

33. Yves Simon, *Philosophy of Democratic Government* (Chicago: University of Chicago Press, 1951), 49.

34. John Paul II, *Rei Sollicitudo Socialis*, 38.

35. *Summa Theologica*, I-II, q. 19, a. 10, Reply. Aquinas points out that "[a]ny part naturally loves the common good of the whole more than its particular and private good. This is clear from the way things behave, for the *chief inclination* of any part is to act on behalf of the whole. We can see this even in the life of society, in so far as citizens are on occasion prepared to spend either themselves or their goods for the commonweal" (Ibid., II-II, q. 114, a. 1 ad 2).

36. See Yves Simon, *The Philosophy of Democratic Government*, 64–66; see also Jonathan Boswell, *Community and the Economy* (New York: Routledge, 1990), 25, and Robert Solomon, "The Corporation as Community: A Reply to Ed Hartman," *Business Ethics Quarterly* 4 (July 1994): 276ff. Simon points out that the common good has a powerful hold on the consciences of people, even when it is radically misunderstood: "People of debased conduct and skeptical judgment still find it natural to die for their country or for such substitute for a country as a gang. And during the golden age of individualism the conscience of men, in spite of what the theorists had to say, often recognized the common good and served it with devotion under such improper names as 'general interest' or 'greatest good of the greatest number'" (ibid., 50).

37. See John Paul II, *Sollicitudo Rei Socialis*, 27. According to Virgil Michel, and following Aquinas, the common good and the individual good are intrinsically connected for two reasons: "The first is that one's own good cannot exist without the common good of the family, or of the state, or of the realm. The second is that man as part of a household or state must also consider what is good for himself precisely as such a part of a larger whole [cf. *Summa Theologica*, II-II, q. 47, a. 10 ad 2]. The goodness of parts is im-

possible without their proper proportionate relation to the whole" (Virgil Michel, *The Social Question* [St. Cloud, Minn.: Parker Printing Company, 1987], 25).

38. In Martin Buber's language, between the "I" and the "Thou" is a moral reality that cannot be exhausted in contracts or self-interests. It is the place where the social development of each of us takes place, where we begin to experience the deep profound truth of interdependence, not in a merely physical way or where we see "others" as instruments of utility (that is, the I-It relationship), but rather an interdependence that sees the other as part of a community of work for the common good. See Martin Buber, *I and Thou* (New York: Charles Scribner's & Sons, 1958).

39. See, e.g., Yves Simon, *Philosophy of Democratic Government*, 50: "Although unity is an absolute perfection, there can be too much of it, inasmuch as, beyond a certain measure, the inappropriate kind forcibly displaces the proper one and destruction results." See also Jacques Maritain, *The Person and the Common Good*, 76–77.

40. Quoted in M. Sherwin, "St. Thomas and the Common Good: The Theological Perspective: An Invitation to Dialogue," *Angelicum* 70 (1993): 324.

41. It should be stressed that nothing in this argument suggests that *any* agency of the temporal common good could make sacrificial demands of individuals' spiritual lives; the spiritual good exceeds the competence of temporal agencies. See Jacques Maritain, *The Person and the Common Good*, 61f.

42. See Michael Naughton and Thomas Bausch, "The Integrity of a Catholic School of Management," *California Management Review* (Summer 1996), which discusses downsizing and the firm's pertinent responsibilities in light of the common good.

43. From personal conversations.

44. Following Aquinas, Ralph McInerny lucidly describes our situation as rational desirers: "To aim at the good is a necessary but not a sufficient condition of an action's being good, but even here there is need to distinguish the real from the apparent good. The will just is the faculty of the good; goodness is its formal object as color is the object of sight. But just as we do not see color in general but some particular color, so too we only will goodness as embodied in a particular end. And the particular thing that is the end is seen or known as good before it can be willed. To see or know it as good is to judge that it is perfective or fulfilling of the kind of agent we are. But we can make mistakes, corrigible mistakes, in thinking that end or course of action is indeed fulfilling and perfective of us" (Ralph McInerny, *Ethica Thomistica: The Moral Philosophy of Thomas Aquinas*, 77).

45. There are those who, with Justice Kennedy in the now famous *Casey* opinion, hold that, contrary to our argument, there is a fundamental right of the individual to define the nature of existence, of the universe, of human life. They will dismiss the suggestion *because* they will. We would ask them to consider: Which of us (to paraphrase the Scripture) can turn one hair on our head from white to black by insisting on our right to self-definition?

46. See Aristotle, *Nicomachean Ethics*, I. iii; Aristotle's terms are *planee* and *epi to polu*, the latter of which we might also translate as "quite probable."

47. Above all, human beings can love God and be drawn into the love of the members of the Trinity, one for another. It is actually to the Trinity that the common good in this life bears a pale analog, and the Trinity is our true common good in the next. "God is not a monad but a Trinitarian communion of 'subsistent relations'." The Trinity is a wholeness composed of wholes. With respect to the Trinity, Jacques Maritain writes: "The Three who compose the society of the Trinity are by no means parts, since they are perfectly identical with it. They are three Wholes who are the Whole." He concludes that created persons in society are, in remote analogy to the Trinitarian Persons, wholes within a whole, and that ". . . the person, as person, requires to be treated as a whole in society" (Jacques Maritain, *The Person and the Common Good*, 57).

48. Consequently, friendship with God is the ultimate end of the organizational common good. As Hollenbach points out, "Everything human beings are to do, in both personal and social life, is directed to one end: union with the God who is their maker and redeemer" (David Hollenbach, "The Common Good Revisited," *Theological Studies* 50 [1989]: 81).

49. Thomas would call those aspects of the human community that help us grow in virtue "common goods." As Sherwin says: "Specifically, the temporal common good is the totality of all those goods which promote virtuous living and which can be shared by all. The 'common good comprises many things' and 'is produced by many actions' (ST, I-II, 96, 1). First, there are bodily goods, such as food and clothing, the resources for which must be present in order for the community to flourish. There are higher goods such as peace, tranquility . . . and the security of the community. . . . There are the goods of the soul such as love and delight. . . . Then there are those goods that are specifically directed to promoting virtue: the laws of the state, the customs and training of the family, and the teaching of the Church. The whole of these goods which make up the cultural heritage of a people and which promote the full human life—the contemplative life which leads to God—this totality is the temporal common good" ("St Thomas and the Common Good"). Hence, there is a sense in which all goods in this life are particular, even those which benefit us all and which we

all need in order to live a good and happy life. This realization is behind the statement of Adler and Farrell that virtue is "essentially common and existentially individual" (M. J. Adler and W. Farrell, "The Theory of Democracy (Part Two)," *Thomist* 3 [1941]: 600).

50. Alternatively, we could say that in making a decision the manager must divide attention between foundational/common and foundational/particular ends.

51. Cargill is a privately held firm in Minnesota and is one of the largest privately held companies in the U.S. Here we must point out that organizations, especially larger ones, experience "gaps" between their stated mission and operational practice.

3. The Virtues

1. G. K. Chesterson, *Orthodoxy* (New York: Image Day, 1990), 30.

2. We are grateful to Deb Lincoln from the University of St. Thomas' Instructional Support Services who created this graphic. This model was developed in a summer seminar on the theme of human development within organizations, coordinated by Robert Kennedy at the University of St. Thomas. Members of the seminar were Deborah Savage, Helen Alford, Chris Thompson, Gary Atkinson, Michael Naughton, David Lutz, and Robert Kennedy. We do not, of course, suppose that this, or any other, single representation can provide a comprehensive picture of human development. Since the question of human development is so important, however, we cannot avoid the task of giving some structure to our attempts to explain it (see also *Human Development Report 1998* [New York: Oxford University Press, 1998]). For the 2000 report, see http://www.undp.org/hdro/HDR2000.html

3. We are grateful to Paul Dembinski for this metaphor.

4. See Paul VI, *Populorum Progressio*, 12.

5. When the *Catechism of the Catholic Church* was first published in 1992, Daniel Seligman, writing in *Fortune* (22 February 1993): 119–120, criticized the Church's social teaching as being "[g]ripped by a communitarian ethic . . . [that] continues to focus on the *motives* of economic players rather than the *outcomes* of economic behavior and remains oblivious of Adam Smith's great insight: that individuals pursuing their own self-interest end up enriching the whole community." Seligman's observations identify the fault line dividing a Christian from a laissez-faire understanding of business.

6. Yves R. Simon, *The Tradition of Natural Law*, ed. Vukan Kuic (New York: Fordham University Press, 1992), 94.

7. The same principle can be expressed in terms of the institution of property. All goods, however possessed, ultimately have a "universal destination." Private ownership of property is thus a secondary institution: it consists in private possession *for the sake* of the goods' "universal destination," that is, for their distribution such that, in their use, they are distributed or allocated fairly. In the Christian tradition, therefore, private ownership is understood to be *for* distribution. Private ownership is the right to possess and accumulate—to manage—goods for use: to satisfy the needs of oneself, of one's family, of one's employees, one's neighbors, and so out into the widest circles of community. The institution of private property is thus recognized as legitimate, not absolutely, but so far as it promotes the best use of the world's resources for the ultimate sake of human development. For a concise overview of the place of private property in the tradition of Catholic social thought, see John Paul II, *Centesimo Annus*, 30–31.

8. See chapter 2.2, "Common and Particular Goods: Developing an Authentic Community."

9. The classic presentation of the principle of subsidiarity appears in Pius XI, *Quadragesimo Anno (On Social Reconstruction)*, nn. 79–80.

10. John Paul II, *Sollicitudo Rei Socialis* 38 (emphases original).

11. We owe the term "patterns of cooperation" and the underlying concept to J. Michael Stebbins

12. See Ralph McInerny, *Ethica Thomistica: The Moral Philosophy of Thomas Aquinas*, rev. ed. (Washington, D.C.: Catholic University of America Press, 1997), 3, 19, 78.

13. The principle is treated in historical, philosophical, and theological detail by John Paul II in *Laborem Exercens*; see especially 12ff.

14. Al Gini, "Work, Identity and Self: How We Are Formed by the Work We Do," *Journal of Business Ethics* 17 (1998): 707–714.

15. As John Paul II put it, "Anyone wishing to renounce the difficult yet noble task of improving the lot of man in his totality, and of all people, with the excuse that the struggle is difficult and that constant effort is required, or simply because of the experience of defeat and the need to begin again, that person would be betraying the will of God the Creator" (*Sollicitudo Rei Socialis*, 30, see Matthew 25: 26–28).

16. See John 3:8.

17. Quoted in Karol Wojtyla (John Paul II), *Toward a Philosophy of Praxis* (New York: Crossroad, 1981), 13ff.

18. We owe this idea to Michael Stebbins, who attributes it to his study of Bernard Lonergan.

19. See William J. Byron, "Ten Building Blocks of Catholic Social Teaching," *America*, 31 October 1998, 9–12.

20. Jonathan Boswell, "Catholic Social Thinking—Is It Under-Developed," background paper for the conference *Whose Ethics? Which Priorities? Catholic Social Thought in Transition*, 11–14 April 1999, Cambridge, England.

21. Joseph Cardinal Ratzinger, "Market Economy and Ethics," in *Ordo Socialis: Making Christianity Work in Business and Economy*, ed. Association for the Advancement of Christian Social Sciences (Philippines: Divine Word Publications, 1992), 67.

22. Dennis Bakke, "Values Don't Work in Business," in *On Moral Business: Classical Contemporary Resources for Ethics in Economic Life*, ed. Max L. Stackhouse, Dennis P. McCann, and Shirley J. Roels, with Preston N. Williams (Grand Rapids, Mich.: Wm. B. Eerdmans Publishing Co., 1995), 716–717.

23. Stephen R. Covey, *The Seven Habits of Highly Effective People* (New York: A Fireside Book, 1989), 15.

24. Ibid., 42–43.

25. John 13:15.

26. The disintegration of social life is a profound problem in society, particularly in the West. This disintegration has many causes, but two of particular note are the decline of cultural institutions such as the family, church, and school, and the belief that the marketplace is an amoral institution that exists merely to satisfy our self-interests. Stephen Carter writes that we consequently enter the realm of work "with flimsy moral armament. We lack the tools to consider what we *should* value or *should* want, to say nothing of how we should act, and thus more and more tend to follow our impulse" (Stephen Carter, *Civility: Manners, Morals, and the Etiquette of Democracy* [New York: HarperCollins, 1998], 16).

27. Robert Solomon, *Ethics and Excellence* (New York: Oxford University Press, 1992). See also Michael Novak, *Business as a Calling* (New York: The Free Press, 1996), chapter 6, where he describes three cardinal virtues of business (creativity, building community, and practical realism).

28. The treatise on the virtues in the *Summa Theologica*, can be found at I-II, qq. 55–67 and II-II, qq. 47–168 (see Thomas Aquinas, *Summa Theologica* [New York: Benziger Brothers, 1947]).

29. In her commentary on Aquinas, Jean Porter explains "the four cardinal virtues are the primary moral virtues because they represent the four fundamental modes, so to speak, by which the individual appropriates the human good as discerned by reason: *Prudence* appropriates that good directly by the action of the intellect, which determines how best to actualize one's specific good; *justice* directs external action in such a way as to conform to rea-

son—it does this by conforming the will to a wider good than that of the individual's own; and *fortitude* and *temperance* moderate the irascible and desiring passions in such a way that the individual spontaneously desires what is truly in accordance with the specific good of the human person and avoids what is not in accordance with the human good. . . . . Temperance and fortitude enable their possessor to moderate her passions in accordance with her larger aims. Justice ensures that her external actions will be in accordance with the norms of a well-ordered community, which harmonizes her private aims with a larger good. Prudence enables her to use her practical intelligence to discern the most appropriate ways of living out her commitment to larger aims, or to pursue them with her community" (Jean Porter, *The Recovery of Virtue* [Louisville, Ky.: Westminster/John Knox Press, 1990], 166–167).

30. Thomas Aquinas, *Summa Theologica*, I-II, q. 65, a. 1.

31. The prudent manager who desires to behave justly toward his employees through a participatory workplace needs the "perfected ability" to make the right decisions toward this end (see chap. 4). Prudence undergirds the other moral virtues by providing the ability to perceive and perform the good that it is possible to achieve in practice in each particular situation. As Pieper states, "Realization of the good presupposes that our actions are appropriate to the real situation, that is, to the concrete realities which form the 'environment' of a concrete human action" (Josef Pieper, *Prudence* [New York: Pantheon Books, 1959], 25). Prudence should not be confused with slyness, trickery, craftiness, etc. Nor should it be seen as a utilitarian calculation for society or, as Pieper writes, for "timorous, small-minded self-preservation" (ibid., 15). The prudent manager is not the calculator, productivity technician, or manipulator; rather, she is the person who has a grasp of the various disciplines of management, perceives the situation as it is, and instantiates the virtues, especially justice, in the particular situation. Prudence is the central virtue for management understood as a practice, since it is able to fuse skills and good ends together in one concrete act.

32. Thomas Aquinas, *Summa Theologica*, II-II, q. 58, a. 12. *Ius* also means "law," in the sense of "natural law."

33. Thomas Aquinas, *Commentary on Aristotle's Nicomachean Ethics* (Notre Dame: Dumb Ox Books, 1993), 302. See also *Summa Theologica*, II-II, q. 58, a. 3.

34. See Servais Pinckaers, *The Sources of Christian Ethics*, translated from the third edition by Sr. Mary Thomas Noble, O. P. (Washington, D.C.: The Catholic University of America Press, 1995), 35–38, for his discussion on justice.

35. Pinckaers explains that "[t]he modern era is characterized by its subjective conception of rights, as formulated by fourteenth-century nominalism. From that time on, rights refer not to what I owe others, but to what others, and society, owe me. Rights have changed hands: I think now in terms of my own rights, not those of others. The fundamental orientation of justice has been reversed: the burden of the debt falls on others, not on me. Justice no longer implies a quality of soul, a movement outward toward others; it concentrates on the defense of external rights. In this sense it is a matter of taking rather than giving. The change accelerated with a new conception of the person's relation to society. This was no longer based on a natural human inclination but became instead an artificial creation, set up to meet human needs and to prevent destructive rivalry" (Ibid., 38–39).

36. To see the goal of the corporation as merely the maximization of profits creates a social vice within the corporation. "It forgets what the Greeks long ago knew: that temperance is a precondition of the social virtue of justice . . . Temperance, whether of individuals or institutions, does not demand the extinguishing of desires, but it does require their restraint. If we are to render justice to another, if we are to render to another his or her due, we must be able to keep our desires regulated, our appetites under control. That restraint translates into the goal of economic performance at a profit" (William F. May, "The Virtues of the Business Leader," in *On Moral Business: Classical Contemporary Resources for Ethics in Economic Life*, ed. Max L. Stackhouse, Dennis P. McCann, and Shirley J. Roels, with Preston N. Williams [Grand Rapids, Mich.: Wm. B. Eerdmans Publishing Co., 1995], 696).

37. Peter Maurin, *Easy Essays* (Chicago: Franciscan Herald Press, 1984), 37.

38. See Aquinas, *Summa Theologica*, II-II, q. 57, a. 1.

39. Aquinas associates the virtue of magnificence with the virtue of courage. Magnificence, like courage, strives "for what is arduous and difficult" (*Summa Theologica*, II-II, q. 134, a. 4). Since the virtue of magnificence directs resources toward the good of the community as well as toward economic return, and not solely toward the return of profits, the person acts courageously by incurring more financial risk (II-II, q. 135, a. 1; this question treats the vices that are opposed to magnificence). The virtue of magnificence is never governed by a mindless heart. It must entail reason and the virtue of prudence. Aquinas explains that "the function of the magnificent man is to use reason well in estimating the outlay involved in a work which is to be done. This is especially necessary in view of the greatness of both work and expense, for without careful calculation there would be a definite

risk of serious loss" (II-II, q. 134, aa. 4, 3). Oswald von Nell-Breuning calls magnificence "a genuinely capitalistic virtue," that is, "a virtue for the entrepreneur" (*Reorganization of Social Economy* [Milwaukee, Wis.: Bruce Publishing Co., 1936], 115, see also 116).

4. JOB DESIGN

1. The article was first published in the *IEEE Control Systems Magazine*, vol. 1, no. 3 (September 1981), and reprinted in the Open University Reader, *The Experience of Work*, ed. Craig R. Littler (Aldershot:Gower/The Open University, 1985), 161–171.

2. See John Paul II, *Laborem Exercens*, 12.

3. John Paul II, *Laborem Exercens*, 4.

4. See Genesis 1:23.

5. See Michael Naughton, *The Good Stewards* (Lanham, Md.: University of America Press, 1992), 5, which points out that people's names often derive from types of work, such as Baker, Smith, Tanner, Farmer.

6. See Robert Bellah, Richard Madsen, William M. Sullivan, Ann Swidler, and Steven M. Tipton, *Habits of the Heart* (New York: Harper and Row, 1985), 66ff.

7. Matthew 25:40 (RSV).

8. John Paul II, *Laborem Exercens*, 6. The translation is unfortunate: the word rendered "man" here is, of course, *homo*—"human being"— in the Latin original.

9. John Paul calls this kind of activity a "happening" in people, to distinguish it from their personal activity.

10. Here, the term "person" incorporates the idea of the agent because, like the agent, the person is not determined by external structures. However, the term agent is associated with rather individualistic approaches to the human person (see N. Abercrombie, S. Hill, and B. S. Turner, *Dictionary of Sociology* [Harmondsworth: Penguin, 1984], 17). Hence, we maintain the use of the term person, intending the concept of agent to be included in it.

11. Karol Wojtyla (John Paul II) says: "Every act of self-determination makes real the subjectivity of self-governance and self-possession: in each of these interpersonal structural relations there is given to the person as the subject—as he who governs and possesses—the person as the object—as he who is governed and possessed. . . . This objectification means that in every actual act of self-determination—in every "I will"—the self is the object, indeed the primary and nearest object" (Cardinal Karol Wojtyla, *The*

Acting Person, trans. Andrzej Potocki [Dordrecht, Holland: D. Reidel Publishing Co., 1979], 108–109).

12. This recognition of the transcendence of the person opens the way to dealing with the spirituality of the person, which we deal with in detail in chapter 8.

13. An interesting insight of Wojtyla's is that the nonmaterial aspect of the person (mind, consciousness, spirituality) is in a real way "integrated" with the material body in action. This integration distinguishes a human person from other nonhuman living beings and also from computers that can simulate "consciousness" but that do not have a human body through which to act. As the subject of our actions, we see ourselves as being physical; however, as self-reflexive beings, we experience the body as something we possess. Because action integrates the material and nonmaterial aspects of the human person, the concept of skill or proficiency so important in the humanization debates takes on a further dimension and links us again with the spiritual dimension: "The term 'skill' as the equivalent of the latin *habitus* seems highly (appropriate) here inasmuch as *habitus* denotes both a skill and a virtue; of these, the latter refers to the *habitus* of the spiritual life and the former, conformably with everyday use, to the body" (Wojtyla, *The Acting Person,* 213). Thus, through a person's actions we see the complementary attributes of integration and transcendence.

14. John Paul II, *Laborem Exercens* 5.

15. This is part of the "mistake of materialism," which makes the personal and spiritual subordinate: "It was largely economism [materialism] that formulated the fundamental question of human work non-humanistically. More particularly, it separated labor from capital resources and opposed one to the other, as though the two were similar factors of production which could be considered from the same point of view. In reality, there need be no real contradiction between capital and labour; both are needed for the successful running of the firm" (Ibid., 13).

16. We are indebted in this section to Elizabeth Garnsey, who worked with Helen Alford on this material for lecture courses in the Engineering faculty of Cambridge University.

17. The economic context in which Taylor developed his system partially accounts for his preoccupations. An economic slump in 1873–74, when Taylor was just beginning his career, and a depression in the 1880s, when he was carrying out some of his experiments, impressed on him both the need to control labor and the dangers of bankruptcy if profits were not made. His earlier career coincided with a national period of relative technical stagna-

tion; design innovation in steam power showed only marginal improvements, while electrical inventions were not yet developed commercially. In such a period of economic stringency and limited technical improvement, labor costs seemed one area in which savings were possible through streamlining the production process (Frederick W. Taylor, *Scientific Management* [New York: Harper and Row, 1947] comprising "Shop Management," "The Principles of Scientific Management," and "Testimony Before the Special House Committee").

18. At the time of Taylor's first publication in 1895, the four main aspects of his approach included (1) the need for the Rate Fixing Department; (2) the need for a "Differential Piece Rate" system, based upon a standard pay for a standard output. Anyone who did more or less than the standard was paid proportionately more or less; (3) the idea that as a principle of political economy under such a system there would be satisfaction between workers and employers because both groups would benefit; and (4) the necessity of understanding the capabilities of machinery in order to set the right rates for jobs (see J. Kelly, *Scientific Management, Job Redesign and Work Performance* [London: Academic Press, 1982], 10).

19. See M. Hammer and J. Champy, *Reengineering the Corporation* (New York: HarperBusiness, 1993), and M. Hammer and S. Stanton, *The Re-engineering Revolution: A Handbook* (New York: HarperBusiness, 1995).

20. Hammer and Stanton, *The Re-engineering Revolution*, 11.

21. Adam Smith, *An Inquiry into the Nature and Causes of the Wealth of Nations: A Selected Edition*, edited with an introduction by Kathryn Sutherland, Oxford: Oxford University Press, 1993), Book V, chap. 1, part III, p. 429.

22. John XXIII wrote, "If the whole structure and organization of an economic system is such as to compromise human dignity, to lessen a man's sense of responsibility or rob him of an opportunity for exercising personal initiative, then such a system, . . . is altogether unjust—no matter how much wealth it produces, or how justly and equitably such wealth is distributed" (*Mater et Magistra*, 83).

23. See H. Alford, "Cellular Manufacturing: The Development of the Idea and Its Practice," *New Technology, Work and Employment* (Spring 1994): 3–18, and H. Alford, "Design of a Cellular Manufacturing System: Applying Catholic Social Thought," *The Journal of Applied Manufacturing Systems* (Fall 1994): 33–46 for published material on this case. The main source is Helen Alford, "Cellular Manufacturing, Business Integration and Humanisation of Work" (Ph.D. diss., Cambridge University, 1992), 112.

24. BAe, British Aerospace, was at the time the biggest single employer in the UK. "PLC" is a designation recognized in UK law for a particular type of corporation, the "public limited company."

25. Eighteen months later, it was decided at the board level that only one of the two final assembly lines should be running and that it was to be the one at Prestwick. Hatfield thus lost its final assembly business, experiencing 250 compulsory layoffs. Just over two years later, 830 middle management and technical staff were moved or laid off. This shows the problem of credibility at its most extreme: the site management did not have the authority to say that there would be no layoffs.

26. See Helen Alford, "Cellular Manufacturing, Business Integration and Humanisation of Work," 112.

27. Ibid., 142.

28. Ibid., 144.

29. Ibid., 141.

30. Ibid., 110.

31. See A. Cherns, "Principles of Sociotechnical Design," *Human Relations* 29, no. 8 (1976): 783–792.

32. The human-centered approach to work and technical design has developed out of the sociotechnical concern for the optimization of both human and technical systems. The basic assumption behind both theories is that within the firm there are interacting social and technical systems. The aim is to optimize the social and technical systems simultaneously, with neither one taking precedence over the other (P. G. Herbst, *Sociotechnical Design* [London: Tavistock, 1974]). Human-centered thinking goes further than this. Since the term "human-centered" is new, it is somewhat fluid in its meaning, but it can include the following assumptions:

1. Human-centered technology cooperates with, fosters, and enhances human skill.

2. Choices of operating strategy should be as numerous as possible (the human worker controls the technology and not vice versa).

3. Human-centeredness implies a reintegration of thinking, planning, and doing—the opposite of the scientific management paradigm.

4. Opportunities for both formal and informal social communication should be fostered. Computer intensive environments in particular need this attention, since they can be designed to reduce the amount of face to face communication (J. Weizenbaum, *Computer Power and Human Reason: From Judgement to Calculation* [Harmondsworth: Penguin, 1976]).

5. In general, human-centered systems will be safe, healthy, and efficient.

6. User involvement in human-centered design is also important but problematic, since users may have conflicting perspectives (F. Rauner, L. B. Rasmussen, and J. M. Corbett,"The Social Shaping of Technology and Work," *AI and Society*, vol. 2, no. 1 [1988]: 47–61). At the level of basic assumptions, Rauner et al. claim that human-centeredness is "ultimately a subjective concept which cannot easily be translated into operational criteria" (50), while Corbett claims that the term human-centered is not "rigorously defined" (J. M. Corbett, "The Design of Human-Centred Technology in Theory and Practice," unpublished SAPU memo 868, 1988).

Theorists see three basic relationships underlying the meaning of "human-centered": work and technology, work and communication, and work and learning. First, work is a "primary form of human life expression." It is not merely a "filling-in," with humans between automated tasks, as it is often treated by production engineers. Work has a more complicated relationship to technology than technocentric design assumptions would imply. Closely related to this view is the recognition of communication as a "fundamental human relation." Communication is an "*act* of commitment and interpretation," an idea which connects this thinking to the position in the Christian social tradition that persons form themselves through their acts. Mechanistic views of communication emphasize the transmission of information, but here we see that communication influences the work process more deeply. It shapes the structures of power, meaning, and norms in the firm. Work is also seen as inextricably bound to learning, such that a human-centered work environment can be evaluated by its "volume of learning opportunities." Just as firms aim to increase productivity from their production systems, this should be translated as the promotion of development of the workers through education and training. These concepts—the fundamental need for work, for communication, and for learning—linked to the interlinking definitions discussed above, comprise the basic ground and scope of the idea of human-centeredness. So far, this approach resembles one that the Christian tradition could endorse.

33. ESPRIT, Project 1217 (1199), *Human-Centered Computer Integrated Manufacturing*, introductory brochure, 1987; ESPRIT, Project 1217 (1199), *Overall System Specification, Deliverable R9*, unpublished, 1987.

34. The technical advantages of designing CIM systems in cells also influenced the project group's interest in this form of CIM.

35. In an earlier, longer (unpublished) version of their 1988 paper, Rauner et al. produce a scenario of a factory using human-centered CIM technology in which the idea of the "cell" as the basic production unit is

used. The factory is split into a production, a planning, and a design division, but within these, organization follows product families in production cells. The idea of the "cell" can be applied to other work systems, including those in services where a particular service is offered and managed by a cell. BICC, in their design for a human-centered factory planning system, speak of the cell as the basic production unit (BICC, *Outline of Human-Centred Nature of BICC Technologies CAM Demonstration System*, unpublished paper, 1988).

36. See P. Slaven, *Application of Social Science to Operator Tasks in CAM*, unpublished paper, 1988.

37. Rauner et al., 56.

38. See J. M. Corbett, "Prospective Design of a Human-Centered CNC Lathe," *Behaviour and Information Technology* 4:3 (1985): 201–14, and "Computer-Aided Manufacturing and the Design of Shopfloor Jobs: Towards a New Research Perspective in Occupational Psychology," in *Psychological Issues of Human Computer Interaction in the Workplace*, ed. M. Frese, E. Ulrich, W. Dzida (Amsterdam: Elsevier Science Publishers B. V., 1987).

39. See Naughton's critique of the Human Relations school: "When the psychological nature of the person dominates as the primary category for understanding work [as it does in the Human Relations school], work can become subservient or hostage to various sets of individual psychological needs at the expense of social needs. Herzberg, for example, writes that the individual is an autonomous being. Although the person participates in social groups, this participation itself is undertaken for extrinsic reasons. He writes: 'There is no organic connection between individuals after the umbilical cord is cut; all connections become the inventions and delusions of man. . . . one of the highest levels of psychological growth is becoming an individual. . . . Cooperation with others becomes a means not only of enhancing some fictitious entity, the group, but also of personal enhancement'" (Michael Naughton, "An Organizational Work Ethic Based on the Papal Social Teachings" [Ph.D. diss., Marquette University, 1991], chap. 1).

40. We are grateful to Deb Lincoln from the University of St. Thomas' Instructional Support Services who created this graphic.

5. Just Wages

This chapter was first presented by Michael Naughton at the John F. Henning Institute's inaugural conference, *Labor, Solidarity and the Common Good*, Saint Mary's College of California, Moraga, Calif., February 1995. See also Michael Naughton, "Distributors of Justice," *America*, 27 May 2000, 13–15.

1. In that year, Green Tree had available approximately $75 million in bonuses, of which $65 million went to Coss. Approximately $7 million went to 118 executives and managers, and approximately $3 million went to 2,300 employees (Ira T. Kay, *CEO Pay and Shareholder Value: Helping the U.S. Win the Global Economic War* [Boca Raton: St. Lucie Press, 1997], 1–2). According to *Business Week's* 1998 annual executive pay survey, Green Tree Financial Corporation's performance was less than stellar in 1997. "In comparing shareholder returns with pay, investors got the least from Green Tree Financial Corp. Chairman Lawrence M. Coss, who has pocketed a breathtaking $179 million since 1995, much of it in company shares. All was well until last November, when the company's ever-soaring earnings ran into a big problem. Hordes of borrowers had repaid their loans to take advantage of lower interest rates. The stock, which was almost at 50, had lost half its value by year end. Green Tree ended up booking a loss for 1997's fourth quarter and restating 1996's final period to show red ink" (Larry Light, "The Good, The Bad, The Ugly of CEO Salaries," *Business Week*, 20 April 1998, 67). See also Scott Carlson, "Done with Disparity," *St. Paul Pioneer Press*, 6 April 1996, 1E–2E.

2. See Frank D. Almade, *Just Wage for Church Employees* (New York: Peter Lang, 1993), which summarizes the Christian tradition on wages; see also John A. Ryan, *The Living Wage* (New York: Macmillan Company, 1906); James Healy, *The Just Wages 1750–1890: A Study of Moralists from St. Alphonsus to Leo XIII* (The Hague: Martinus Nijhoff, 1966), chapter 1; Michael Naughton, *The Good Stewards* (Lanham, Md.: University Press of America, 1991), 18–21, 45–47, 73–77 and 97–103; and Jean Yves Calvez and Jacques Perrin, *The Church and Social Justice* (Chicago: Henry Regnery Company, 1961), 239–245.

3. Jeremiah 22:13 (RSV).

4. James 5:4 (RSV).

5. S. A. Ali, *Social and Economic Aspects of the Islam of Mohammed* (Lewiston, N.Y.: Edwin Mellen Press, 1993), 103.

6. John Paul II, *Laborem Exercens*, 19. For an excellent discussion on the history and modern implications of a "family wage," see Bryce Christensen ed., *The Family Wage: Work, Gender, and Children in the Modern Economy* (Rockford, Ill.: Rockford Institute, 1988). (NB: The Rockford Institute is now called The Howard Institute.) See also Allan C. Carlson, "Gender, Children, and Social Labor: Transcending 'The Family Wage' Dilemma," *Journal of Social Issues* 52 (1996): 137–161.

7. The Hay Group, leaders in compensation consulting who owe their beginnings to a devout Quaker, offer a distinct counterexample (see

Thomas P. Flannery, David A. Hofrichter, and Paul E. Platten, *People, Performance and Pay* [New York: The Free Press, 1996], xv).

8. For a more extensive treatment of this topic, see John Paul II, *Laborem Exercens*, especially nn. 6–9. Our account of the subjective dimension as it relates to wages was influenced by Josef Pieper's analysis of an *honorarium*, which was pointed out to us by Ernest Pierucci. Pieper explains, "An honorarium implies that an incommensurability exists between performance and recompense, and that the performance cannot 'really' be recompensed" (Josef Pieper, *Leisure, the Basis of Culture* [New York: Random House, 1963], 52). Pay thus becomes the token of a moral and spiritual relationship. S. A. Cortright, in his paper "Quinquagesimo Anno: Pieper's 'Leisure, the Basis of Culture Revisited,'" comments, "the just wage conforms more to the character of the honorarium than to the character of the wage proper: an honorarium makes no pretense of compensating commutatively the 'service' rendered . . . it takes the character rather of a contribution to the cost of living, intended ultimately to support the recipient in activity which is of intrinsic value: which is rather already a part of, as opposed to a means to, a common good. A wage in the narrower sense supposes, on the other hand, that the service of good rendered can be determined through the relation of a commutation, that it has a price, irrespective of the needs of the provider" (this paper was delivered at the John F. Henning Institute Conference, *The Person in Catholic Social Thought*, Saint Mary's College of California, Moraga, Calif., 18 March 1998).

9. As James Murphy puts it, "action is immanent (that is, perfects the self) only because it is transitive (perfects the world); self and world are jointly articulated in the act of labor" (James Bernard Murphy, "A Natural Law of Human Labor," *American Journal of Jurisprudence* [1994]: 71–95). The subjective dimension of work is not easily discernible when we are used to seeing only the objective dimension of work. At first sight, the work done in organizations can look as if it involves people merely busy with objects. "But on reflection it appears that deeds, decisions, discoveries affect the subject more deeply than they affect the objects with which they are concerned. They accumulate as dispositions and habits of the subject; they determine him; they make him what he is and what he is to be" (Bernard Lonergan, "*Existenz* and *Aggiornamento*," in *Collected Works of Bernard Lonergan*, ed. Frederick E. Crowe and Robert M. Doran [Toronto, Canada: University of Toronto Press, 1988], 223).

10. John Paul II, *Laborem Exercens*, 6.

11. Thomas Aquinas, *Summa Theologica* (New York: Benziger Brothers, 1947), II-II q. 58, a. 12.

12. See Aquinas, *Summa Theologica*, II-II, q. 57, a. 1. Within the Christian and western classical traditions, justice is considered the most excellent (and complete) of the cardinal virtues, precisely because it is other-regarding.

13. In the Christian social tradition, being just requires us not only to think of what we should do, but of *what sort of people we want to become.* The two are intimately linked: what we do significantly shapes what we become. Without the basic solidarity formed through right relationships with their colleagues, employees shrivel into small-minded "strategic maximizers," persuaded that their sole concern lies with their own narrow advantage, blind to the common good. Neither managers nor employees can be dispensers of justice, unless (in the words of Aquinas) their souls are entirely possessed by justice, whereby their intentions are converted to the common good (Thomas Aquinas, *Commentary on Aristotle's Nicomachean Ethics* [Notre Dame: Dumb Ox Books, 1993], 302; see also *Summa Theologica*, II-II, q. 58, a. 3).

14. These three principles are an adaptation of Ryan's six canons of distributive justice (John Ryan, *Distributive Justice*, 3d ed. [New York: Macmillan Company, 1942]; see also John Finnis' discussion of distributive justice in *Natural Law and Natural Rights*, 174ff.).

15. A special thanks to Kimberley Wise and Deb Lincoln from the University of St. Thomas, St. Paul, Minn., who designed the graphic. It is clear that contingency increases as we move outwards through the circles, but that does not mean it becomes impossible to determine which pay systems are more just than others; this is exactly where the virtues come in. The problem with most managers is not that they become too concrete and programmatic in their application of their faith but rather that many never reach the point of putting their faith into practice. Gainsharing, skill-based pay or ESOPs cannot be moral imperatives in every situation, yet something resembling them would normally be appropriate.

16. See Robert Kennedy's reflections on just wages at www.stthomas.edu/cathstudies/faculty/kennedy/compensation.htm (1/28/01). See also Michael Naughton and Robert Kennedy, "Executive Compensation: An Evaluation from the Catholic Social Tradition," *Social Justice Review* (Summer 1993).

17. Unfortunately, we will not be able to examine all the complexities involved in a living wage. The issue raises many questions. Do all jobs require living wages? If not, which do and which do not? What role does the state have in determining living wages? Must temporary employment pay a living wage? Does international competition call for an international

living wage? These questions are not treated here, but are important nonetheless.

18. Richard B. Freeman and Lawrence F. Katz, "Rising Wage Inequality: The United States vs. Other Advanced Countries," in *Working
Under Different Rules*, ed. Richard B. Freeman (New York: Russell Sage
Foundation, 1994), 32–33. Despite these statistics, household income is up
because hours worked per household have increased through dual-income
parents, multiple jobs worked by parent, or increased hours per job. In 1973
for example, Germans and Americans worked approximately the same
number of hours. In 1992, average Americans worked the equivalent of one
month per year more than Germans (see Freeman, *Working Under Different
Rules*, 3). Although Americans have achieved a high standard of living, they
have done so at the expense of the "quality of life," working more, spending less time on family, church, school, and community. It is worth recalling
that the Catholic social tradition defines a living wage as a family wage
based on *one* working parent, not two, because of the conviction that working life must not be permitted to dominate family life. The lack of a fam-
ily/living wage forces both spouses to work, thus upsetting family stability as
well as social cohesion (see John Paul II, *Laborem Exercens*, 19). In telling
contrast, "[In] Japanese companies, each person's total situation will influence the amount of his income. The number of family members, his
housing needs, the distance from his home to the plant, and other person-
centered factors are given consideration" (Arthur M. Whitehill, *Japanese
Management: Tradition and Transition* [New York: Routledge, 1991], 173).

19. While U.S. workers in high-paying jobs do better than those in
Japan and Germany, U.S. workers in low-paying jobs—less skilled and less
educated—do worse (Freeman, *Working Under Different Rules*, 13; see table,
38). U.S. wage inequality increased in the 1980s and 1990s with a redistribution of wealth that shifted more wealth to the top 20% and less to the bottom 20%, although surveys in 1998 and 1999 seem to indicate some relief to
the bottom quintile. This redistribution stems from a decentralized labor
market and wage setting practices, weak unions, a low minimum wage, shifts
from goods to service production, as well as weak government protection for
labor in the U.S. compared to that in Europe (ibid., 30, 45). Other reasons
for the decline in wages include import competition from low wage countries, an increase in single parent households, increased demand for highly
trained workers with higher levels of education, and an increase of younger
workers. The bottom line is that during the 1990s, low-wage Americans saw
lower living standards "than low-wage workers in virtually all other advanced countries," while the rich were far better off in the U.S. than they

were in other advanced countries (see ibid., 226; these comparisons use purchase power parity to measure the value of foreign currencies).

20. For example, "the difference earned by American university-
educated workers over those who stopped their education at high school
rose from 37% in the late 1970s to 53% in 1989" ("Rich Man, Poor Man," *The
Economist*, 24 July 1993, 71; NB: statistics were taken from OECD forecasts).
It should be pointed out that less skilled workers in Europe have not suffered
as greatly because they have greater union representation. See Dean Baker,
"The U.S. Wage Gap and the Decline of Manufacturing" (http://www.
uswa.org/heartland/2manuf.htm) (1/28/01).

21. See Lisa M. Lynch, "Payoffs to Alternative Training Strategies at
Work," in Freeman, *Working under Different Rules*, 71.

22. Jeffery Pfeffer, "Competitive Advantage Through People," *California Management Review* (Winter 1994): 20; see also Clair Brown et al., *Work
and Pay in the United States and Japan* (New York: Oxford University Press,
1997), 76.

23. Thomas P. Flannery et al., *People, Performance and Pay*, 15.

24. It should be pointed out that workers in the U.S. receive much of
their training informally through learning on the job. While informal learning initially raises productivity, in the long run it fails to have a substantive
effect "Three recent studies show that formal training has a high payoff" in
the United States, but that the payoffs differ by type of training" (Freeman,
Working under Different Rules, 82; see Clair Brown et al., *Work and Pay in the
United States and Japan*, 75, 78–79, and Clair Brown and Michael Reich, "Developing Skills and Pay through Career Ladders," *California Management
Review* [Winter 1997]: 124–145, who argue that on-the-job training in the
U.S. is too informal and, consequently, inefficient).

25. Lynch, "Payoffs to Alternative Training Strategies at Work," in
Freeman, *Working under Different Rules*, 74.

26. E. E. Lawler, S. A. Mohrman, and G. E. Ledford, Jr., *Creating High
Performance Organizations* (San Francisco: Jossey-Bass Publishers, 1995), 15.
Motorola's training program, which requires one week of training for all
employees yearly, has been seen as exemplary in the U.S.

27. John Paul II notes that a mark of contemporary developed
economies is that "*the possession of know-how, technology and skill*" (emphasis
original) has displaced ownership of land as the foundation of wealth (*Centesimus Annus*, 32), a development anticipated by John XXIII in 1961. Hence,
the kind of work one has to offer increases in importance. Those who are
unskilled can no longer afford to remain so, and those who are skilled need
to continually develop their skills.

28. John Paul II observes: ". . . many people, perhaps the majority today, do not have the means which would enable them to take their place in an effective and humanly dignified way within a productive system in which work is truly central. They have no possibility of acquiring the basic knowledge that would enable them to express their creativity and develop their potential. They have no way of entering the network of knowledge and intercommunication which would enable them to see their qualities appreciated and utilized" (*Centesimus Annus*, 33). Although such workers may not be actually exploited, they are nonetheless unjustly marginalized.

29. Richard B. Freeman, "The Facts about Rising Economic Disparity" in *The Inequality Paradox: Growth of Income Disparity*, ed. James A. Auerbach and Richard S. Belous (Washington, D.C.: National Policy Association), 22.

30. See Robert L. Rose, "A Productivity Push at Wabash National Puts Firm on a Roll," *The Wall Street Journal*, 7 September 1995. Skill- and knowledge-based systems of compensation focus on the development of three classes of skills: vertical, upward skills, usually exercised by management (e.g., inventory control, quality control, scheduling, and team leadership); horizontal or trade skills, which include learning the various jobs upstream and downstream on the production line; and depth or technical skills, such as in apprenticeship programs for carpentry, accounting, tax preparation, etc. (see E. E. Lawler, *Strategic Pay* [San Francisco: Jossey-Bass, 1990], 155 ff.; see also E. E. Lawler and G. E. Ledford, "Skill-Based Pay," *Personnel* [1985]: 30).

31. For example, high-tech companies with highly skilled employees have the highest revenues per employee, while food markets, with generally low-skilled employees, have some of the lowest revenues per employee. Of course, if revenues are not available to pay a living wage, the point is moot.

32. Skill-based pay systems increase organizational effectiveness by building in flexibility. When employees can perform multiple jobs, organizations have room to maneuver as they face product change, parts shortages, and the like (see Lawler and Ledford, "Skill-Based Pay," 33; Lawler, *Strategic Pay*, 160ff.). Skilled workers require fewer supervisors, and multiskilled employees with a more detailed understanding of the overall production system are more likely to solve problems on the spot, rather than pass them to others (see Lawler, *Strategic Pay*, 163). Typical disadvantages of skill-based pay include high pay rates, high training costs, higher costs as the learning curve rises, and administration costs (see Lawler, *Strategic Pay*, 166ff.). Lawler comments, "In most cases, skill-based pay tends to produce somewhat higher pay levels for individuals, but these costs usually are offset by greater workforce flexibility and performance. Flexibility often leads to

lower staffing levels and less absenteeism or turnover, both of which may drop because employees appreciate the opportunity to utilize and be paid for a wide range of skills" (E. E. Lawler, "The New Pay: A Strategic Approach," *Compensation and Benefits Review* [1 July 1995]: 17).

33. Lynch, "Payoffs to Alternative Training Strategies at Work," 77. The obvious danger with skill-based systems is that they may increase pay rates ahead of gains in productivity or quality. Management plays a critical role in proportioning resources. Keeping production gains in line with gains in pay may require, for example, an initial period of consistently low or marginal wages traded against future, substantial raises. For example, German apprentices are paid substantially less than apprentices in the U.S. and Britain, but later payoffs for the training are far greater, because the training is more comprehensive, professional (that is, less industry-specific), includes general education and broader skills, is nationally recognized, and overall is simply more competent. The Japanese practice is similar to the German. Brown et al. point out that "the initial training appears to be paid at least in part by employees, who collect the return on their investment in the form of higher wages later. Since employers in Japan are not paying the full cost, they can provide more training" (Brown et al., *Work and Pay in the United States and Japan*, 91).

34. Lynch, "Payoffs to Alternative Training Strategies at Work," 83–85. To date, such studies have worked from small samples, and despite their encouraging results, organizations seem to hesitate when adopting skill-based systems because of doubts over whether the initial, relatively high investment in employees can be justified, considering employee turnover in a highly mobile society and the relatively long time period required to recoup the investment. Yet, Robert Reich points out, "Average length of stay in the job is in direct proportion to the amount of training provided young employees on the job" ("Companies Are Cutting Their Hearts Out," *The New York Times Magazine*, 19 December 1993, 54–55). This is truer for smaller organizations, where 11% of the workforce is trained as compared to 26% in larger companies (see Lynch, "Payoffs to Alternative Training Strategies at Work," 65–66). In a report from the Office of Technology Assessment to Congress, it was stated that "[g]ood training pays off—for the individual worker whose skills are upgraded, for the company seeking a competitive edge, and for the Nation—in overall productivity and competitiveness" (Margaret Hilton, "Shared Training: Learning from Germany," *Monthly Labor Review* [March 1991]: 33). For discussion of the "free rider" problem, "where a firm can pay for investments in training only to have competitors benefit if workers quit," see Brown et al., *Work and Pay in the United States and Japan*, 75 and 78 (the authors point out that in Japan, "free-riding" presents less of a problem

because of the stability of the labor force and the norm of lifetime employment with a single company).

35. "It is our intent, under normal business conditions, to pay people hired below this RPM Living Wage *accelerated* increases until the Living Wage is reached" (*Reell Precision Manufacturing Corporation Salary System Overview*).

36. Although Reell did not initially consider the change as an element in its program for promoting the "target wage," the manufacturing line was redesigned from a Command-Direct-Control system to a Teach-Equip-Trust system. The resulting savings in setup and supervisory times, and improvements in quality, contributed materially to the economic feasibility of Reell's just-wage policies.

37. See, e.g., Pius XI, *Quadragesimo Anno,* 72–73, and John XXIII, *Mater et Magistra,* 71.

38. See Pfeffer, "Six Dangerous Myths about Pay," *Harvard Business Review* (May–June 1998): 109–119. Pfeffer distinguishes between *labor rates*, determined as total salary divided by time worked, and *labor cost*, which is a function of labor rates and productivity. As Pfeffer points out, in many cases among competing organizations, a firm with a higher labor rate may nevertheless experience lower labor costs than its competitor, because its employees are significantly more productive than its competitors' employees. For example, General Motors requires 46 employee-hours to assemble a car, Ford 37.92 hours, Toyota 29.44 hours and Nissan only 27.36 hours (ibid., 114). GM's problem is not its labor rate but its labor cost, which is influenced by its culture, quality controls, and production processes. Pfeffer concludes that "only labor costs—and not labor rates—are the basis for competition . . . [and] that the issue is not just what you pay people, but also what they produce" (117).

39. For a discussion of the term "indirect employer" and of the just or living wage as the achievement principally of the political community as a whole, see John Paul II, *Laborem Exercens,* nn. 16–20, and *Centesimus Annus,* 40, 42; cf. John XXIII, *Mater et Magistra,* 51–58, 71; *Gaudium et Spes,* 67–68, and Naughton, *The Good Stewards,* 20–21 and 102–103. When the market system is so competitive and so dysfunctional that paying a living wage is penalized, rather than rewarded, employers and managers cannot expect to be totally responsible for paying a just wage. This right to a living wage is the responsibility of all people, not just direct employers. If a particular company is in a highly price-sensitive market, such as a commodity market, pressures to reduce labor costs may become so great that an employer may be forced to pay the "market wage," which may be below a living or family wage (see John

Paul II, *Laborem Exercens*, 17). An employer in such a system may be forced to pay lower wages, provide fewer benefits, and let working conditions deteriorate in order to compete with others in the industry. To do otherwise would place the company at a competitive disadvantage. No matter how much direct employers may want to pay a living or a family wage, they may be forced to pay the going rate or risk going out of business. This scenario is most evident in developing countries where labor protection is nonexistent, labor unions are suppressed, and labor markets are flooded. This is why indirect employers are so critically important in the determination of pay. Indirect employers include institutions and persons such as suppliers, customers, states, educational systems, employer associations, financial institutions, health care systems, unions, and other intermediary groups in the community that can have some effect on wages. The most obvious and influential indirect employer is the state. The policies and regulations of the state have a tremendous influence on whether direct employers can pay a living wage, and whether workers are able to keep the wages they earn. By creating wage and safety standards, government creates a level playing field for all companies, where employees are given basic safeguards. The state plays a critical role in helping organizations fulfill their obligations when competitive pressures would otherwise prevent them from doing so. As John A. Ryan put it, the state "has both the right and the duty to compel all employers to pay a living wage" (*A Living Wage*, 301). The critical question for state regulation of a living wage is its expediency. That is, can the state, in today's international economy, require a living wage without raising inflation, decreasing demand, and increasing unemployment to such an extent that it causes more harm than good? These are large, complex, and contentious questions. Yet, if the state does not take partial responsibility for ensuring a living wage, it places undue burden both on organizations and on families, particularly on large families. John Paul II explains that paying a family wage in a particular industry or company may be impossible because of either financial inability or because of the various needs of different families—sizes, medical care, special education, and so forth. Consequently, John Paul II advocates allowances by the state to "mothers devoting themselves exclusively to their families" (*Laborem Exercens*, 19.2). He explains that family wages are basic human rights that are the responsibility both of the employer, whom he refers to as the "direct" employer, and also of the state, which he refers to as the "indirect" employer. As many commentators throughout the Catholic social tradition have noted, to expect the business organization alone to carry the duty of paying a family wage would give economic incentives to organizations to discriminate against large families. If the state fails to supplement family wages, it also ignores the complexity of the economy and the social responsibility of society as a whole to guarantee a family wage. Managers tend to be suspect of government interference, especially as it relates to regulating organizations. But few would disagree that the state serves to protect people against violence and injustice so they may enjoy life and property. As Ryan puts it, "To compel a man to work for less than a Living Wage is as truly an act of injustice as to pick his pocket. In a wide sense it is also an attack upon his life. An ordinance prohibiting this species of oppression would, therefore, be a measure for the protection of life and property" (*A Living Wage*, 301). The European Union, notably influenced by the Christian social tradition, has within its Social Charter that the government is committed to ensure "all workers have the right to a fair remuneration sufficient for a decent standard of living for themselves and their families" (Jesuit Centre for Faith and Justice, "A Fair Day's Pay," *Doctrine and Life* 38 [April 1988]: 20). See Christensen, *The Family Wage*, and Carlson, "Gender, Children, and Social Labor," for some creative public policy solutions to the problems of paying family wages.

40. Lawler, *Strategic Pay*, 185.

41. Ibid., 185.

42. Lawler, "The New Pay": 18.

43. Pius XI states that "[t]he just amount of pay, however, must be calculated not on a single basis but on several, as Leo XIII already wisely declared in these words: 'To establish a rule of pay in accord with justice, many factors must be taken into account.'" (*Quadragesimo Anno*, 66).

44. Thomas Aquinas, *Commentary on Aristotle's Nicomachean Ethics*, 296; see also 342ff. on equity.

45. See Ryan, *A Living Wage*, 75.

46. In *Mater et Magistra*, 71, John XXIII added the term "equity" to "justice" to tie the discussion of compensation more directly to its second ground, namely, what portion of the whole good or service made or achieved derives from the contribution of the worker. A wage based on "justice and equity" should derive not only from the worker's material needs (distributive justice) but also from how much the worker has contributed to the business expansion (commutative justice). On equity, see also Douglas M. Cowherd and David I. Levine, "Product Quality and Pay Equity between Lower-Level Employees and Top Management: An Investigation of Distributive Justice Theory," *Administrative Science Quarterly* (2 June 1992): 303.

47. Ernest Bartell, "*Laborem Exercens*: A Third World Perspective," in *Co-Creation and Capitalism*, ed. John W. Houck and Oliver F. Williams (Lanham, Md.: University of America Press, 1983), 187. John A. Ryan, for

example, systematically captured this link in his six canons of distributive justice (Ryan, *Distributive Justice*).

48. Robert Reich captures a near-universal suspicion: "There is something wrong with rising profits, rising productivity and a soaring stock market but employee compensation heading nowhere" (*Minneapolis Tribune*, 1 November 1995). Indeed, one has to wonder where excess profits are going when various stock markets are at all-time highs and employee wages are flat. See also Margaret M. Blair, "CEO Pay: Why Such a Contentious Issue?" *The Brookings Review* (Winter 1994): 23–27.

49. Incentives allocated to top executives have boosted executive pay to previously unheard of heights, leaving, as *The Wall Street Journal* (11 April 1996) put it, "everybody else further and further behind." Executive pay has grown four times faster than the pay of the average worker and three times faster than corporate profits. The reason: *stock options*. Stock options have created what has been popularized as "the winner-take-all markets." Part of the cause of the disproportionate income distribution in U.S. organizations is that traditionally, financial incentives and bonuses such as profit sharing, stock options, and the like have remained exclusively at the top of the organizational structure (see *Fortune* [18 September 1995]: 230). Corporate executives and upper-level managers in the U.S. are the most highly paid among Western industrial countries. While in Japan the level of pay of lower-ranked employees has increased faster than the level of top executives, the opposite trend is true in the U.S. (James Abegglen and George Stalk, Jr., *Kaisha: The Japanese Corporation* [New York: Basic Books Inc., 1985], 192). This phenomenon led Edward Lawler to quip that since U.S. CEO salaries are so high, corporations should move their headquarters to other countries and tap into the efficient, low wages of foreign CEOs.

50. Among the *Fortune* 1,000 companies, 24% use no pay-for-performance program widely, "and only 14 percent use three or more widely. The results clearly establish that most organizations do not make a significant effort to reward most individuals for their performance. The opportunity therefore exists for most organizations to reward many more individuals for performance and, as a result, to increase their level of involvement in their organizations" (Lawler, Mohrman, and Ledford, Jr., *Creating High Performance Organizations*). In an earlier survey, Lawler found that among the *Fortune* 1,000 companies, 13% offered no form of incentive pay; among the remaining 87%, 49% involved 1% to 20% of their employees in an incentive program, and of those employees a fair majority were salespeople and executives (Lawler, *Strategic Pay*, 57ff.). A Hay Group report on more than

500 companies found that "only 19 percent had implemented profit sharing, only 16 percent gainsharing, and only 13 percent had long-term incentives below the executive level. Yet more than 80 percent of those same organizations said they believed that they needed to revamp both their short- and long-term incentive programs" (Flannery et al., *People Performance and Pay*, 106).

51. Michael Novak, "The Executive Joneses," *Forbes*, 29 May 1989, 95. See Adolf A. Berle and Gardiner Means, *The Modern Corporation and Private Property*, rev. ed. (New York: Harcourt, Brace and World, 1968), xii–xiii and 299–302, for the traditional rationale for allocating incentives primarily to executives, which is that incentives substitute for the rewards (profits) of ownership in spurring management to care zealously for the economic well-being of joint-stock property. It is argued that increased stock ownership by executives will result in better management and thus enhance corporate performance. One study reported in the *Wall Street Journal*, however, suggests strongly that significant stock ownership by executives has little effect on the economic order and health of the company. On the contrary, companies where employees own more than 10 percent of the stock do far better. What may not be true of executive ownership may indeed be true if ownership is more broadly distributed (*Wall Street Journal*, 23 March 1993, 1).

52. Erik Gunn and John Fauber, "Pay at Top Is Raising Questions," *The Milwaukee Journal*, 5 May 1991, D12. The argument is made that simple market pressures, regardless of individual contribution or merit, fuel disproportionate increases in top executive pay. For example, the ice-cream manufacturer Ben and Jerry's had attempted to hold CEO compensation to a "just" ratio of 5 to 1, but has abandoned the policy owing to an inability to attract and retain the desired talent. Graef Grystal, an executive compensation consultant turned critic holds a darker theory. He argues that since many CEOs handpick their boards of directors, the boards' compensation committees are heavily laden with CEOs' colleagues, creating a set of incestuous relationships and cozy, inflationary effects. Whatever the actual case, the phenomenon would seem to have a corrosive effect on employee morale, yet "[t]here have been over 250 studies of the consequences of the top pay of corporate executives, but none have examined the effects of pay differentials between upper-echelon managers and lower-level employees. . . . Future studies of executive pay should consider not only the effects of top managers' pay on their own motivation but also how executive pay levels affect the motivation of lower-level employees" (Cowherd and Levine, "Product Quality and Pay Equity," 317).

53. Companies that fail to distribute financial incentives and rewards lead employees to disconnect their job performance from the exercise of cre-

ative effort, perseverance, and other characteristics associated with high achievement. In one rather dated survey, Japanese and U.S. workers were asked in a poll who would profit from an increase of productivity and quality in the plant. Only 9% of the U.S. workers felt they would accrue the benefits compared to 93% of the Japanese (Robert Bachelder, "Japan and the U.S.: The Economics of Equity," *The Christian Century*, 26 August 1987, 719–723). If executives aspire to foster enhanced organizational teamwork and a sense of corporate purpose, how can they expect to motivate the managers and workers when their own compensation is widely viewed as excessive, possibly four hundred times more than the average worker of a particular firm? (see Sheldon Friedman, "The Compelling Case for Limiting Executive Compensation," *California Management Review* 77 [March 1988]: 61–62).

54. Companies that push pay-for-performance incentives farther down into the organization must face the question of "internal equity." When labor and middle managers are receiving 2–3% merit increases and executives are receiving 20–40% increases on the single basis of performance by the organization overall, the "incentive" begins to look to those in the lower echelons like ridicule from above. As one quality control supervisor put it, such disparities "mock the concept of teamwork needed to compete in today's markets" (Michael A. Verespej, "Pay for Skills: Its Time Has Come," *Industry Week* [15 June 1992]: 22–30). In an *Industry Week* survey, middle level managers erupted in anger over increasing executive compensation, with 62% believing that executives are overpaid. That middle-level managers' responsibilities are closer to those of executive managers makes it all the more transparent that executives' contributions do not translate into 75–150 times more pay. It should be pointed out that the discrepancy in pay increases as the size of the organization increases (see Flannery et al., *People, Performance and Pay*, 188–189).

55. Pay-for-performance plans involve three basic variations: individual (merit pay, bonuses, executive stock options, etc.), team and/or departmental (gainsharing), and divisional or organizational (profit sharing, stock ownership—ESOPs). These levels and their corresponding programs are variable pay elements that depend on the performance of the individual, group, division, and firm.

56. Verespej, "Pay for Skills," 22–30. Another survey indicated that 72% "of blue collar workers, and 56% of white collar workers, would prefer straight wages over any type of incentive plan" (Bureau of National Affairs, *Changing Pay Practices: New Developments in Employee Compensation*, 1988).

57. For more detailed considerations of gainsharing's advantages and disadvantages in comparison to the more familiar profit-sharing system, and for discussion of gainsharing's role in comprehensive pay-for-performance

systems, see Brian Graham-Moore and Timothy L. Ross, *Gainsharing: Plans for Improving Performance* (Washington, D.C.: Bureau of National Affairs, 1990); Lawler, *Strategic Pay*, 125–128; M. L. Weitzman, *The Share Economy* (Cambridge, Mass.: Harvard University Press, 1984); and Flannery et al., *People, Performance and Pay*, 109.

58. See Lawler, *Strategic Pay*, 110ff.

59. Ibid., chapter 9.

60. Some theorists call this connection "a strong line of sight," since the employees can perceive a strong correlation between cause (hard work) and effect (higher pay). Gainsharing programs will often fail because of their lack of clarity of what is being measured.

61. The Scanlon plan, the oldest and most popular gainsharing plan, originated in the 1930s when Joseph Scanlon, a local union president, attempted to prevent the shutdown of a steel mill and the accompanying massive layoffs. The Scanlon plan would define the costs of production in a given month, and if there were savings, workers would receive a percentage of it. Today, the Scanlon plan distributes approximately 75% of corporate gains to employees and the other 25% to the organization (Lawler, *Strategic Pay*, 157–162). If workers are to improve the effectiveness of the organization, they need to understand its workings, and must trust management to reward their work. In order to build this trust, the practice of equity must pervade the firm. This may mean the demise of executive dining rooms, special parking lots, executive health clubs, and so forth. Although these may be small gestures, they can symbolize the move to a more equitable organization.

62. See Thomas P. Flannery, David A. Hofrichter, and Paul E. Platten, "Using Culture to Bring Pay Objectives into Focus," *ACA Journal* [Autumn 1996]: 44–53. For an opposing view on incentive-based pay, see Jeffrey Pfeffer, "Six Dangerous Myths about Pay," 114ff. Pfeffer is particularly critical of individual incentive plans on the grounds that they cause far more problems than they solve.

63. "Gainsharing is considered a good idea not simply because it has organizational value or enhances effectiveness, but because it is the right way to treat people. It is seen as returning to the employee much of the control and income-enhancement opportunity that began to decline with the advent of scientific management and modern manageralism. . . . It is, therefore, not simply a compensation system or even a way of paying people more fairly. Rather, it is seen as a better way of organizing and managing people. For a few companies—including Herman Miller, and Lincoln Electric in Cleveland—gainsharing is a core management principle for the whole organization" (Rosabeth Moss Kanter, "The Attack on Pay," *Harvard Business Review*

[March and April 1987]: 81). See Laura Nash, *Believers in Business* (Nashville: Thomas Nelson Publishers, 1994), 149ff., on Herman Miller.

64. John Byrne et al., "Is the Boss Getting Too Much?" *Business Week,* 1 May 1989, 48. Ben and Jerry's Ice Cream observed a similar distribution scale, originally set at 5:1, then increased it to 7:1, and finally dropped altogether. Crucial to the success of Herman Miller was their CEO, Max De Pree, who embraced the goal of building a "covenant" within his organization.

65. Charles R. Day, "Kerm Campbell: 'We Need to Change the Meaning of Management,'" *Industry Week,* 7 November 1994, 39.

66. John XXIII, *Mater et Magistra,* 72. Labor costs as a percentage of total costs vary from industry to industry, yet trends seem to indicate that the percentage for labor is decreasing.

67. See Servais Pinckaers, *The Sources of Christian Ethics* (Washington, D.C.: The Catholic University of America, 1995), 83ff.; see also John Paul II, *Laborem Exercens,* 5–6.

68. See P. A. Zingheim and J. R. Schuster, "Introduction: How Are the New Pay Tools Being Developed?" *Compensation and Benefits Review* (July–August 1995): 10.

69. There is some literature on the integration of ethics and strategy: see R. Edward Freeman, Daniel R. Gilbert, and Edwin Hartman, "Values and the Foundation of Strategic Management," *Journal of Business Ethics* 7 (1988): 821–834; see also John Paul II, *Redemptor Hominis,* 15.

70. Pinckaers, *The Sources of Christian Ethics,* 84 and 87.

71. See John B. Matthews, Kenneth Goodpaster, and Laura Nash, *Policies and Persons: A Casebook in Business Ethics* (New York: McGraw-Hill, 1991), 111. See also Lynn Sharp Paine, "Managing for Organizational Integrity," *Harvard Business Review* (March–April, 1994): 107–108, on how Sears automotive division's overemphasis on sales quotas pressured and "incentivized" mechanics into selling unnecessary parts and services.

72. See the classic article by Steven Kerr, "The Folly of Rewarding A and Getting B," *Academy of Management Journal* 18 (1975): 769–783.

73. An overemphasis on quantifiable goals is hardly limited to business. The academy practices its own version of an opaque paper chase, e.g., the elevation of publishing (counted by the page and the refereed journal) over teaching (reckoned by the development of minds and spirits), which has produced its own distortions in higher education.

74. Pinckaers, *The Sources of Christian Ethics,* 87.

75. Moreover, when sacrifices are not distributed equitably throughout the workforce, organizations become downright dysfunctional. When GM

demanded wage concessions from labor, then awarded executive bonuses, employees were outraged by the display of executive egoism. Unlike Ford and Chrysler, whose management shared in the economic hardships, GM has had more strikes, poorer morale, higher levels of distrust, and lower quality. As Pfeffer ("Six Myths," 118) observes, "When Southwest Airlines asked its pilots for a five-year wage freeze, CEO Her Kelleher voluntarily asked the compensation committee to freeze his salary for at least four years as well. The message of shared, common fate is powerful in an organization truly seeking to build a culture of teamwork."

76. Interestingly, Reell once instituted salary freezes in anticipation of a revenue shortfall that never materialized. This generated some ill will among employees who saw the freeze as unnecessary. Management learned that they could ask people to make sacrifices when problems actually occurred, but not because they would be likely to occur.

77. Business Executives for Economic Justice position paper, "Not Just a Just Wage" (Chicago, 1999), unpublished. See also Robert Kennedy's insightful paper on just compensation (http://www.stthomas.edu/cathstudies/faculty/kennedy/compensation.htm [1/28/01]).

78. Lawler, *Strategic Pay*, 40.

79. Lawler, *Strategic Pay*, 53; see also Pfeffer, "Six Myths," 118.

6. Corporate Ownership

1. Peter S. Grosscup, "How to Save the Corporation" in *Curing World Poverty*, ed. John H. Miller, C.S.C. (St. Louis: Social Justice Review, 1994), 43. We are indebted to many people for the content of this chapter, in particular, Norman Kurland of the Center for Economic and Social Justice in Washington, D.C., and Jeff Gates, whose book *The Ownership Solution: Toward a Shared Capitalism for the* 21st Century (Reading, Mass.: Addison-Wesley, 1998) served us as an essential resource on the importance of capital ownership. *The Ownership Solution* (as policy-makers from Bill Bradley to Jack Kemp and analysts from Michael Novak to Mikhail Gorbachev have testified) is "must" reading. Kurland and Gates are on the front lines of the movement to "repeopleize" corporate property for the twenty-first century. We are grateful for their insights and experience. See also Robert Ashford and Rodney Shakespeare, *Binary Economics* (Lanham: University Press of America, 1999).

2. *Human Development Report* 1998 (New York: Oxford University Press, 1998), 30; see also Gates, *The Ownership Solution*, 7. Xabier Gorostiaga

discerns the emergence of a "Champagne Glass Civilization, in which flexible capital—a product of the revolution in management and electronics—allows power to be centralized and concentrated as never before in history. Five hundred years ago, the metropolises and empires, which were founded on the basis of colonial exploitation, never achieved this level of concentration and centralization of power. Nor did they achieve the abysmal differences between the standards of living of the metropolis and the colonies, as exists today between a small group of privileged countries in the North and the great majority of nations of the South" ("The Universities of Christian Inspiration and the Catholic Social Thought Confronting the New Millennium," a paper delivered at the Second International Symposium of Catholic Social Thought and Management Education, Antwerp, Belgium, July 1997. Papers from the conference can be found at www.stthomas.edu/cathstudies/mgmt/antwerp) (1/28/01).

   3. See Gates, *The Ownership Solution*, 3–5, and "Capitalism and Human Dignity: The Ownership Imperative," *America*, 19 October 1996, 17. It is important to note, however, that since 1993 there has been a reversal in income growth patterns: "From the early 1970s through 1993, the trend of increasing income inequality was clear and pervasive. Since 1993, however, this seemingly relentless trend has apparently stalled" (Janet L. Yellen, "Trends in Income Inequality" in *The Inequality Paradox: Growth of Income Disparity*, ed. James A. Auerbach and Richard S. Belous [Washington, D.C.: National Policy Association, 1998], 12). In the same collection of readings, Robert Reich argues that this "reversal" appears in part because more people are employed working longer hours and because retirees are better off (*The Inequality Paradox*, 1). See also Edward N. Wolff, "Recent Trends in Wealth Ownership" a paper for the conference on "Benefits and Mechanisms for Spreading Asset Ownership in the United States," New York University, 10–12 December 1998; Richard B. Freeman, ed., *Working Under Different Rules* (New York: Russell Sage Foundation, 1994); Michael Hout, "Inequality by Design: Myths, Data, and Politics," at www.russellsage.org/publications/working_papers.htm (1/28/01); John H. Hinderaker and Scott W. Johnson, "The Truth about Income Inequality," a policy paper for the *Center of the American Experiment;* Karen Pennar, "A Helping Hand, Not Just an Invisible Hand," *Business Week*, 24 March 1997, 70–72; Joseph Spiers, "Why the Income Gap Won't Go Away," *Fortune* 132 no. 12 (11 December 1995): 65; Aaron Bernstein, "Inequality, How the Gap Between Rich and Poor Hurts the Economy," *Business Week*, 15 August 1994, 78–83; "Slicing the Cake," *The Economist*, 5 November 1994, 13–14; "Inequality; For Richer, for Poorer," *The Economist*, 5 November 1994, 19–21; "Rich Man, Poor Man," *The Economist*, 24 July 1993, 71;

Robert B. Reich, "As the World Turns," *The New Republic,* 1 May 1989, 23–28; Dean Baker, "The U.S. Wage Gap and the Decline of Manufacturing," at www.Uswa.org/heartland/2manuf.htm (1/28/01); J. Stacy Adams, "Toward an Understanding of Inequity," *Journal of Abnormal and Social Psychology* 67 (1963): 422–436; Gary Burtless, "Worsening American Income Inequality," *The Brookings Review* (Spring 1996): 26–31; "Income Disparity," *Credit Union Magazine* (April 1997): 38–42; Aaron Bernstein, "Sharing Prosperity," *Business Week,* 1 September 1997, 64–70.

4. "Politics into economics won't go," *The Economist,* 11 May 1996, 26, cited in Gates, *The Ownership Solution,* 5. Richard B. Freeman reports that "Virtually all of the past decade's economic growth has gone to the upper 5 percent of families. Since the early 1970s, while the income of the top 1 percent of households has doubled, family and household incomes have stagnated or declined for 80 percent of the population" (Richard B. Freeman, "Solving the New Inequality," at http://bostonreview.mit.edu/BR21.6/Freeman.html [1/28/01]. This web site hosts a vibrant discussion on income disparity).

5. James M. Poterba and Andrew A. Samwick, *Stock Ownership Patterns, Stock Market Fluctuations and Consumption,* Brookings Papers on Economic Activity, vol. 2 (Washington, D.C.: Brookings Institution, 1995), 295–357, 368–372, cited in Gates, *The Ownership Solution,* 4. Michael Hout reports that "from March 1973 and March 1994 Current Population Surveys show a drop in pension coverage from 62 percent to 46 percent of U.S. employees" ("Inequality by Design").

6. See Gates, *The Ownership Solution,* 6.

7. Ibid.

8. Ibid., 5.

9. See Hout, "Inequality by Design" (these numbers come from the *Economic Report of the President,* 1996). "The gains in productivity fueled executive compensation, the stock market, and corporate profits. But not wages." See Corey Rosen, "Legislative Proposals of the Capital Ownership Group" (unpublished, National Center for Employee Ownership, www.nceo.org. [1/28/01]), who reports that real wages have dropped 8% since 1973: "In the 1990s, productivity is up 7%, but wages and benefits are only up 1%." Richard B. Freeman argues, "That the United States has distributed the gains from economic growth more unevenly than any other advanced country should make every American uneasy about the nation's economic performance" ("The Facts about Rising Economic Disparity," in *The Inequality Paradox,* 20).

10. Gates, *The Ownership Solution,* 3. "Disconnection" is a major theme for Gates and bears a relation to our idea of the divided life.

11. Peter Drucker, "Peter Drucker Takes the Long View" (an interview), *Fortune*, 28 September 1998, 169.

12. Gates, *The Ownership Solution*, 8. Richard B. Freeman explains that "If labor's capital [pensions and ESOPs] were more firmly under the control of its worker owners, we would expect it would be used to help foreclose the 'low road' on industrial restructuring that has disrupted American labor markets and depressed family incomes; to reduce domestic investment's sensitivity to speculative international capital flows; and to increase the willingness of management to undertake policies that benefit a wider range of enterprise stakeholders than short-term owners of shares" ("The New Inequality").

13. The statistics are taken from Jeff Gates, "From Containment to Community" to appear in a future issue of *Perspectives* by World Business Academy. See Gates' web site, www.sharedcapitalism.org (1/28/01).

14. John A. Ryan, *A Better Economic Order* (New York and London: Harper & Brothers Publishers, 1935), 171. He saw three major evils of U.S. capitalism at the time: subliving wages, excessive wealth disparity between rich and poor, and concentration of capital ownership. It was the third evil that Ryan saw as particularly problematic: "the narrow distribution of capital ownership is more fundamental than the other two evils because it threatens the stability of the whole system" (Marvin L. Krier Mich, *Catholic Social Teaching and Movements* [Mystic, Conn.: Twenty-Third Publications, 1998], 53). Kelso's two-source theory emphasizes the fact that those who are dependent for income on their labor alone are *ipso facto* economically vulnerable (Louis O. Kelso and Mortimer J. Adler, *The Capitalist Manifesto* [New York: Random House, 1958], chapter 2). For example, according to figures released by the Bureau of Labor Statistics for the first half of 1994, the average hourly earnings for private workers, adjusted for inflation, declined from $8.03 in 1970 to $7.40 in 1994. In 1995 corporate profits increased 22% due in part to a meager 2.9% increase in benefits and wages. "'What's going on is a straight redistribution of income from labor to capital,' says James Annable, economist at First National Bank of Chicago" (Bill Montague, "Wages rose 2.9%; lowest in 15 years," *USA Today*, 14 February 1996, 1; see also "Inequality; For Richer, for Poorer," 20).

15. For Kohlberg, the objective of a leveraged buyout is to use a little equity and a lot of debt to buy companies. With this, one can run the company more efficiently than before, sell off parts of the company, and use the excess cash to pay off debt as soon as possible. When reselling the streamlined company, the highly leveraged aspect of the deal maximizes the profits of investors and executive managers whose compensation is directly tied to the price of stock. Since the investor and manager in the LBO put up so

little of their own money to buy the company, the return on investment is maximized in light of the relatively short period during which the company is held. It should be noted that KKR receives a portion of its leveraged buyout fund from pension funds. As William Greider put it, "The time has come, perhaps, to ask the question modern liberalism has always ducked: Who owns America?"

16. Kohlberg himself had difficulties with his partners on the direction of KKR: see Sarah Bartlett, "The Inside Story of the Rise of KKR," *Fortune,* 3 June 1991, 172.

17. Kohlberg is agnostic on the issues of wealth distribution and income disparity. His concern with financing corporations deals only with the control of property, not with any social vision of distribution. It matters little who owns the corporation as long as whoever owns it also controls it. Actually, in Kohlberg's vision of the corporation, there is an advantage in having only a few people own a company, since this guarantees greater participation on the board of directors and control over executive management.

18. Paul H. Dembinski, "The Financialisation of the World and the Risks of Not Making Sense," in *Living in the Global Society,* ed. Roberto Papini, Antonio Pavan, and Stefano Zamagni (Aldershot: Ashgate Publishing Ltd., 1997), 156. As increasing amounts of property take the financial form of shares, financialization conditions us to see property in general, and corporations in particular, as mere opportunities for individual gain.

19. Charles Avila, *Ownership: Early Christian Teaching* (Maryknoll, N.Y.: Orbis Books), 3. He continues, "ownership is a relation, but not so much a relation between a person and the thing owned as between the owning person and other people, whom the owner excludes from, or to whom the owner concedes, possession."

20. ESOPs are defined as qualified retirement plans. A trust is established, to which a company contributes either by direct payment or through a profit-sharing plan or by borrowing money. The trust is converted into stock by purchase from current shareholders. That stock is, in turn, held under the names of the individual employees. When employees retire, they usually sell their stock back to the ESOP, from which new employees can then purchase it. Approximately 15,000 U.S. firms have broad employee ownership, with 10,000 of them organized through ESOPs. "Companies with broad-based stock option plans, ESOPs, or other employee ownership arrangements accounted for 47 of the "Best 100 Companies in America to Work For" ("Employee Ownership Companies Top 'Best 100 List'," *Employee Ownership Report* 19 [March/April 1999]: 1).

21. We are grateful to the insights of Robert Ashford here. For Kelso the economy is undergoing an historic shift from a predominantly labor

economy to a labor-capital economy. Thus, to rely solely or principally on wages for wealth distribution is like relying solely on two cylinders of a four-cylinder engine: you get half the power, and the system is driven to breakdown. See also Oswald von Nell-Breuning, S. J., "The Formation of Private Property in the Hands of Workers," in *The Social Market Economy: Theory and Ethics of the Economic Order*, ed. Peter Koslowski (Berlin: Springer Verlag, 1998), 295; see also Antoine de Salins and François Villeroy de Galhau, *The Modern Development of Financial Activities in the Light of the Ethical Demands of Christianity* (Vatican City: Libreria Editrice Vaticana, 1994), 35.

22. Peter Davis explains that many of the people involved with the original cooperative enterprises were alarmed by the increasing concentration of ownership of the means of production and by the negative effects that concentration had on the working masses ("Co-operative Management and Co-operative Purpose: Values, Principles and Objectives for Co-operatives into the 21st Century" [unpublished, January 1995]: 7). In Europe, cooperatives, and in particular the Mondragon cooperatives in Spain, were inspired by a social vision of corporate purpose; see William Foote Whyte and Kathleen King Whyte, *Making Mondragon* (New York: ILR Press, 1988). They make the important point that the choice "between considering the pursuit of profits as the sole or primary driving force or considering profits as a necessary limiting condition—a means to other ends" differentiates a shareholder-driven organization from a worker-owner organization. See also Greg MacLeod, *From Mondragon to America* (Sydney: University College of Cape Breton Press, 1997). See Mondragon's web site www.mondragon.mcc.es (1/28/01).

23. David Kirkpatrick, "Avis: How the Workers Run Avis Better, *Fortune*, 5 December 1988; reprinted in *Curing World Poverty*, ed. John H. Miller, C.S.C. (St. Louis: Social Justice Review, 1994), 221 (emphasis added). Kohlberg and Roberts were asked to respond to Kelso's accusations but offered no comment.

24. Frederick Ungeheuer, "They Own the Place," *Time*, 6 February 1989, 51.

25. See Lewis Hyde, *The Gift: Imagination and the Erotic Life of Property* (New York: Vintage Books, 1983), 3–4.

26. As Augustine explains, "all privation is a diminution" (Avila, *Ownership*, 117, and Augustine, *De Genesi* 11, 15, PL 34:436). Private property has a legal meaning, but theologically, there is no such thing as private property, private sector, private lives, private choices, private spirituality, or private affairs. Privacy is an illusion, since everything we have is formed in the context of our social relationships and has meaning in that context. The word

"private" brings us to the theological and philosophical fault line between an individualistic (Kohlberg) and a Christian (Kelso) view of property/ownership.

27. We are indebted to our colleague Jeanne Buckeye for this story.

28. T. S. Eliot, "Choruses from 'The Rock'," in *The Complete Poems and Plays, 1909–1950* (New York: Harcourt, Brace and World, 1971), 103. Within the Christian as well as in most religious traditions, "A man who owns a thing is naturally expected to share it, to distribute it, to be its trustee and dispenser." (Hyde, *The Gift*, 15, 138–139).

29. Quoted in Avila, *Ownership*, 67. See also Luke Timothy Johnson, "Wealth and Property in the New Testament," *Priests and People* (May 1998): 181–184.

30. That is, the Christian concept of property-ownership is intrinsically linked to stewardship; see Avila, *Ownership*, 116.

31. J. Irwin Miller provides an example of this absolute understanding of private property: "In Victorian England the prevailing sentiment was for the sanctity of property rights. When, therefore, in 1846 at the height of the potato famine, Mrs. Gerrard in County Galway, Ireland, evicted on one day all 300 of her tenants, none of whom was in arrears, so that her holdings might be turned into a grazing farm, Lord Brougham, speaking, in the House of Lords, felt she was acting most ethically indeed. Said he, 'Property would be valueless and capital would no longer be invested in cultivation of land if it was not acknowledged that it was the landlord's undoubted, indefeasible, and most sacred right to deal with his property as he wishes.' His Lordship asserted this to be a most ethical act, indeed a 'sacred right,' because it was in accord with the prevailing tone and sentiment of the ruling class at that time" (J. Irwin Miller, "How Religious Commitments Shape Corporate Decisions," in *On Moral Business: Classical Contemporary Resources for Ethics in Economic Life,* ed. Max L. Stackhouse, Dennis P. McCann, and Shirley J. Roels, with Preston N. Williams [Grand Rapids, Mich.: Wm. B. Eerdmans Publishers, 1995], 709).

32. Aquinas saw individually possessed, productive property as the most expedient means of promoting the common use of created goods. Thus, for Aquinas, ownership means "private possession *for the sake of common use.*" With this formula, however, Aquinas merely reformulates in a clearer way the major strand of thought on property descended from Christian antiquity and informed by Jewish teaching. To regard property as a merely private object which one uses as one likes is as antithetical to a Judeo-Christian understanding as seeing the Sabbath as a day for doing whatever one wants. Clement of Alexandria said that property creates "unrighteous" or wrong re-

lationships "when a man [or organization] for personal [or private] advantage regards it as being entirely his [their] own" (Avila, *Ownership*, 44). The Christian social tradition understands the institution of ownership as a social institution with a social purpose (see Herbert Vorgrimler and Oswald von Nell-Breuning, "Socio-Economic Life" in *Commentary on the Documents of Vatican II*, vol. 5, ed. Herbert Vorgrimler [New York: Crossroad, 1989], 306; and John A. Ryan, *A Living Wage* [New York: Macmillan Company, 1910], 71–72). Kelso and Adler treat the social dimension of ownership under their participative principle. In order to establish right relationships in the economy, it is imperative to create conditions that allow people to participate in the economy. That is, conditions must allow fair access to productive activities, both through capital (acquired property) and labor (innate "property"). If this participative principle is to have any meaning, it must be followed by the distributive principle (output), which is defined in relationship to the individual's labor and capital inputs, so that an economic system is created which links distribution to participation, and incomes to productive contribution (Kelso and Adler, *The Capitalist Manifesto*, 66–86).

33. John Paul II, *Laborem Exercens*, 14. One of the first calls from the popes on worker ownership came from Pius XI in 1931: "We consider it more advisable in the present condition of human society that, so far as possible, the work-contract be somewhat modified by a partnership-contract. . . . Workers and other employees thus become sharers of ownership or management or participate in some fashion in the profits received" (*Quadragesimo Anno*, n. 65; see also *Mater Magistra*, nn. 77 and 92, and *Gaudium et Spes*, n. 68).

34. See Thomas Aquinas, *Summa Theologica* (New York: Benziger Brothers, 1947), II-II, q. 66, a. 2.

35. Ibid.

36. See John Paul II, *Laborem Exercens*, 15. The personalist criterion in Catholic social teaching shifts the emphasis regarding worker ownership from ownership as a means of meeting physical needs to ownership as a condition of full and responsible participation in economic life. This is particularly evident in John Paul's writings concerning worker ownership, although it is also found in John XXIII's *Mater et Magistra*. See also Johannes Messner, *Social Ethics* (St. Louis: B. Herder Book Co., 1949), 822–823; and, on economic freedom, see Hiliare Belloc, *The Restoration of Property* (New York: Sheed and Ward, 1936), 21ff.

37. Quoted in Dawn Brohawn, "Value-Based Management," in *Curing World Poverty*, ed. John H. Miller, C.S.C. (St. Louis: Social Justice Review, 1994), 207.

38. Pius XII declared, "Wealth is like the blood of the human body, it ought to circulate around all the members of the social body" (Quoted in Jean-Yves Calvez, S.J., and Jacques Perrin, S.J., The Church and Social Justice [Chicago: Henry Regnery Co., 1961], 149). Once blood fails to circulate and is concentrated in one area, the whole body is in danger.

39. Brohawn, "Value-Based Management," 190.

40. Luke 11:17.

41. John Paul, *Laborem Exercens*, 14.

42. Jack Stack, "Springfield Remanufacturing Corporation" in *Curing World Poverty*, ed. John H. Miller, C.S.C. (St. Louis: Social Justice Review, 1994), 237.

43. Jack Stack, *The Great Game of Business* (Doubleday: New York, 1992), chapter 4.

44. Aquinas, *Summa Theologica*, II-II, q. 66, a. 2; see also Leo XIII, *Rerum Novarum*, 36, and Avila, *Ownership*, 45.

45. Aquinas, *Summa Theologica*, I-II q. 19, a. 10.

46. Luke 12:16–21 (RSV).

47. What should become abundantly clear in this discussion is that techniques such as leverage financing, when embodied in different philosophies (Kelso's democratic communitarianism vs. Kohlberg's individualistic liberalism), lead to radically different outcomes. Everyone works within a philosophical worldview. Everyone has first principles or starting points. Reflection on these first principles is of utmost importance both for one's own moral character as well as to the health and well-being of society. Financing the capital structure of organizations is embedded within a philosophical view of *what a corporation is for*. Kelso and Kohlberg represent two competing moral philosophies of property manifested in the modern corporation. One could only imagine what might have happened if, in the 1980s, investors and management had adopted Kelso's leveraged ESOPs rather than Kohlberg's leveraged buyouts on behalf of investors dedicated solely to maximizing return.

48. 1 Timothy 6:10.

49. John Paul II, *Sollicitudo Rei Socialis*, 37.

50. Teleopathy is "a habit of character that values limited purposes as supremely action-guiding, to the relative exclusion not only of larger ends, but also moral considerations about means, obligations, and duties." Goodpaster goes on to explain that "the manifestations of teleopathy are the manifestations of a decision maker that has sacrificed perspective and balance to a goal or a series of goals over time. . . . By turning over balanced judgment to the pursuit of purpose, purpose becomes a kind of idol. Teleopathy can thus be seen as a secularized form of idolatry (see Kenneth

Goodpaster, "Ethical Imperatives and Corporate Leadership," in *Ethics in Practice: Managing the Moral Corporation*, ed. Kenneth R. Andrews [Boston: Harvard Business School Press, 1991], 217). See also the entry "Teleopathy" in *Blackwell Encyclopedic Dictionary of Business Ethics*, ed. Patricia Werhane and R. Edward Freeman (Oxford: Blackwell Publishers, 1997), 627–628.

51. Quoted in Aquinas, *Summa Theologica*, II-II, q. 141, a. 6.

52. See de Salins and Villeroy de Galhau, *The Modern Development of Financial Activities*, 27, and Paul J. Wadell, C.P., *The Primacy of Love* (New York: Paulist Press, 1992), 135.

53. Information on this case comes from Emma Lou Brent, "The Evolution of an ESOP Company," in *Our Journey to an Ownership Culture*, ed. Dawn K. Brohawn (Washington, D.C.: The ESOP Association; Lanham, Md.: The Scarecrow Press, 1997), 16–27. For a practical managerial philosophy of ESOPs, see Norman G. Kurland, Dawn K. Brohawn, and Michael D. Greaney, "Value-Based Management: A System for Building an Ownership Culture," available from the Center for Economic and Social Justice (www.cesj.org) (1/28/01). Approximately 12,000 U.S. corporations, covering some 12% of the workforce, have implemented ESOPs, including United Airlines (55% ESOP), Polaroid (25%), and Cargill (17%).

54. Two ways for an ESOP to be established are by self-finance and leverage: self-financed ESOPs usually draw on a profit-sharing program; in a leveraged ESOP, capital is created with credit, and if competently invested, will pay for itself out of future earnings.

55. The following text comes from Norm Kurland, The Center for Economic and Social Justice.

56. Or as Weirton Steel does, the company can create a market for the stock by keeping a minority percentage of shares on the public market.

57. "When men have become wage-slaves they think in terms of income. When they are economically free, they think in terms of property. Most modern men living under industrial conditions regard economic reform as essentially a redistribution of income; property for them means only an arrangement whereby a certain income is secured. Free men look at it just the other way. They think of income as the product of property" (Belloc, *The Restoration of Property*, 103).

58. Myron S. Scholes and Mark A. Wolfson, "Employee Stock Ownership Plans and Corporate Restructuring: Myths and Realities," *Financial Management* (Spring 1990): 17. Nevertheless, the National Center for Employee Ownership (NCEO) reports that pay and benefits are higher in ESOP companies than comparable non-ESOP companies (Peter A. Kardas, Adria L. Scharf, and Jim Keogh, *Wealth and Income Consequences of Employee*

Ownership [Oakland, Calif.: The National Center for Employee Ownership, 1998], 20ff.). See also "Pay and Benefits are Higher in ESOP Companies, *Employee Ownership Report* (July/August 1998): 1, 3.

59. This distribution of "capital" wealth has multiplying effects for both the organization and the employee. As Rosen explains, "the more funds that are contributed to an ESOP each year, the more committed the employees are to their company. They also are more satisfied with their work and more concerned with the company's financial performance. And they are much less likely to leave. . . . they would be willing to give up their next wage increase for a share in their companies" (Corey Rosen, "Using ESOPs to Boost Corporate Performance," *Management Review* [March 1988]: 30–33).

60. Brent, "The Evolution of an ESOP Company," 25.

61. Ibid., 22.

62. ESOPs, like all organizational techniques, carry with them difficulties that the prudent manager must examine. Among the more noteworthy problems: ESOPs involve a tax subsidy for capitalists (and nascent capitalists) that increases tax rates for others, especially the poor; "ESOPs assume extremely high growth rates that doom the plan on ecological grounds alone" (John B. Cobb and Herman E. Daly, *For the Common Good: Redirecting the Economy toward Community, the Environment, and a Sustainable Future* [Boston: Beacon Press, 1994], 301); redeeming shares might be costly, depending on the condition of the company (hence, Weirton Steel makes 20% of its shares public, creating a market through which employees can redeem their shares); ESOPs may encourage employees to entrust too much of their retirement investment in one instrument (see also Ellen E. Schultz, "Workers Put Too Much in Their Employer's Stock," *The Wall Street Journal,* 13 September 1996, A9); finally, the problem of valuation, i.e., determining the price of the stock at the time of the sale to employees: employees must take care not to pay too much for a firm, particularly those who are buying a company under economic duress.

63. Brent, "The Evolution of an ESOP Company," 23.

64. See Gates, *The Ownership Solution,* 50ff.

65. Avila, *Ownership,* 44.

66. See Virginia Vanderslice, "Creating Ownership When You Already Have Participation," *Employee Ownership Report,* NCEO Newsletter 18 (November–December 1998): 5.

67. As Hilaire Belloc pointed out in 1936, if "we regard economic freedom as a good, our object must be thus to restore property. We must seek political and economic reforms which shall tend to distribute property more and more widely until the owners of sufficient Means of Production . . .

are numerous enough to determine the character of society" (*Restoration of Property*, 21).

7. MARKETING COMMUNICATION AND PRODUCT DEVELOPMENT

1. Quoted in R. Mackenzie, "Selling Dreams: Catholicism and the Business Communicator," paper delivered at the Second International Symposium on Catholic Social Thought and Management Education, Antwerp, Belgium, July 1997, (http://www.stthomas.edu/cathstudies/cstm/antwerp/p13.htm) (1/28/01).

2. Regis McKenna, *Relationship Marketing* (London: Century, 1991), 3.

3. Ibid., 3.

4. Ibid., 5.

5. Ibid., 4.

6. Other classification systems are more complex. For instance, Sheth et al. describe four schools of thought concerning how the marketing function is perceived by marketers themselves (see J. N. Sheth, D. M. Gardner, and D. E. Garrett, *Marketing Theory: Evolution and Evaluation* [New York: Wiley, 1988]).

7. For example, see McKenna, *Relationship Marketing* and T. Takala and O. Uusitalo, "An Alternative View of Relationship Marketing: A Framework for Ethical Analysis," *European Journal of Marketing* 30 (1996): 45–60.

8. See A. Fuat Firat, N. Dholakia, and A. Venkatesh, "Postmodern Marketing," *European Journal of Marketing* 29 (1995): 40–56.

9. Ibid.

10. McKenna, *Relationship Marketing*, 12 (emphasis added).

11. For example, see Takala and Uusitalo, "An Alternative View."

12. C. Grönroos, *Service Management and Marketing* (Lexington, Ky.: Lexington Books, 1990), 12.

13. Takala and Uusitalo, "An Alternative View," 46.

14. Michael Piore and Charles Sabel, *The Second Industrial Divide* (New York: Basic Books, 1984).

15. Obiora Ike, *Value, Meaning and Social Structure of Human Work* (Frankfurt am Main: Peter Lang, 1986), 243–244.

16. John Paul II, *Sollicitudo Rei Socialis*, 38.

17. Cardinal Karol Wojtyla, *The Acting Person*, Analecta Husserliana Series, vol. 10, ed. Anna-Teresa Tymieniecka (Boston: D. Reidel Publishing Co., 1979), 285.

18. S. Fournier, S. Dobscha, and D. G. Mick, "Preventing the Premature Death of Relationship Marketing," *Harvard Business Review* (January–February 1998): 42–51.

19. Don E. Schultz, Stanley Tannenbaum, and Robert F. Lauterborn, *Integrated Marketing Communications* (Lincolnwood, Ill.: NTC Business Books, 1992).

20. Mackenzie, "Selling Dreams."

21. We are grateful to Deb Lincoln from the University of St. Thomas Instructional Support Services, who created this graphic.

22. See Schultz et al., *Integrated Marketing Communications.*

23. See Fournier, Dobscha, and Mick, "Preventing the Premature Death of Relationship Marketing." A case that might lead one to endorse the death of IMC involved a credit card company that sent reminders to cardholders each year of the gift purchases they had made in the previous year. A customer who had purchased "thank you" gifts for the doctors who had treated his sick mother duly received reminders of that painful incident, even after he had—with explanation—requested that the "service" be suspended.

24. Ibid., 55. The "category network" involves analyzing where a particular product is placed in the hierarchical, psychological model that, according to the authors, captures the way we store information on products. For example, when customers think about buying something to drink, the "superordinate" level they refer to is their idea of a "drink" or a "beverage." The next level of distinction they refer to are the basic categories of drink that they could choose from, such as "fruit juice," "soft drink," "alcoholic drink," and so on. At the subordinate level, these basic categories split further into categories such as "diet cola," "orange juice," "all-natural soft drink," and so on. The "category network" is thus composed of these superordinate, basic, and subordinate levels. The marketer needs to know where in the category structure the customer holds information about the company's product. Clearly, the nearer the superordinate level, the more likely the customer will buy the product repeatedly. As Schultz et al. say: "We hypothesize that the goal of most marketing communications is to move the marketer's brand from the subordinate to the basic level in the hierarchy" (*Integrated Marketing Communications,* 52–53). This clearly displays the manipulative undertone in their work.

25. As Schultz and his colleagues show, the ad agency "went one step further. The[y] created a selling line that tied in directly with the point the strategy was trying to make. These models were more than a '10'—the popular denominator for good looks. These models were 'Definitely a 15.' This selling line was a memorable promise to the consumer" (*Integrated Marketing Communications,* 189).

26. There is also the troubling problem of the existence of large databases created by companies about their customers. Legislation is designed to protect customers from the grossest misuse of this information, but unless regulatory regimes are backed up by a genuine intention and effective methods to maintain confidentiality (in other words, a virtuous group of people pursuing the genuine common good of both the company and the customers), the potential for abuse of private information is worrisome.

27. St. Augustine, *De Magistro*, 8, quoted in Mackenzie, "Selling Dreams," 35.

28. St. Augustine, *On the Trinity*, XII, quoted in Mackenzie, "Selling Dreams," 35.

29. See Pope Leo XIII, *Rerum Novarum*, 50–51.

30. See R. B. Kennard, "From Experience: Japanese Product Development Process," *Journal of Product Innovation Management* 8 (1991): 184–188. The impact of this kind of language is tempered by the fact that studies continue to show that firms do not treat the customer as king, even though they may use that rhetoric. Edgett et al. show that in only 18.9% of cases of Japanese companies operating in the UK and 29.1% for British companies, do new products arise from ideas originating with customers or distributors. Such low figures suggest that more could be done to make the customer/supplier relationship more influential in the NPD process. Better communication with the customer is needed, especially because the number one factor identified by all companies is the need for a product to satisfy the customer. However, the role of the marketing department in this does not seem well appreciated. An analysis of NPD failure in Edgett showed that firms did not rate skillful marketing and good marketing research very highly as factors for success. Clearly, there is room for development in the relationships here, so they can have the effect on NPD they should (S. Edgett, D. Shipley, and G. Forbes, "Japanese and British Companies Compared: Contributing Factors to Success and Failure in NPD," *Journal of Product Innovation Management* 9 (1992): 3–10).

31. Philip Land, "The Earth Is the Lord's: Thoughts on the Economic Order," in *Above Every Name*, ed. Thomas E. Clarke (Ramsey, N.J.: Paulist Press, 1980), 227.

32. Edmund Morris, *The Rise of Theodore Roosevelt* (New York: Coward, McCann and Geoghegan, 1979), 193.

33. Oswald von Nell-Breuning, *Reorganization of the Social Economy* (Milwaukee, Wis.: Bruce Publishing Co., 1936), 115.

34. Bob King, *Better Designs in Half the Time: Implementing QFD in America*, "Goal/QPC," 3rd ed. (Methuen, Mass., 1989), 1–9. Here our discussion is based on the work of Bob King, who has made available in

English perhaps the most advanced version of the QFD process developed in Japan by Yoji Akao. King integrates other elements from Western thinkers into Akao's work that enhance the process.

35. Ibid., 1–9.

36. The charts are organized in the following way:

> Chart A (4 parts): Customer demands are linked to "substitute quality characteristics" and through these to function, quality character, and component parts of the product;
>
> Chart B (4 parts): Function, cost, breakthrough targets, and quality plan against critical parts;
>
> Chart C (4 parts): Mechanisms (that form part of the product) in relation to new technology, functions, substitute quality characteristics, and component parts;
>
> Chart D (4 parts): Failure modes in relation to customer demands, functions, substitute quality characteristics, and component parts;
>
> Chart E (4 parts): New concepts in relation to customer demands, functions, substitute quality characteristics, and also in relation to a summary of the process so far;
>
> Charts F&G (4 parts and 6 parts): various elements charted, such as equipment deployment, process planning, and fault tree.

All these categories are probably self-evident, with the exception of the idea of the "substitute quality characteristic." These are characteristics the product must have in order to satisfy customer requirements for that product. For instance, customers may require that a roll of paper should be wrinkle- and tear-free. Product research may show that the key factor in achieving this is a round central tube supporting the paper roll. Therefore, as King indicates, the roundness of the inner tube is the substitute quality characteristic for paper with no wrinkles or tears.

The first of the set of charts may be the key to the rest. The first of the subcharts that make up the total chart A is called the "Quality Table." The Quality Table in Akao's more developed form of QFD is like the simpler "House of Quality" idea in other simpler versions of QFD. The walls of the house of quality are the "customer attributes" required in a product, while the ceiling is composed of the engineering characteristics of the product which provide these attributes. In the roof of the house, the interactions between changes in the engineering characteristics are explored and their effects on the fulfillment of required customer attributes. The simple structure of the "House of Quality" and the powerful metaphor of building the house ensure that this tool has often been very useful in the breakthrough phase of a design project. Both Akao's more complex chart and the "House of Quality" provide the foundation on which to build the rest of the QFD program.

At least two other tools are of great importance: those associated with understanding the customer and the "quality table." Everyone knows that it is central to the design process to understand what the customer wants and to serve customer needs. However, knowing how to get this information is not that easy. In many ways, the problems associated with getting the right information from the customer resemble those associated with getting responses from users in the human-centered design process. Both customers and users often are not consciously aware of the benefit they derive from some particular aspect of a product or system. It is only when it is no longer there that they realize what they gained from it. In other words, this is a kind of "taken-for-granted" quality, what Herzberg would have called a "hygiene" factor in the workplace. To deal with these problems, Kano, another Japanese professor of quality, has devised a kind of questionnaire in which customers could indicate whether a factor was expected, whether they actively liked or disliked some attribute, or whether some aspect had what he calls "exciting quality," a positively attractive attribute.

More difficult still is the fact that both customers and users are often unaware of new possibilities for a product, things that they can only experience and evaluate after the product is designed. There is no easy solution to this problem, so it is still necessary to test the product with customers at a very late stage in the design process.

8. Faith, Hope, and Charity

1. Teilhard de Chardin, *The Divine Milieu* (New York: Harper and Row, 1960), 32.

2. "The Latin root of the word 'spirituality,' *spiritualitas*, attempts to translate the Greek noun for spirit, *pneuma*, and its adjective *pneumatikos*, as they appear in the New Testament Pauline letters. Thus, 'to be united to Christ is to enter into the sphere of the Spirit' (1 Cor. 6:17). . . . The 'spiritual person' (e.g., 1 Cor. 2:14–15) is *not* someone who turns away from material reality but rather someone in whom the Spirit of God dwells" (Philip Sheldrake, *Spirituality and History* [New York: Crossroad, 1992], 34–35. Albert Dalfovo points out that St. Paul "opposes *spirit* to *flesh* or *animal*, not to *body* or *matter*. The spiritual person is one whose life is ordered by the Spirit

of God, whereas the person who is carnal (fleshly) or animal is one whose life is opposed to God's Spirit . . . the body can be spiritual if led by the Spirit, and spirit can be carnal if opposed to the Spirit" (from "Contextualizing Spirituality and Work in Africa," delivered at The Third International Symposium on Catholic Social Thought and Management Education, Goa, India, 10–12 January 1999; see www.stthomas.edu/cathstudies/cst/mgmt/research/goa/DALFOVO.html [1/28/01]). As Henri de Lubac puts it, "the *pneuma* that is 'in man', ensures a certain hidden transcendence of man beyond himself, a certain openness, a certain received continuity from man to God. . . . it is a privileged place of their encounter, a place that lies at the very heart of man and remains forever intact. . . . There is the vague feeling that there exists in each of us, be it the greatest of sinners, a hidden nook that no one but God can penetrate, 'a sacred point within us wherein we speak the *Pater noster*' . . . a point that is unable to hide from love" (quoted in Eric de Moulins-Beaufort, "The Spiritual Man in the Thought of Henri de Lubac," *Communio* 25 [Summer 1998]: 290). As we will see, this human spirit can develop only through participation in the Holy Spirit. For a discussion of the fluidity of spirituality, see Walter Principe, "Toward Defining Spirituality," *Studies in Religion* 12 (1983): 127–141. Sandra Schneiders ("Spirituality in the Academy," *Theological Studies* 50 [1989]: 676–697) observes, "It is truly remarkable that a term which only 20 years ago connoted suspect enthusiasm or mindless piety in Protestant circles and was virtually unknown to Judaism, Eastern traditions, Native American religion, the new religious movements, or secular systems of life integration is now used freely within all of these circles" (691).

3. David Whyte, *A Heart Aroused* (New York: Currency Doubleday, 1994), 13.

4. Sandra Schneiders defines spirituality as "'the experience of consciously striving to integrate one's life in terms not of isolation and self-absorption but of self-transcendence toward the ultimate value one perceives.' The generally agreed-upon characteristics included in this definition are the notions of progressive, consciously pursued, personal integration through self-transcendence within the horizon of ultimate concern" (see Schneiders, "Spirituality in the Academy," 684; see also her "Theology and Spirituality: Strangers, Rivals, or Partners?" *Horizons* 13 [1983]: 266).

5. Here it is important to distinguish, but not separate, an ethic of work from a spirituality of work. An *ethic of work* is concerned with the conditions within which work is carried out and the ethical norms on which those conditions are based. Our argument in the chapter on the common good, for example, was an exercise in business or organizational ethics in which we considered how the conditions of work (wages, ownership struc-

tures, job design, product development, and so forth) affected human development. However, our discussions of ethics were animated throughout with an implicit spirituality of work, which we here make explicit. A *spirituality of work* touches the deepest motivations we have behind our work; it helps us to understand how work is connected to our soul and to our ultimate end. Unlike an ethic of work, a spirituality of work concentrates on the hard questions of *ultimacy*. Nevertheless, the two are inextricably linked. Paul Wojda observes, "[E]thical questions are ultimately intelligible only within a spiritual context, and spiritual questions inevitably press upon moral concerns" ("Ethics, Spirituality, and the End of Life," unpublished). Much of conventional business/organizational ethics assumes that we can speak of ethical issues distinct from their connections with spiritual issues. Conventional ethics frequently leave our spiritual questions dangling, perhaps because these questions aim to expose our work-a-day routines to the illumination of our final end (see Johan Verstraeten, "Beyond Business Ethics: Spirituality and the Quest for Meaning," presented at The Third International Symposium on Catholic Social Thought and Management Education, Goa, India, 10–12 January 1999: www.stthomas.edu/cathstudies/cst/mgmt/research/goa/johan.html [1/28/01]).

6. This arrangement of levels is adapted from Maximus the Confessor, a spiritual writer in the early church, who described contemplation as a threefold activity: natural (contemplation of natures), spiritual (contemplation of scriptures), and mystical (contemplation of God himself); see Lars Thunberg, "The Human Person as Image of God," in *Christian Spirituality: Origins to the Twelfth Century*, ed. Bernard McGinn, John Meyendorff, and Jean Leclercq (New York: Crossroad, 1989), 304.

7. From a conversation with Robert Kennedy. In an article in the *New York Times* (12 November 1997), "Searching for Spirituality in Silicon Valley," engineers and managers lamented that their organizations had no soul and embodied no transcendent meaning beyond the pursuit of self-interest (www. nytimes. com/ library /cyber / week/111297spiritual. html) (1/28/01). While many of those interviewed in Silicon Valley work for companies that pay great salaries, make employees owners, empower workers, and produce great products, they found that even the satisfaction of their professional interests still left them empty. This deprivation of meaning had created for many of them "a spiritual crisis." As the article put it, employees wanted "to infuse the workplace with more meaning, to uplift the spirits of a generation of workers whose bible is no longer the Old Testament, but the Dilbert Principle."

8. John Paul II, *Laborem Exercens*, 24.

9. These are also John Paul II's questions in *Fides et Ratio*, 1.

10. Whyte, *The Heart Aroused*, 114.

11. From a talk by Richard Leider at St. Olaf's Faith and Work Breakfast Series, Minneapolis, Minn., 19 February 1998.

12. "How I Flunked Retirement: An Interview with Lee Ioccoca," *Fortune*, 24 June 1996, 50–61. The disease of those who come to this stage in their lives is that they are unprepared for it. Their failure to act, their refusal to develop other habits, brought them to a place they would prefer not to be.

13. Whyte, *The Heart Aroused*, 183.

14. Ibid., 277.

15. Our identity is particularly linked to our response to suffering. For suffering will make us either bitter or better, but it will never leave us the same. "The soul's ability to experience heaven or joy, in the corporate workplace, then, is commensurate with our ability to feel grief" (ibid., 108).

16. Thomas Aquinas, *Summa Theologica* (New York: Benziger Brothers, 1947), I-I q. 1, a. 1. See also Romans 1:20ff., John Paul II, *Fides et Ratio*, 82–83, and *Gaudium et Spes*, 15. Spirituality without a *telos*, an end, leaves us in a "ceaseless motion of self-discovery" (L. Gregory Jones, "A Thirst for God or Consumer Spirituality? Cultivating Disciplined Practices of Being Engaged by God," *Modern Theology* 13 [January 1997]: 4). Thus David Whyte's work, which we used in the first part of this chapter, is very helpful, but he arouses a sense of mystery in us without explaining it in a way that directs us toward a greater participation in its truth. Basil Willey makes this critique of poets in general (see Basil Willey, *The Seventeenth Century Background* [London: Chatto & Windus, 1950], 13).

17. See John Paul II, *Fides et Ratio*, 13.

18. We owe this insight to Jeff Gates. *Religio* for Aquinas is a habit of participating in practices of the church, both communal and individual, to reconnect ourselves to God. The common act of worship makes present both our origin and destiny through the presence of God. Moreover, religion is at once a kind of justice, whereby we give to God what is due to Him alone as Creator, and a communion, since through its practices we unite ourselves with others as participants in spiritual goods. Among the latter, of course, is a tradition of spiritual wisdom, which can serve to make up what we lack. In every way, religion restores the defects of merely personal spiritual experience. See Joseph A. Komonchak, *Foundations in Ecclesiology*, supplementary issue of the *Lonergan Workshop*, vol. 11, ed. Fred Lawrence (1995): 145ff.

19. Alasdair MacIntyre, *Three Rival Versions of Moral Enquiry: Encyclopaedia, Genealogy and Tradition* (Notre Dame: University of Notre Dame Press, 1990), 140. See also D. Stephen Long, "Charity and Justice: Christian

Economy and the Just Ordering of the Commandments," *Communio* 25 (Spring 1998): 16–17.

20. It is important to note the centrality of virtue to the Christian spiritual life: it involves a sustained cooperation with God's grace. In the end, it is God who attains us, not we who attain God, which is why we speak of theological virtues and not just cardinal virtues. If we cooperate with this grace, we begin to see in each moment God's creative and redemptive designs. In his discussion on a spirituality of work in *Laborem Exercens*, John Paul explains that "an inner effort on the part of the human spirit, *guided by faith, hope and love*, is needed in order that through these points the work of the individual human being may be given the meaning which it has in the eyes of God and by means of which work enters into the salvation process on a par with the ordinary yet particularly important components of its texture" (24, emphasis added).

21. See Schneiders, "Spirituality in the Academy," 684.

22. Genesis 1:27–28, 31. Our belief in God's creation and our role in it affirm the fundamental goodness of the world, without which human suffering and sin and divine salvation make no sense.

23. "Image represents not only a status but also a potentiality, and this potentiality blossoms only when human beings are set free by Christ from enslavement to sin and are able to develop the potential capacities given at creation to their full maturity. . . . Human beings are created in the image of God, in order that they may become like God" (Thunberg, "The Human Person as Image of God," 298–299). Henri de Lubac observes, "God reveals himself continuously to man by continuously impressing upon him his image; and it is precisely this continuous divine activity that constitutes man" (quoted in de Moulins-Beaufort, "The Spiritual Man," 292).

24. Talmud, *Sotah* 14a, in Jeffrey Salkin, *Being God's Partner: How to Find the Hidden Link Between Spirituality and Your Work* (Woodstock: Jewish Lights Publishing, 1994), 64. In this imitation theme, Salkin recounts one of the final scenes in the film *Manhattan*, where Woody Allen tells his friend, Yale, to reflect more deeply about his own moral life. Offended, Yale retorts, "You are so self-righteous! We're just people. We're just human beings. You think you're God." Woody Allen shrugs and responds, "I gotta model myself after someone."

25. That we work always and only on God's property is supported by the Christian doctrine of stewardship. As we mentioned in chapter 6 on ownership, Christian stewardship is led to the most radical theory of property through the recognition that everything we have is a gift; properly speaking, we own nothing, since we create nothing. "I have been asked to

give an account of what has been given to me." In traditional language, human dominion over things is for the sake of executing the intention of the Creator, who exercises primary dominion. That intention is expressed in the fact that the world and its goods are given to meet human need, and not the need of this one or that, but of *all*. Hence, dominion or possession of goods is rightly exercised only for the sake of meeting the proximate, common need. In terms of dominion language, it should not be forgotten that "dominion of human beings is dependent on their mastering their own passions, and that, in turn, depends on a proper development of their spirituality" (Thunberg, "The Human Person as Image of God," 302).

26. Lawrence Welch, "*Gaudium et spes*, the Divine Image, and the Synthesis of *Veritatis splendor*," *Communio* 24 (Winter 1997): 804.

27. Wadell, *The Primacy of Love*, 103. See Josef Pieper, *On Hope*, trans. Sr. Mary Frances McCarthy, S.N.D. (San Francisco: Ignatius Press, 1986), 13, and Josef Pieper, "Future without a Past, Hope with No Foundation," in *Josef Pieper: An Anthology* (San Francisco: Ignatius Press, 1989), 210.

28. The idea of over- and underinvesting in our work comes from John Haughey, S. J., *Converting 9 to 5: Bringing Spirituality to Your Daily Work* (New York: Crossroad, 1994), 126.

29. Josef Pieper, *On Hope*, 67.

30. In other words, hope inspires us to magnanimity which Aquinas and Aristotle called "'the jewel of all the virtues,' since it always—and particularly in ethical matters—decides in favor of what is, at any given moment, the greater possibility of the human potentiality for being" (Pieper, *On Hope*, 28).

31. See Wadell, *The Primacy of Love*, 103–105. "There are two things that kill the soul, despair and false hope" (Augustine, quoted in Pieper, *On Hope*, 48).

32. A less obvious, but perhaps more common expression of despair is "workaholism," which is summed up in the slogan, "Keep at it, and don't despair." If that slogan expresses our hope, we have already despaired. For, ". . . an individual in the last stages of despair can, by reason of the natural and cultural forces in the penultimate regions of his soul, appear to others and even to himself to be an 'optimist.' He has only to seal off the innermost chamber of his despair so radically that no cry of pain can escape to the outer world" (Pieper, *On Hope*, 49). To throw oneself exclusively into work (or into *any* temporal activity) is to have lost, in Pieper's words, "the courage for the great things that are proper to the nature of the Christian" (55).

33. The cynic never sees himself as part of the problem. Unlike Durenberger, the cynic cannot "confess." He thinks himself too smart to be part of the problem and no one will fool him into thinking otherwise. Yet, in the end the cynic fools only himself, because he refuses to be what he was meant to be. While he appears to know many things, he is incapable of fixing his gaze on the things that truly matter. "Therefore, he can neither order his mind (see Prov. 1:7) nor assume a correct attitude to himself or to the world around him" (see John Paul II, *Fides et Ratio*, 18).

34. 1 Corinthians 13:13.

35. Thomas Aquinas defines charity as friendship with God which begins "in this life by grace, but will be perfected in the future life by glory" (*Summa Theologica*, I-II, 65.5; see also II-II, 23.1; quoted in Wadell, *The Primacy of Love*, 63).

36. John Paul II, *Fides et Ratio*, 12.

37. John 15:15.

38. Quoted in Basil Pennington, "The Cistercians," in *Christian Spirituality: Origins to the Twelfth Century*, ed. Bernard McGinn, John Meyendorff, and Jean Leclercq (New York: Crossroad, 1989), 210. *Gaudium et Spes*, 12, states, "[O]nly in the mystery of the incarnate Word does the mystery of man take on light."

39. Paul Wadell reminds us that, besides benevolence, *mutuality of shared commitment* is critical to friendship: "Every friendship is forged around some good that brings the friends together" (Paul Wadell, *The Primacy of Love*, 69–70). Thus, if the good of an organization is common, as we discussed in chapter 2, and if the virtues that we discussed in chapters 4 through 7 are present in the relations of its members to one another, the organization becomes a "school of virtue," a community of friends.

40. Walter Burghardt, *Preaching the Just Word* (New Haven, Conn.: Yale University Press, 1996), 82.

41. Basil Pennington, "The Cistercians," 208.

42. John D. Zizioulas, "The Early Christian Community," in *Christian Spirituality: Origins to the Twelfth Century*, ed. Bernard McGinn, John Meyendorff, and Jean Leclercq (New York: Crossroad, 1989), 24.

43. Philippians 2:7.

44. See E. Glenn Hinson, "Praying without Ceasing," *Weavings* 13 (May/June 1998): 34–43.

45. Bernard Lonergan, *Topics in Education*, in *Collected Works of Bernard Lonergan*, vol. 10, ed. Robert M. Doran and Frederick E. Crowe (Toronto, Canada: University of Toronto Press, 1993), 67; quoted in Richard Liddy,

"Bernard Lonergan on Work," presented at The Third International Symposium on Catholic Social Thought and Management Education, Goa, India, 10–12 January 1999: www.stthomas.edu/cathstudies/mgmt/research/goa/BLONWORK.html (1/28/01).

46. Michael Buckley, S. J., *The Catholic University as Promise and Project* (Washington, D.C.: Georgetown University Press, 1998), chapter six.

47. Quoted in Verstraeten, "Beyond Business Ethics."

48. "The discipline of praying daily at fixed times not only discloses the sacramental character of time itself, but guarantees that one's engagement with God is not limited to moments of crisis or exultation. Spiritual growth presupposes dedication to the lengthy transformation by which one becomes less self-centered and self-driven and more God-centered and God-empowered. The deliberate decision to make time for God at regular intervals whether or not one 'feels' drawn to prayer concretely manifests the choice to make the relationship with God one's highest priority" (Jan M. Joncas "The Church at Prayer," in *Spirituality and Morality: Integrating Prayer and Action,* ed. Dennis J. Billy, CSS.R., and Donna Lynn Orsuto [New York: Paulist Press, 1996], 88).

49. This phrase comes from Brother Lawrence, a seventeenth-century Carmelite lay brother (see E. Glenn Hinson, "Praying without Ceasing," 35).

50. Teilhard de Chardin, *The Divine Milieu*, 67.

51. I (Naughton) have learned this form of prayer from my pastor, Fr. Michael Papesch. I have found these rhythms of prayer helpful in developing my own spirituality of work.

52. Silence is necessary to Christian spirituality *because* it is a condition for attentiveness to the "other," to God and other persons. This silence can be found in many places. "When Evelyn Underhill, a brilliant Oxford graduate, . . . sought Baron von Hugel as her spiritual guide, he told her to go first and spend two afternoons a week in a ghetto. 'If properly entered into and persevered with,' he explained, it will 'discipline, mortify, deepen, and quiet you. It will, as it were, distribute your blood—some of your blood—away from your brain, where too much is lodged at present.'" (Evelyn Hopper, *Life of Evelyn Underhill* [New York: Harper & Bros., 1958], 75; quoted in E. Glenn Hinson, "Praying without Ceasing," 42).

53. See Josef Pieper, *Leisure, the Basis of Culture* (New York: Mentor Books, 1963). John Henry Newman stated it well: "He is still here; He still whispers to us, He still makes signs to us. But His voice is too low, and the world's din is so loud, and His signs are so covert, and the world is so restless, that it is difficult to determine when He addresses us, and what He says."

54. John Michael Talbot, from his album, *Come to the Quiet.*

55. On kenosis see Verstraeten, "Beyond Business Ethics." It is in silence that grace fills our empty places. Whyte notes that in silence we can "meet creation on its own terms, we are able to stop our interminable self-occupied monologue for one precious moment and hear creation speaking to someone greater and larger than the person indicated by our job description" (*The Heart Aroused*, 293–294). Joseph Pieper points out that "[u]nless we regain the art of silence and insight, the ability for non-activity, unless we substitute true leisure for our hectic amusements, we will destroy our culture—and ourselves" (Pieper, *Leisure, the Basis of Culture*, 41).

56. See Kallistos Ware, "Ways of Prayer and Contemplation" in *Christian Spirituality: Origins to the Twelfth Century*, ed. Bernard McGinn, John Meyendorff, and Jean Leclercq (New York: Crossroad, 1989), 395–414. See also George Mantzaridis, "Spiritual Life in Palamism," in *Christian Spirituality: High Middle Ages and Reformation*, ed. Jill Raitt (New York: Crossroad, 1988), 208–222; and Philip Sherrard, "The Revival of Hesychast Spirituality," in *Christian Spirituality: Post-Reformation and Modern*, ed., Louis Dupré and Don E. Saliers (New York: Crossroad, 1989), 417–431.

57. Ware, "Ways of Prayer and Contemplation," 400.

58. An image given to us by Debashis Chatterjee. See Ware, "Ways of Prayer and Contemplation," 407–410, for a fuller description of the *hesychia* method, which has three main features: body posture, breathing, and focus on the heart.

59. Verstraeten, "Beyond Business Ethics."

60. The wording of this prayer can take many different forms. In the Greek Orthodox tradition, the most common form is "Lord Jesus Christ, Son of God, have mercy on me." This prayer should also "be said in a 'free' way as we go about our daily work. . . . The monk who prays only when he stands up to say his prayers is not really praying at all" (Ware, "Ways of Prayer and Contemplation," 403–404).

61. This form of prayer safeguards the "personalization of the spiritual life," but it must be set in the context of an ecclesial life if it is to avoid the excess of individualism (see Sherrard, "The Revival of Hesychast Spirituality," 422).

62. The *Magnificat* is a monthly magazine that provides a simplified way to pray the office along with the daily readings in the Catholic tradition; see www.magnificat.net (1/28/01).

63. From a conversation with Haughey.

64. Mother Teresa did not think that God was only in the poor. A journalist, in his attempt to recognize Mother Teresa's special qualities, dismissed her relevance to the world as too holy, too saintly, too extraordinary for ordinary folk by stating, "Oh Mother Teresa, you are so holy, how can

any of us be like you?" Her response: she had been called to be holy as a nun, and the journalist had been called to be holy as a journalist.

65. See Dennis Hamm, S.J., "Rummaging for God: Praying Backward through Your Day," *America,* 14 May 1994, 23.

66. See John Haughey, *Converting 9 to 5.* Our three rhythms are one spiritual practice to develop a spirituality of work. Spirituality is not only for monks, but for all Christians, regardless of profession. We can become an "'urban hesychast,' preserving inwardly a secret center of stillness in the midst of outward pressures, carrying the desert with us in our hearts wherever we go" (Ware, "Ways of Prayer and Contemplation," 412). To participate in an ongoing conversation over the Internet on spirituality and work, contact Gregory Pierce at Gfapierce@aol.com.

67. From a talk by Rabbi Jeffery Salkin at the University of St. Thomas, September 1998.

68. Matthew 5:8; see also Michael Buckley, S. J., "Seventeenth-Century French Spirituality: Three Figures," in *Christian Spirituality: Post-Reformation and Modern,* ed. Louis Dupré and Don E. Saliers (New York: Crossroad, 1989), 58.

69. See James T. Fisher, "The Priest in the Movie: *On the Waterfront* as Historical Theology," in *Theology and The New Histories,* ed. Gary Macy, The Annual Publication of the College Theology Society, vol. 44 (New York, Orbis Press, 1998): 167–185.

9. LITURGY

1. Dom Virgil Michel, "The Liturgy the Basis of Social Regeneration" in *American Catholic Religious Thought,* ed. Patrick Carey (New York: Paulist Press, 1987), 282. See also Dorothy Day, "Liturgy and Sociology," *The Catholic Worker* (December 1935): 4 (this essay is also available on line at http://www.catholicworker.org/dorothyday/) (1/28/01). See also Pope John Paul II, *Dies Domini* (The Lord's Day) (Chicago: Liturgy Training Publications, 1998), and Michael Baxter, "Reintroducing Virgil Michel: Towards a Counter-Tradition of Catholic Social Ethics in the United States," *Communio* 24 (Fall 1997): 499–528.

2. In Greek civic usage, "leitourgia," combining "laos" (the people) and "ergon" (work or energy) could mean something done by the citizens of the polis (as opposed to free women and children, and slaves), like voting in a trial, or by a particular citizen on behalf of the polis (like a rich person outfitting a fighting ship in time of war). In Christian adapted usage it means the work done by the "citizens of the Kingdom" (catechumens and

the baptized) on behalf of nonbaptized humans and the nonhuman created order, as well as the work done by Christ Jesus on behalf of the church and the created order. We are grateful to Jan Michael Joncas for reminding us of this.

3. Michael Skelley, "The Liturgy of the World and the Liturgy of the Church: Karl Rahner's Idea of Worship," *Worship* 63, no. 2 (March 1989): 112–131.

4. Ibid., 125.

5. Ibid., 128–129.

6. Karl Rahner, "The Eucharist in Our Daily Lives," *Theological Investigations,* vol. 7 (New York: Seabury, 1977), 226; quoted in Skelley, "The Liturgy of the World," 130.

7. Peter Fink, "Liturgy and Spirituality: A Timely Intersection," in *Liturgy and Spirituality in Context: Perspective on Prayer and Culture,* ed. Eleanor Bernstein, C.S.J. (Collegeville, Minn.: Liturgical Press, 1990), 51.

8. See John Baldovin, "The Liturgical Year, Calendar for a Just Community," in *Liturgy and Spirituality in Context: Perspective on Prayer and Culture,* ed. Eleanor Bernstein, C.S.J. (Collegeville, Minn.: Liturgical Press, 1990), 102–103.

9. See Fink, "Liturgy and Spirituality," 61.

10. Acts 2:42 (RSV).

11. See *Sacrosanctum Concilium,* 10.

12. Particularly important in this list is the first element, the liturgy of the hours. An ancient form of communal prayer involving psalms, canticles from the scriptures, scripture readings, and intercessions, it provides an increasingly important element in the liturgy of parishes and cathedrals, as well as in the life of religious and lay communities. Much research has been done this century on this ancient form of communal prayer, and shows that from early times there were two traditions of the liturgy of the hours, or what modern researchers now call the "cathedral" and "monastic" traditions. Historical reasons led to the disappearance of the simpler, cathedral tradition, which normally involved only morning and evening prayer. The more complex and extensive monastic form gradually supplanted it. One of the important projects of the liturgical reform after Vatican II was an attempt to recover more of the cathedral tradition of prayer, in order to make the liturgy of the hours more accessible and make it the normal mode of prayer of every Christian. Although further reform is needed to realize that aim, we are already witnessing a revival of the liturgy of the hours for every member of the church. This involves the gradual grounding for the prayer of all the church's members in the psalms and canticles of the Jewish and Christian traditions. Some of the greatest poems and prayers ever written

are found among these scriptural writings, and doubtless a tremendous enrichment of the prayer of the church will occur if many members come to
know, love, and pray them.

13. This theological idea expressing a reality of faith is influenced by
the Jewish tradition, though the meaning we use is altered. In the traditional
Jewish Passover celebration, the original Passover event is recalled through
reading the Biblical account, and that recollection is understood to make
present and new the reality of the release of the Jewish people from slavery.

14. We are not giving a full account here of the theology of the sacraments, nor do we wish to imply that there are not other ways to explain
theologically the nature of the sacraments (such as the scholastic formula-
tion of the "form" and "matter" of a sacrament and the idea of "transub-
stantiation" as a way of understanding how Christ can be truly present
under the form of the bread and wine of the Eucharist). We chose the
threefold approach because it is simple, it is has a long tradition of use in the
church, and because it makes particularly clear the connection between
liturgy and our daily lives.

15. See Jan M. Joncas, "The Church at Prayer," in *Spirituality and
Morality: Integrating Prayer and Action,* ed. Dennis J. Billy, CSS.R. and
Donna Lynn Orsuto (New York: Paulist Press, 1996), 80–96.

16. Baldovin, "The Liturgical Year," 108.

17. In *Laborem Exercens* (26), John Paul cites some of the occupations
mentioned within the scriptures. The books of the Old Testament contain
many references to human work and to the individual professions: for example, the doctor [Sir. 38:1–3], the pharmacist [Sir. 38:4–8], the craftsman
or artist [Ex. 31:1–5; Sir. 38:27], the blacksmith [Gn. 4:22; Is. 44:12]—we
could apply these words to today's foundry workers—the potter [Jer. 18:3–4;
Sir. 38:29–30], the farmer [Gn. 9:20; Is. 5:1–2], the scholar [Eccl. 12:9–12; Sir.
39:1–8], the sailor [Ps. 107(108):23–30; Wis. 14:2–3], the builder [Gn. 11:3;
2 Kgs. 12:12–13; 22:5–6], the musician [Gn. 4:21], the shepherd [Gn. 4:2, 37:3;
Ex. 3:1; 1 Sm. 16:11; et passim], and the fisherman [Ez. 47:10]. The words of
praise for the work of women are well known [Prv. 31:15–27]. In His Parables on the Kingdom of God, Jesus Christ constantly refers to human work:
that of the shepherd [Jn. 10:1–16], the farmer [Mk. 12:1–12], the doctor [Lk.
4:23], the ower [Mk. 4:1–9,] the householder [Mt. 13:52], the servant [Mt.
24:45; Lk. 12:42–48], the steward [Lk. 16:1–8], the fisherman [Mt. 13:47–50],
the merchant [Mt. 13:45–46], the laborer [Mt. 20:1–16]. He also speaks of
the various forms of women's work [Mt. 13:33; Lk. 15:8–9]. He compares the
apostolate to the manual work of harvesters [Mt. 9:37; Jn. 4:35–38] or fish-
ermen [Mt. 4:19]. He refers to the work of scholars too [Mt. 13:52].

18. See Michel, "The Liturgy the Basis of Social Regeneration," 280.

19. The Argentinean representatives of UNIAPAC (ACDE) are promoting the case of a businessman for canonization, Enrique Ernesto Shaw.

20. Baldovin, "The Liturgical Year," 105.

Epilogue

1. Quoted from Marvin L. Krier Mich, *Catholic Social Teaching and Movements* (Mystic, Conn.: Twenty-Third Publications, 1998), 98.

2. Stephen R. Covey, *The Seven Habits of Highly Effective People* (New York: A Fireside Book, 1989), 95 144.

Index

About the Authors

HELEN ALFORD, a professor in the Faculty of Social Sciences at the Pontifical University of Saint Thomas (the "Angelicum"), Rome, has also served as a research assistant and lecturer in the Engineering Department of the University of Cambridge, where she received her Master's in Engineering and Ph.D. in Management and Engineering. Her dissertation employed central elements of the Catholic social tradition to assess and evaluate the system known as "cellular manufacturing." She has done significant field research at British Aerospace, with the high-technology manufacturing and subcontracting industries in and around Cambridge, and has also participated in the project "Design of the Human Centered Computer Integrated Manufacturing Cell," under the aegis of the European Strategic Program of Research in Informational Technology (ESPIRIT), sponsored by the European Community. A former Visiting Fellow of the John A. Ryan Institute for Catholic Social Thought, University of St. Thomas, she is currently carrying out studies with small, high-technology industries in central and northeastern Italy. Numerous technical papers offered to the Engineering Department of the University of Cambridge are complemented by her articles in such journals as *New Technology, Work and Employment, Journal of Applied Manufacturing Systems, Journal of General Management* and *Journal of Human Values.*

MICHAEL NAUGHTON is associate professor at the University of St. Thomas in St. Paul, Minnesota, where he holds a joint appointment to the Department of Theology and to the Graduate School of Business. He is director of the university's John A. Ryan Institute for Catholic Social Thought of the Center for Catholic Studies, an organization that examines the relationships of Catholic social thought to business, Catholic education, and urban issues. As director of the institute, he has organized international conferences in the United States, Belgium, Mexico, and India on the theme of Catholic social thought and management. Professor Naughton received his doctorate in Theology and Society from Marquette University, and his M.B.A. from the University of St. Thomas. He is the author of *The Good Stewards: Practical Applications of the Papal Vision of Work,* coeditor of *The Dignity of Work: Pope John Paul II Speaks to Managers and Workers,* and the author of articles for such journals as *California Management Review, America, Logos, Commonweal, Journal of Business Ethics, The Thomist, Current Issues in Catholic Higher Education, Review of Social Economy, Journal of Applied Manufacturing Systems, Journal of Human Values* and *Social Justice Review.* He has delivered papers, presentations, and has conducted workshops on organizational issues in light of the Christian social tradition throughout the United States and in Europe, Latin America, Asia, and Africa.